Jamaica's Evolving Relationship with the IMF

Christine Clarke · Carol Nelson

Jamaica's Evolving Relationship with the IMF

There and Back Again

palgrave
macmillan

Christine Clarke
Department of Economics
University of the West Indies
Mona, Jamaica

Carol Nelson
Department of Government
University of the West Indies
Mona, Jamaica

ISBN 978-3-030-59203-5 ISBN 978-3-030-59204-2 (eBook)
https://doi.org/10.1007/978-3-030-59204-2

This Palgrave Macmillan imprint is published by the registered company Springer Nature Switzerland AG
The registered company address is: Gewerbestrasse 11, 6330 Cham, Switzerland

Wishes to dedicate this book to her parents and grandparents from whose shoulders she was able to reach the sky. Anaelle, reach even further!

—Christine Clarke

This Book is dedicated to my family for their support -Alex and Rashida especially, during the writing of this book. This book also recognizes colleagues- past and present- who gave and still give public service to engender Jamaica's growth and development- their experiences are reflected in what we write.

—Carol Nelson

Preface

During the year 2009, the Government of Jamaica took a critical look at its structure, modus operandi, and size in order to empower it to make decisions that would enable the reduction of the wage-to-GDP ratio to the recommended 9% whilst not curtailing or hampering the ability of the state to provide the goods and services that it must. In rethinking the role of the Jamaican state, Office of the Prime Minister (2009) acknowledged that whilst the goal of the public sector reform is to improve its performance metrics, these goals must contend with the nuances of the country context and that, given the failures of pursuing one or other type of state architecture, there was no fail-safe organisational structure that a state could simply select and leave to deliver the desired results on autopilot. Instead, regardless of the position taken by the state, the state will have to be pragmatic in making choices based on the broader interests and goals of the nation that are required to generate growth and support its development agenda. The failures of the interventionist state are well-known and led to a more laissez-faire approach to state operations whose monumental failure was observed in the occurrence and aftermath of the 2007 financial sector crisis.

It is in this context, and with a background of a very tumultuous relationship between Jamaica and the International Monetary Fund (IMF) that had been patched up partially in the 1990s after which the country amicably said "ta-taa" (Matherson, 2013) in 1995, that Jamaica returned to the IMF in 2009 in an attempt to shore up its resources to deal with any fallout from the global financial sector crisis. The preliminary assessments of the challenges being faced by the country forced the government to focus more intently on one of the five basic areas that the World Bank (1997) highlighted that the state must do: maintaining a non-distortionary policy environment including macroeconomic stability. The difficulties Jamaica has faced regarding macroeconomic stability are encapsulated in its 2010 rank of 131 among the 133 countries included in the annual Global Competitiveness Index (GCI). This macroeconomic stability in Jamaica's case was largely in relation to the rules and management of the fiscal affairs of the country. There was ministerial authority to provide discretionary waivers that were largely unbounded in value, unbudgeted for, and for which there was very little accountability. Debt-to-GDP was becoming too large in the context of anemic rates of economic growth and no sign of economic growth on the horizon in the context of the global economic crisis. The need to establish and entrench fiscal discipline was high on the agenda and the Fund was the perfect partner along with the development partners who rallied around the need for the Fund to opine on and oversee the government's economic policy arrangements.

Whilst Jamaica was able to overcome the challenges of accessing support from the IMF and, simultaneously, to attract historical levels of support from its two major development partners—the Inter-American Development Bank and the World Bank—the government was unable to hold the fiscal line. Promises of wage increases to the two largest public sector groups—teachers and nurses—were deathknells to the spirit of the signed agreement and trust in the government's ability to continue within its boundaries. As a result, only three of eight planned reviews were conducted and Jamaica soon found itself without the economic anchor necessary to validate its operations. Given the country's aspirations to become *"the place of choice to live, work, raise families and do business"* (Planning Institute of Jamaica, 2009) it was impossible for this impasse to continue indefinitely. The Fund itself had expended significant amounts of effort to reconcile with the Jamaican people and had ensured that complementary programmatic and policy funding would accompany its own interventions to support the social and other dimensions in which the effects of the crisis could be felt.

As in the first volume, our exploratory methodologies include quantitative and qualitative analytical techniques with the use of primary and secondary data. The theoretical framework of Actor Network Theory

(ANT) is utilized, juxtaposed with Critical Discourse Analysis (CDA) to explore how Jamaica's engagement with the various IMF Agreements emerge. What is also considered is the interplay and interactions between and within the networks created, looking at their dynamics and how various actors coalesced, converged and diverged in relational interplay.

Discourse shapes society and culture from the perspective that every single instance of language use reproduces, shapes or transforms society and culture, including power relations. Critical Discourse Analysis (CDA) explores the relationship between talk and text, discourse practice and their sociological manifestations in such contexts, probing the underlying power relations. Discourse as a form of social behaviour has associated social processes, being embedded in economic, political and institutional contexts from within which the discourse originates. Discourse and other elements of social practices, including semiosis, implicates how discourse is factored or is engaged within the processes of change and contours the power relationships between all social elements involved within the network of practices.

Under the ANT construct, IMF is an actor and the respective Agreements each become actors or actor networks soliciting the enrolment of other actors/institutions, or Governments to the point of representing them, indicative of power which is derived relationally and through the ebbs and flows of the struggle that ensues in furthering the adoption of new discourses and practices from the Agreements. This begins a process of displacing the former-practices, methods and mental approaches, manifested now in the inculcation, ideationally and relationally of new 'IMF' discourses and practices. These interactions altogether, implicate the degree of change and the nature of social relations within the ongoing network and processes, shaping the circumstances and outcomes, all being framed at the nexus of Jamaica's evolving relationship with the IMF.

This volume now presents what happens next.

It takes us from the point of the impasse in 2011 right up to the struggles in 2020 against the COVID-19 virus that threatens to shake the foundations of fiscal stability as governments are tempted to intervene, intervene, intervene. Whilst Jamaica's rank on the GCI has improved to 110 out of 141 countries, it is clear that the price paid through multiple debt exchanges and landscape changes by the fiscal authorities, the changes though necessary are not sufficient to bring us below 100. The extensive IMF programme implemented in 2013 not only set the stage for recovery but also sought to address some of the longstanding challenges that needed to be addressed to support the achievement of Vision 2030 Jamaica. It also addressed the concerns of the domestic and international private sector interests who were concerned that the break in the relationship spelt irreparable damage to the functioning of the economy. What both the Jamaican authorities and the private and other interests would learn is that, consistent with global experience, building and improving state capacity to function as well as to implement reforms is a function of long-term political commitment, good policies and state institutions that have the capacity to implement changes. A successor agreement had to be inked and implemented successfully by whichever political party formed the administration.

The private sector and other stakeholders were not so sanguine on the results from the 2013 EFF and suggested that the government re-engage the IMF as a means of ensuring that its hands were "held to the wheel" of reform. The IMF also expressed concerns given the nascent nature of the fiscal discipline that had been instituted especially in the context of the need to generate growth and to address the persistent social challenges. The government and IMF would select a precautionary SBA (PSBA) which enabled access to balance of payment support that the IMF can attest that the government did not draw down on. With no prior actions, the government embarked upon its reform agenda and there were formal and informal celebrations when the ink dried on the final review of the PSBA. The remarkable feats encompassed in Jamaica successfully completing two consecutive agreements with the IMF, particularly, after the early derailing of the hardwon 2010 SBA is noteworthy and in stark contrast to the relationship between the IMF and Jamaica in the 1970, 1990s and 2000s. Albeit, this was not only due to a more pragmatic approach to IMF agreements by the government and the wide range of technocrats who delivered on the benchmarks, as the IMF itself had been through its own series of internal reforms that altered the way it viewed the impact of the economic reforms and its allowances for governments to build buffers into the programme to protect the poor and vulnerable. As Jamaica closed the chapters on its borrowing relationships with the IMF, the question on everyone's mind is—would there be a third return to the IMF? What would 2020 and the new decade it heralded bring and would the provisions made to improve the resilience of the nation's economy be sufficient to prevent such a return? We close this volume by providing insights into the impact of the COVID-19 disease and the various policy responses on the Jamaican economy and confirm that

Jamaica has returned to the IMF for a third time as the most far-reaching and deadly crisis wreaks havoc globally.

Mona, Jamaica

Christine Clarke
Carol Nelson

References

Matherson, N. (2013, January 5). *IMF no Panacea for Jamaica's economic woes.* The Jamaica Gleaner, p. Editorials.

Office of the Prime Minister. (2009). *Strategy for restructuring the public sector.* Government of Jamaica.

Planning Institute of Jamaica. (2009). *Vision 2030 Jamaica – National development plan.* Planning Institute of Jamaica.

The World Bank. (1997). *The state in a changing world: World development report.* New York: Oxford University Press.

Acknowledgments

This book benefitted from the exceptional efforts of Ms. Romae Finegan, Christine's research assistant who unpacked the three IMF agreements and provided insight into the coding required for the multiple analytical perspectives used throughout the volume in this regard. Gabriel Smith and Anna Kay Hall also provided support to the collation of various pieces of information to support the drafting of Chapters 4 and 9.

We also wish to thank Clovis Brown for granting us the liberty to utilize some of his cartoons published in the Jamaica Observer in this volume as we believe they reflect a window into perspectives held by the general populus and provide insight. Moreover, Clovis' ability to capture the essence of personal as well as public sentiment about a prevailing issue and creatively express it through the medium of cartoon imagery is unique-conveying political, socio-economic, experiential and cultural truths about *'Jamaicaness'* enabling their digestion with humour and candour.

Praise for *Jamaica's Evolving Relationship with the IMF*

"'There and Back Again' by Nelson and Clarke

Continues, the exploration from 2010, of the IMF Jamaica relationship, traversing the ebb and flow within Jamaica's socio-political economy, as well as the discourse, practice and governance of both.

Bridging the political divide, Vision 2030, engenders dimensions of ownership, multipartite partnership, and modalities of social governance within the IMF programme.

Completing the IMF lending relationship, Covid-19- as a fly in the proverbial ointment leaves the jury out, on Jamaica going 'Back again'."

—Lloyd George Waller, *Ph.D., Waikato, New Zealand*

Contents

Abbreviations

AGRO 21	Agricultural Programme 1970s
ALCAN	Aluminium Company of Canada
ALCOA	Aluminum Company of America
ASYCUDA	Automated System for Customs Data
Bauxite MOU	Bauxite Memorandum of Understanding
BFE	Blaise Financial Entities
BITU	Bustamante Industrial Trade Union
BOJ	Bank of Jamaica
CARE	COVID-19 Allocation of Resources for Employees
CARICOM	Caribbean Community
CARPHA	Caribbean Public Health Agency
CARTAC	Caribbean Technical Assistance Centre
CAST	College of Art Science & Technology
CBI	Caribbean Basin Initiative
CD	Certificate of deposit
CEM	Country Economic Memorandum
CFE	Century Financial Entities
COVID-19	Coronavirus Disease
CPI	Consumer Price Index
CPU	Central Planning Unit
CTMS	Central Treasury Management System
DfID	Department for International Development
DLP	Democratic Labour Party
EFF	Extended Fund Facility
EPI	Environmental Performance Index
ESAF	Enhanced Structural Adjustment Facility

EU	European Union
FAA Act	Financial Audit and Accountability Act
FAO	Food and Agriculture Organisation
FINSAC	Financial Sector Adjustment Company Limited
FRF	Fiscal Responsibility Framework
FRL	Fiscal Responsibility Law
FSC	Financial Services Commission
FSSF	Financial Sector Security Fund
GATT	General Agreement on Tariffs and Trade
GCI	Global Competitiveness Index
GDDS	General Data Dissemination System
GDP	Gross Domestic Product
GEF	Global Environment Fund
GOJ	Government of Jamaica
HEART	Human Employment and Resource Training
HIPC	Heavily Indebted Poor Countries Initiative
IAEA	International Atomic Energy Agency
ICU	International Clearing Union
IDB	Inter-American Development Bank
IDP	International Development Partner
IFS	International Financial Statistics
ILO	International Labour Organisation
IMF	International Monetary Fund
JAMPRO	Jamaica Promotions Corporation
JCSA	Jamaica Civil Service Association
JDX	Jamaica Debt Exchange
JHTA	Jamaica Hotel & Tourist Association
JLP	Jamaica Labour Party
JRC	Jamaica Railway Corporation
JTA	Jamaica Teachers' Association (JTA),
JUPOPE	Jamaica Union Public Officials Public Employees
KPH	Kingston Public Hospital
LTO	Large Taxpayer Office
MDA	Ministries, Departments and Agencies
MDG	Millennium Development Goals
MFI	Multilateral Financial Institution
MLGCD	Ministry of Local Government and Community Development
MNCs	Multinational Corporations
MoEYC	Ministry of Education Youth & Culture
MOF	Ministry of Finance
MOH	Ministry of Health
NAJ	Nurses Association of Jamaica
NDP	National Development Plan

NGO	Non-Governmental Organisations
NIR	Nominal Interest Rate
NIS	National Insurance Scheme
NO	National Outcome
NPA	National Planning Agency
NPIMD	National Policy on International Migration and Development
NTA	National Training Agency
NWU	National Workers Union
OAS	Organization of American States
OPP	Obligatory Passage Point
OTI	Omnibus Tax Incentive Law
PAHO	Pan-American Health Organisation
PATH	Programme of Advancement through Health and Education
PDP	Plan Development Process
PDU	Plan Development Unit
PIOJ	Planning Institute of Jamaica
PNP	People's National Party
PRC	People's Republic of China
PSBA	Precautionary Standby agreement
SAF	Structural Adjustment Facility
SAL	Structural Adjustment Loan
SBA	Stand-By Arrangement
SCF	Standby Credit Facility
SDG	Sustainable Development Goals
SDR	Special Drawing Right
SEPROD	Soap & Edible Products
SET Cash	Supporting Employees with Transfer of Cash
STATIN	Statistical Institute of Jamaica
T21	Threshold-21 Jamaica Model
TVET	Technical and Vocational Training
UAWU	University and Allied Workers Union
UDC	Urban Development Corporation
UN Women	United Nations Entity for Gender Equality and the Empowerment of Women
UN	United Nations
UNAIDS	Joint United Nations Programme on HIV/AIDS
UNDP	United Nations Development Programme
UNEP	United Nations Environmental Programme
UNESCO	United Nations Educational, Scientific and Cultural Organisation
UNFPA	United Nations Population Fund
UNICEF	United Nations Children's Fund
USA	United States of America

USAAW	Union of Schools Agriculture and Allied Workers (USAAW)
USAID	United States Agency for International Development
USD	United States Dollar
UTASP	Union of Technical, Administrative and Supervisory Personnel
WB	World Bank
WIF	The West Indies Federation
WIFLP	The West Indies Federal Labour Party
WISA	The West Indies Sugar Association

List of Figures

List of Tables

CHAPTER 1

Introduction

Context

The Jamaican economy was burdened with a legacy of debt originating from the resolution of the 1990s financial sector crisis and compounded by the cumulative effect of high fiscal deficits, public enterprise-related contingent liabilities, and tightened international credit markets that required higher and higher rates of interest on marginal loans. Compared to other Caribbean nations which were growing between 4 and 12% annually, Jamaica's exhibited a low economic growth of 1% annually with multiple years of negative growth. The situation was exacerbated by the spillover from the impact of the global food price crisis and the global economic and financial sector crisis which sent economies across the world into deep recession. This further stymied the growth prospects in Jamaica and, in fact, instigated concerns regarding the viability of the Jamaican economy. The economic fallout severely impacted the Jamaican diaspora and severely curtailed the flow of remittances which has proven to be a major coping mechanism for many Jamaicans. In turn, the decline in remittance flows implied reduced foreign exchange inflows into Jamaica. Fluctuations in and the eventual decline of the global price of alumina on the world market compelled the Russian owners of the West Indies Alumina Company (Windalco), United Company RUSAL (UC RUSAL) to take the decision to close their least profitable plants which had direct implications for Windalco in Jamaica. Since the 1970s, UC RUSAL's

C. Clarke and C. Nelson, *Jamaica's Evolving Relationship with the IMF*,
https://doi.org/10.1007/978-3-030-59204-2_1

investments which were made into three plants in Jamaica, served to re-energize and revitalize the sector. The resultant closure signalled the rolling back and a declining trend (Foster, 2010). Windalco managed by UC RUSAL, consisted of two bauxite producing plants and a port in Jamaica, which when the closure was imminent, advised that it would send home its workforce of 760 employees, by the end of March 2010. This was against the backdrop of Jamaica's largest bauxite and alumina production company Alumina Partners of Jamaica (ALPART) also closing its doors, six months earlier in July 2009, making redundant 1000 salaried employees. With the decline in real income and an increase in unemployment, domestic demand became weakened with inflation reaching 7.5% by the end of 2010/2011.

Specific to the months prior to 2010, the global economic conditions and financial fallout caused by the 2008 financial crisis, served to only worsen Jamaica's situation, as the door to access resources from financial markets used to fund budgetary and fiscal gaps was albeit closed. The closing of the financial markets in the aftermath of the global economic crisis essentially unraveling the access by Jamaica to resources which served to provide a means to fund its fiscal gaps. There were severe challenges displayed in the inability to serve his high debt levels of up to 135% of GDP.

The foreign exchange receipts from tourism remittances and mining received a severe hit in terms of inflows. The triumvirate of insecurity in the job market which affected the revenue flows from tourism, uncertainty in the foreign exchange flows from the diaspora due to the economic impact of the financial crisis, as well as falling price in the global market for bauxite combined, significantly curtailed the income and foreign exchange inflows to enable Jamaica to finance its programmes.

Why Debt Restructuring?

The accumulation of Jamaica's debt was attributed in part to the domestic financial crisis whereby the Jamaican government sought to mitigate its effect by absorbing the debt burden which formed the bulk of the debt overall. The cost of the financial sector crisis and bailout added 40% of GDP to the debt (GOJ, 2011).

Further, Jamaica's high debt levels resulted in the closure of international capital markets to Jamaica from 2008. In prior decades, public expenditure had been supported by extensive external borrowing which enabled the provision of foreign exchange to mitigate fiscal shortfalls and external account deficits (King & Richards, 2008). The current account deficit persisted due to accessing local and international bond markets during the 1990s, in order to provide resources for the Government to service and maintain a large debt load in the most part, being a public contingent liability. The aggregation of the interest rate payments and their variations over the years depending on the terms and conditions imposed by international credit markets, upon the accumulated debt, exposed the Government to wide-ranging vulnerabilities as well as exacerbating the costs incurred. Government's borrowing in the volatile markets overseas and in the domestic market increased the portion of the debt attributed to interest rate payments.

This variability of interest rate payments exposed the Government to difficulties in managing the debt portfolio. Concomitant with the use of public resources to mitigate the financial crisis there was growth also occurring in non-interest current expenditures whereby Jamaica's average debt to GDP ratio was 143% between 2009 and 2013 (Schijman et al., 2014). Reinhart and Rogoff (2010) find that public debt to GDP in excess of 90% has a negative impact on economic growth. Blake (2015) determined from his study that the impact of public debt on economic growth was negative using quarterly data from 1990 to 2014.

Hudson and Stennett (2003) opined from their study concerning the sustainability of the current account, that the economy's net external liabilities would grow, alongside the risk of a growing investor perception that the debt was unsustainable. Jamaica's external debt consisted of commercial debt (mostly global bonds) and debt to official creditors (bilateral and multilateral). Domestic debt comprised of GOJ securities and direct commercial debt. By 2009 Jamaica's debt was 140% of GDP the bulk of which was owed to domestic creditors. Summers (1996), intimates that current account deficits in excess of 5.0% of GDP are excessive which was supported in the wake of the Asian Financial crisis whereby the countries prone to contagion were those that had large current account deficits during the 1990s. However, this militated against the country's real exchange rate and the degree of excess would be relative to an 'optimal benchmark'. Total public sector debt also included domestic and external publicly guaranteed debt. The challenges and difficulties that the legacy of debt exerted on the development prospects for the Jamaican economy was a contentious area of debate between the two political parties, at various points of in time, according to the outcomes of electoral cycles over time, whereby each would be put in office and be tasked, in terms of treating with the debt. Remedial measures policies and approaches exercised by each administration that could be used to curtail debt accumulation, close the gaps and address weaknesses within the structure of the economy over the years had limited and sometimes converse effects, by further increases.

One recourse, that was heavily debated by both political parties, in the 2006/2007 Budget Debate was the suggestion to recourse to the use of the recently signed Petrocaribe Agreement. This Agreement initiated by Venezuela, allowed countries in the region to finance a portion of their petroleum consumption needs at preferential interest rates. It was highlighted by the Leader of the Opposition, in the debate, that the savings from these purchases could be invested and used to retire the more expensive debt commitments. Proceeds from the arrangement were estimated to yield 18 billion dollars by the end of the fiscal year that could be utilized to reduce the debt stock as well as have a corollary effect of reducing the revenue required for debt servicing.

Adjuncts from this, was that resources could also be separated and securitized creating bonds which would be backed by these flows to receive interest rates at levels below that at which resources are being borrowed where by the bond proceeds would repay more expensive debt and lower the interest rate burden. Another option suggested was to loan resources from multilateral institutions which would also have a lower interest rate cost differential to replace expensive instruments as they reached their maturity and consequently limit the demand to resolve to the international capital markets for high-cost instruments. The economy, due to the constraints and limited access to financing, resorted to measures involving short-term pro-cyclical fiscal and monetary policy in their respective approaches.

Broader Economic Concerns

The status of the economy was such that real GDP per capita had remained flat since the 1990s and the debt accumulation served to perpetuate low growth which in turn led to the deterioration of the fiscal accounts leading further to reductions in the standard of living. Overall macroeconomic uncertainty, weak infrastructure and institutions, compounded by bureaucratic red tape resulted in business processes being retarded and developments thereunder being impacted heavily by limitations in accessing finance. In the broader society, pressing social issues such as rising poverty, crime and violence further contributed to an unsavoury business environment which in addition to other features of the economy, resulted in high failure rates for businesses. Prefaced against the background of a private sector that lacked dynamism, there were some successes in some sectors namely tourism and agriculture and niche markets however these had very few linkages with the rest of the economy.

Some studies (IDB, 2016) have shown that the economy suffers from hysteresis, reflecting a reduced growth in productive capacity, whereby certain structural factors contribute to weak economic performance. Commensurate with this the public sector demonstrated low efficiency and effectiveness which has contributed to inadequate allocations of resources as well as weak public financial management practices. This diagnosis has been further compounded but the impact of accumulated debt has exerted further constraint in infrastructural development as well as impacting social investments, which further challenges the provision of public services overall.

It was determined that there were heightened complexities and multi sectoral linkages in the areas of crime which surfaced as a major problem in Jamaica with widespread impact. Overall crime and violence have been highlighted as a major deterrent for investments, compounded by indicators that the outstanding challenge for boys and young men that underperform in education simultaneously the victims and perpetrators of crime (World Bank, 2003; UNODC, 2007). Connected with this were corollary concerns relating to public sector employment and an increase in the police and security forces, comprising a large percentage of the public sector workforce with implications for the public sector wage bill and responding to the challenges presented by criminal activities.

Additional vulnerabilities in the economy had also been signalled, related to extreme weather events in addition to climate change effects which have broad brush impacts on the economy overall. Consequently, adequate supplementary provisioning was required to further economic resilience to climate shocks which translate across sectors, thus the agenda to respond requires a cross sectoral approach. Climate change has had a debilitating influence on the Jamaican economy requiring enhanced measures towards climate resilience due to the risks which have the potential to impact the Jamaican economy in varying dimensions. There are risks, given the vulnerability of the human population in terms of health and potential for loss of life and livelihoods. Overall well-being can be impacted negatively, especially of the rural population and human settlements due to the type of physical infrastructure or lack thereof. The economic effects on agriculture as well as the risks for the loss of income especially for those rural populations that are highly dependent on the sector are factors that need to be considered. Given Jamaica's commitment to the achievement of the Sustainable Development Goals (SDGs) there was the need to increase productivity and foster the domestic drivers of growth, engendering heightened competitiveness towards support for the development and sustainability of strategic investments (See Chapter 11 of this volume) to undergird these objectives.

Contextualizing the IMF Stand-by Agreement 2010

The JLP administration took office in September 2007 and after seven months in office they embarked upon a "new framework for development' involving fiscal consolidation, debt management and tax reform. Critical pillars of focus involved reforming the financial system and implementing a comprehensive debt management strategy. Other supporting objectives included furthering greater efficiency, by reforming the public sector, divesting public bodies as well as streamlining efficient levels of expenditure. The calendar year for 2009 however, saw the economy contracting by 2.7% attributed to declining trend for Mining, Quarrying, Manufacturing and Construction, although there was a positive growth of 12.1% for Agriculture Forestry and Fisheries sectors. The contraction by 1.5% of real GDP in FY2008/2009 had the expected projection that there would be an additional reduction of 3.5% in FY2009/2010. This was attributed to the severe weakening of the largest revenue earners to the economy such as tourism and mining as well as the rising incidents of crime reflected by a peak in the homicide rate of 62.8 per 100,000 inhabitants becoming severe deterrents of two business investments and consumer confidence in 2009.

Measures were taken to enhance revenues but with limited success however improvements in the balance of payments of 7.3% of GDP were the outcome of a reduction in the merchandise trade deficit which was complemented by increases in the surplus with respect to services sub accounts which had realized improvements compared to the four years prior. Experiencing significant shortfalls in foreign exchange earnings led to the Government drawing down heavily on the Net International

Reserves to help minimize the impact, leading to a sharp decline in this stock. The impacts on the economy included Treasury bills trending downward from 20.51% and 21.77% at the end of March 2009 to 15.95% and 16.8% respectively by the end of December 2009. Inflation was 10.2% in 2009 compared to 16.8% in 2008 which was influenced by higher international commodity prices especially fuel and oil as well as the impact of government revenue measures. Inflation was projected to be 13.5% for the next fiscal year. The Jamaican dollar had depreciated by 22%, interest rates were raised above 20%, the debt to GDP ratio was around 150%, investor confidence weakened and access to credit was drying up (IMF, 2010).

Stand-by Arrangement (SBA) 2010

In early 2010, Jamaican authorities, under the leadership of Prime Minister Bruce Golding of the Jamaica Labour Party (JLP) negotiated and reached an agreement with the IMF on a 27-month Stand-by Arrangement (SBA), being the first such arrangement in 14 years. The objectives of the SBA of 2010 reiterated that the Government:

- firmly committed to implementing policy reforms to fundamentally transform the Jamaican economy and create the conditions for strong and sustained growth.
- sought to put the public debt/GDP ratio firmly on a downward trajectory,
- had the intent to entrench fiscal discipline and accountability within Government,
- aimed to significantly increase real GDP growth rates.

Notably, the IMF's instrument of a Stand-by Agreement (SBA) has been frequently accessed by middle income or even advanced countries, which allows for flexibility in the arrangement as the Fund respond to their needs and to address balance of payments problems. The SBA framework, upgraded in 2009, allowed access to Fund resources with a degree of flexibility and responsiveness to evolving issue. It also allowed for the provision of short-term financing, in the case of Jamaica in 2010, for a period of 27 months, to support country adjustment policies.

The Agreement embodied commitments by the Government of Jamaica to pursue reformation in terms of its economic policies and to access resources with a view to remedy the weaknesses in policy and structural elements that heightened Jamaica's macroeconomic vulnerabilities. At March 2010 the Net International Reserves stood at USD1.75 billion representing enough coverage for imports of goods and services for 17.4 weeks. The current account deficit on the other hand was 8.5% of GDP which was an improvement in previous fiscal year. The IMF SBA targets were also revised to J$106.7 billion dollars or 9.6% of GDP. In the first quarter of the Agreement January to March 2010, the prior actions were achieved which included a debt reduction measure, the Jamaica Debt Exchange (JDX) package which demonstrated a commitment to enter the SBA arrangement initially, coupled with tax reform and divestment commitments. At that time, it was estimated that the entire debt exchange operation, relative to the securities, would yield savings of over 3% of GDP in FY2010/11 which would enable a reduction in the amount of debt maturing during 2010–2012 by at least two-thirds.

Jamaica Debt Exchange (JDX) 2010

There were a number of contributing factors that precipitated the Jamaica Debt Exchange (JDX) of 2010, one of which, was the need to bring debt servicing closer to a sustainable level, in terms of the Government's ability to service it, given the context of worsening macroeconomic conditions. These measures were also undertaken against the backdrop of an assessment which suggested that the financial sector would respond positively and there would be no adverse impact. The JDX, aimed to lower the interest burden and lengthen the maturity profile (Johnston, 2015) of the Government's outstanding debt. Consequently, the Jamaica Debt Exchange (JDX) was structured with a degree of stress testing, with the provision of centralized support measures to mitigate against any risks to ensure the maintenance of the stability of the financial sector.

The JDX was designed to support complementary actions aimed at financial stability through the execution of a comprehensive liability management programme consisting of Jamaica's domestic debt, marketed as the Jamaica Debt Exchange (JDX). The integrity of the financial system overall was buttressed with cost savings for the Government at the expense of the bondholders. The JDX was also a pre-condition for approval of the Stand-By Arrangement being negotiated with the International Monetary Fund with a view to provide public accounts with some degree of space so that more growth enhancing public investments could be pursued as well as reducing borrowing costs for the private sector. The closing date for bondholders to respond to the offer was 26 January 2010. Through the JDX, the Government sought to consolidate some 350 domestic instruments into 23 fresh bonds and extend their maturities which would reduce the coupon rates from as high as 28% towards an average coupon rate of 12%. The government also engendered a cut in interest payments by stretching the maturities on JMD700bn (US$7.8bn) worth of domestic securities and extending their tenures by just over two years. One of the incentives and support for participation was the creation of the Financial System Support Fund (FSSF) which was funded jointly by the IMF, World Bank and IDB in the event that—despite the rigour of the stress testing applied to the system to assess its susceptibility to market risks—there was deep and widespread need to support domestic financial institutions with liquidity if the eventuality arose. The liquidity would only be available if an institution participated in the JDX and exchanged in excess of 90% of their debt holdings (Grigorian, et al. (2012).

The benefits envisaged from the JDX included fulfilling prior conditions enabling the finalizing of a US$1.25bn Stand-by Arrangement (SBA) that was being negotiated with the IMF as well as support from other multilaterals of about US$1.1bn. It was envisaged that the reduced debt service costs as well as the support received in the context of commitment to an SBA programme, would position Jamaica to be better able to engineer its economic recovery. After the successful debt exchange, Treasury bill auctions in March saw market rates declining from 10.18% on the 3 months and 10.49% on the six-months instruments. On the other hand, average interest rates declined and interest payments as a share of GDP declined from 17% in FY 2009/10 to 9.3% in FY 2011/12.

Quantitative targets involving tax administrative reform as well as with respect to the execution of capital spending, signalled the commitment to the Programme. Supporting efforts to achieve the primary balance targets as well as the debt targets, the idea was to engender contributions to an overall comprehensive balance towards furthering the achievement of the targets.

The economic platform of the SBA, involved fiscal consolidation, based on wage freezes, reduced expenditure and increasing revenues. Some of the measures under the SBA entailed an ambitious programme of fiscal consolidation which was preceded by the prior actions such as the JDX a comprehensive debt management strategy was developed in addition to a number of reforms to further strengthen the financial system. Other measures included strengthening the safety net to ensure that the adjustment burden which should effectively across society and economic agents buttressed by the strengthening of the social safety net to suffer the negative impact on the poor as well as programmes being more targeted and expansive.

Actions had been completed that enabled positive movements with respect to the structural reform agenda with all structural benchmarks achieved by the end of March. Quantitative targets with respect to the primary balance, public sector balance and debt under the programme were met and the Programme resided upon three central and interrelated pillars:

1. Streamlining expenditure fiscal consolidation strategy, focused on of non-core public bodies; and reforming the public sector divestment
2. Debt management strategy that decisively addresses the debt overhang (Schmid, 2016); and reforms to further strengthen the financial system.
3. Monetary policy will aim at bringing inflation down to mid-single digit levels and maintaining it at those levels within the context of exchange rate flexibility.

The overall fiscal policy agenda involved the Government committing to a reduction of the public sector deficit by 12.75% of GDP in 2010 to 5% in FY 2011/2012. The intention was to curtail rising public debt and to entrench methods concerning fiscal discipline and accountability and at the same time, enable fiscal consolidation by streamlining expenditures. Other areas included negotiate and concluding an agreement on the divestment of Air Jamaica or initiate plans to liquidate the airline by June 2010.

Structural Benchmarks

These included passing a Fiscal Responsibility Framework and accompanying legislative amendments. There was also a requirement to review and revise the Bank of Jamaica's (BOJ's) concept paper for an Omnibus Banking Law and the related legislative and regulative framework to strengthen the oversight of the financial sector. Additional to a temporary freeze on issuing new licences for security dealers was put into effect for those whose business model was based on repos and other short-term liabilities for February 2010.

Several pilot projects were to be launched to help assess the costs, savings, and efficiency gains expected from the reform proposals. Staff noted the importance of ensuring that the objective of reducing the wage bill is highlighted in this process.

In the financial sector, the authorities were moving ahead with reforms to strengthen the supervisory and regulatory frameworks. Although still weak, the economic activity was better than originally anticipated as a result of better than projected performances in agriculture and tourism. Investor sentiment improved significantly since the approval of the SBA and the JDX which was more successful than assumed in the programme. No financial institution needed to access the Financial Sector Support Fund (FSSF)

There existed a risk to the Programme's performance being adversely impacted by the deteriorating security situation from the Tivoli Incursion which had the potential risk to filter over to impact tourism as well as negative investor sentiment.

Spillovers from the Eurozone debt crisis risk also constituted a major risk. Any loss of momentum in the global recovery and/or increase in sovereign risk premia could threaten programme objectives, by weakening economic activity and contributing to revenue shortfalls; increasing interest expenditures; and putting pressure on the current account

Fiscal Responsibility Agenda

Governments experience challenges with respect to spending excesses beyond budgetary limits as well as excessive borrowing.Consequently fiscal rules are implemented to rein in spending in excess of budgetary caps, as well as excessive borrowing, which has implications for the debt stock. As a result, successive budgetary cycles reflect the receipt of debt as a legacy from previous administrations, so the agendas of successive governments are undermined and the country overall, with respect to development and economic growth.

The objective of the Fiscal Responsibility Framework (FRF) was to enable public financial management to be improved by extending the coverage of the budget to all government institutions. Consequently, forms of spending had to be undergirded by the principle of obtaining budgetary appropriations prior to spending, which was endorsed by Parliament especially with respect to self-financed public bodies. Paragraph 15 of the FRF recognized that despite the positive impact of the JDX that there was still a risk for fiscal sustainability because of the stock of debt and the nature of its structure, which would require a strict adherence to the fiscal targets in the programme to adequately manage (GOJ, 2011)

The Fiscal Responsibility Framework (FRF) was approved in March 2010 along with measures and other structural targets, such as the transfer of Air Jamaica to Caribbean Air, a freeze on licences for security dealers and the presentation of a framework paper for the Omnibus Banking Act which were accomplished. The Fiscal Responsibility Framework (FRF) therefore, strengthens sanctions applicable for non-compliance in terms of;

- deferred financing mechanisms which are prohibited;
- internal consistency between the medium-term fiscal strategy and the annual budgets;
- comprehensive audits of tax incentives to be completed;
- ensuring a comprehensive revenue administration and Central Treasury Management System (CTMS) which are to be implemented.

The passing of fiscal responsibility legislation was therefore of great importance in an effort to increase certainty and a degree of predictability in fiscal performance, which has a direct relationship to the degree of institutional and managerial reforms which appear to place fiscal responsibility in the hands of the institutions and public sector. However, in this legislative context, what was apparent was that the powers of the minister increased in terms of responsibility and accountability. This is a necessary component, which now holds the political directorate responsible for fiscal performance and also holds them accountable. Some fiscal targets may be legislated in the context of fiscal responsibility laws that enhance operational transparency and the exchange of information. Nevertheless, the accountability of the minister is strengthened with the powers provided (Bullock, 2009).

To enable coherence between the plans and policies of Government to support activities for economic development, the fiscal management strategy employed had to further this, as well provide for assessments of the required Government finances needed to accomplish them. Altogether these had to possess conformity overall to the Fiscal Responsibility Statement (FRS). The Auditor General had a role to make comments on the Fiscal Policy Paper (FPP) to Parliament, in terms of efficacy, any anomalies, deviations, the premises and conventions which informed decision-making.

Financial Sector Reforms

Reforms in the financial sector entailed strengthening the supervisory and regulatory framework with respect to collection investment schemes as well as the revision of the Prudential framework for security dealers. a concept paper which targeted measures to combat unregulated financial organizations were also commissioned. The legislation committee considered two bills: The Financial Administration and Audit (FAA) (Amendment) Act; and the Public Bodies Management and Accountability (PBMA) (Amendment) Act, 2010.

The amendments to the PBMA Act appear to be less substantial. There are adjustments to the requirements for the presentation of corporate plans with explicit responsibilities for 'the responsible' (sector) Minister and for the Minister to table consolidated budgets of selected public bodies along with the central-government budget. There was a stronger articulation of the role of boards, executive management (performance agreements recommended) and auditors and a requirement for the Minister to table an annual report of action taken by the attorney general for remedies for any breaches of the PBMA Act.

The Act to Amend the FAA Act spoke to refining, and making explicit, definitions of credit agreements and deferred financing on 29 January 2010. A Further Amendment the FAA Act, on February 23, substantively addressed the sharpening of the powers and responsibilities of the Minister of Finance, the Financial Secretary (FS) and the Auditor General (AG). Central to this amendment was the insertion of a new Part VII—'Fiscal Responsibility Framework' (FRF.) whereby the Minister became responsible for presenting, with the budget, a Fiscal Policy Paper (FPP) to include a macroeconomic framework, a Fiscal Responsibility Statement (FRS) and a Fiscal Management Strategy (FMS).

These Acts in concert, sought to establish the legal framework for the FRF, and to empower the Minister to improve the management of public finances by addressing current weaknesses in the fiscal policy and improve the efficiency and transparency within administrative systems in the country. The FAA Act provides explicitly for a Fiscal Responsibility Statement reflecting the minister's opinion of prudent levels of fiscal balance and debt, proposed fiscal-policy measures and a declaration that he will adhere to the principles of prudent fiscal management. The law will provide for:

a. Specific principles of fiscal management and the fiscal targets to be achieved in the medium term;
b. The annual tabling of a fiscal policy paper with the national budget,
c. The presentation of an accompanying debt management strategy;
d. Commitments towards fiscal discipline in budget preparation and execution;
e. Prior approval from the Minister for borrowing by public bodies; and
f. Independent assessment by the Auditor General on the Government's adherence to the principles of fiscal prudence.

A report on economic and public financial performance is to be laid in the House twice per year, inclusive of a tax-expenditure statement, showing waivers, exemptions and other revenue foregone, to be presented with the Budget. Wage agreements were to be consistent with the state of public finances.

Given the challenging economic environment, Staff emphasized the importance of remaining vigilant on containing spending and developing contingency plans in the event of revenue shortfalls. The authorities considered that new tax policy measures would have limited benefits in the event of revenue shortfalls, given their uncertain yields in a low-growth economic environment. Despite the authorities' plans to introduce new legislation aimed at implementing a formal policy on dividend and profit transfers by public bodies, the capacity to generate additional revenues to the government in FY2010/11 was small under the programme design.

Primary expenditure containment was the main instrument towards achieving fiscal targets if revenue did not perform as anticipated. The staff therefore urged the government not to waiver on its commitment to keep the wage bill within the budgetary envelope. Staff fully supports the authorities' initiative to restrict the use of tax incentives, waivers and exemptions which were complicating and undermining tax administration and compliance. Fund Staff noted the preparation of action plans to implement key reforms in revenue administration and Central Treasury Management (CTM). Staff noted that public sector reform initiatives were moving forward on schedule. The commission set up by the Prime Minister on public sector reform had submitted its preliminary recommendations to the Cabinet.

Contributions to Achievements of Targets?

Overall performance was strong, with all March 31st quantitative targets being met. Performance increased in relation to tax administration efforts, restrained spending on goods, services and capital, which facilitated meeting the primary balance and debt targets for the central government. The March 31st structural benchmarks were met and in the fiscal arena, a new Fiscal Responsibility Framework (FRF) was approved by Parliament in March 2010 and it contained several provisions to improve the Public expenditure management system. A freeze was introduced in February on the issuance of new licences for securities dealers whose business model was based on repos which persisted. In March, the concept paper for an Omnibus Banking Act was to be initiated.

Improvements were also considered with respect to rationalizing the antiquated system of tax incentives and the numbers dating back to the 1950s. This system consisted of outdated perspectives and procedures which encapsulated impediments to increasing the diversity and dynamism of the Jamaican economy. This was outside of the significant loss of potential revenue that these outdated incentives and modalities served to forestall for the economy. Consequently, improvements in tax administration more so, given the expenditure constraints, were considered vital with respect to possible revenue coupled with enhanced fiscal performance.

SBA Programme Reviews

Under the First Programme Review it was discussed that even though economic activity was better than expected with respect to tourism and agriculture, the outcome was weak, as growth was minus 2.5% instead of

3.5% resulting in the growth target for fiscal year 2010 to 2011 being revised to 0.5%.

The Quantitative targets with respect to the primary balance and expenditure ceilings were all achieved.

Another observation was that activity bolstered by the SBA approval following the JDX, gave credence to the view that there was an improved investor sentiment implicated by the reopening of the WIDALCO alumina plant in June 2010. Other positive indicators were the lowering of the 30-day policy rate to 9.5% as compared to 12.5% in December 2009 and the issuance of six months Treasury bills at 9.9% which was the lowest rate since the 1980s. The minimum of 90% of existing government paper was to be captured by the design and implementation of modalities of Debt Exchange with the targeting of institutional holders of government paper to maximize participation and involvement. There were efforts to contain expenditure by the under execution of capital spending, divestments and more efficient tax administration efforts. Air Jamaica airlines was sold to Caribbean airlines in May 2010 and the sale of Clarendon Alumina Partners (CAP) was not finalized.

On May 1, Caribbean Airlines assumed full financial responsibility for Air Jamaica's operations. The agreement with Caribbean Airlines allowed for a transition period of 6–12 months to enable the seamless continuation of operations and service and provide the Government of Jamaica with a 16% share of the Trinidad and Tobago airline company. Staff commended the authorities for their hard work in bringing about the divestment of Air Jamaica and their plans to divest Clarendon Alumina Production (CAP) and Petroleum Corporation of Jamaica (Petrojam).

However, there were concerns that the divestment of entities that were unprofitable and made losses, could result in additional expenditure that would impact the direct debt ceilings of central government. Given the proclivity for debt indicators to be impacted and the challenge to limit this, it was highlighted that although the JDX was a progressive measure that improved the debt stock, vulnerabilities persisted with respect to high interest rates, exchange rate shocks with risks for fiscal sustainability, which were ever present. Consequently, this reinforced the need for full adherence to the fiscal targets and the development and implementation of an effective debt management strategy that would buffer the exposure to unforeseen shocks as well as insulate debt dynamics. Despite the positive developments, the debt stock remained vulnerable to exchange rate shocks as well as interest rate variability.

Consequently, it was noted that there were macroeconomic improvements required to sustain the benefits of the JDX to avoid an erosion or reversal of the benefits in terms of interest rate reductions. It was noted that the fall in interest rate costs, making up a considerable share of revenues in recent years would not exclude the need for deleveraging in the future, as the country's stock of debt still remained at over 100% of GDP, with challenges to manage. Notably, an efficient debt management framework and prescribed practices were required to insulate the debt dynamics from such unforeseen shocks.

The Fiscal Responsibility Framework (FRF) was approved in March 2010 with elements to manage public expenditure. In addition, a concept paper for the Omnibus Banking Act, was to be revised and developed with technical assistance from the Fund to strengthen the oversight of the financial sector. Global political economy risks entailed the potential widening of the external current account deficit FY2010/2011 attributed to spillovers from the Eurozone debt crisis with the potential to dampen global recovery and weaken domestic performance.

For the Second Review period, structural benchmarks included the completion of a plan, by June 2010, to establish a central treasury management system by end-2010. In addition, a concept paper to address legislation and other measures required to manage unregulated financial organizations, was to be developed in consultation with the IMF with the same timeline. Fiscal performance was enhanced by improvements in tax administration and the exercise of continued expenditure restraint. GCT inflows came in well about projections despite lower inflation and appreciation of the currency NIR target was exceeded by approximately US$300 million.

The Government was cautious enabling expenditures to fall within the budget and primary spending was contained within programme projections and all quantitative criteria for the end-June review were met. Overall, the economic performance continued to be positive although economic activity remained weak but showed signs of recovery and tourism continued to perform well, not impacted by unrest in Kingston.

Domestic financial markets remained stable. The BOJ lowered policy rate to 8.0% accommodating market trends as the exchange rate stabilized. Non-performing loans (NPLs) continued to rise but at a decreasing rate and the FSSF remained untapped. While declining interest rates had an overall positive impact on the fiscal and debt sustainability indicators, their short-term impact on the primary surplus had been negative as a result of the adverse impact on the withholding tax on interest income.

There was an improved growth outlook reflecting better prospects in growth in agriculture, mining and quarrying and construction in FY 2010/11 to 0.5% and inflation projected to decline to about 6%. However, with respect to social indicators, the unemployment rate was still high and poverty rates were increasing.

In the context of the Second Review, there were events unfolding that had their genesis in 2009 when the Government of Jamaica had received an extradition request from the United States (US) for the Jamaican drug lord Michael Christopher 'Dudus' Coke which stoked the flames of a diplomatic crisis which emerged between the two countries. (Esposito et al., 2010) as well as the Tivoli Incursion.

Prime Minister Bruce Golding, over a period of about nine (9) months, resisted the extradition request, on the grounds of the validity of the process used by the United States to obtain the evidence underlying the request, which contravened rights under the Jamaican Constitution, given that the methodology used, abridged the right of citizens' privacy which would deny its admissibility in criminal proceedings. Golding's prolonged resistance and 'hold' on responding to the United States, pivoted upon being seemingly 'bullied' (Schwartz, 2012) compounded by the apparent US dismissal of Jamaica's request for the resubmission of the extradition request in conformity with the Jamaican Constitution. (Esposito et al., 2010).

The context was clearly compromising for the Prime Minister, in that Mr Coke the alleged "drug lord' in the US extradition request, was incumbent in the West Kingston constituency that had been, according to Spaulding (2011) '*forcefully bequeathed'* to Golding by Edward Seaga', the former leader of the JLP, when he relinquished his post as party leader and MP for West Kingston in 2005.

(Thompson, 2007).

Issues were raised in Parliament by the Opposition in March 2010 and the public thereafter with respect to the role of the international law firm, Manatt, Phelps & Phillips, (MPP), from Los Angeles, California as to whether their services were;

- Being paid for by the Government of Jamaica with public resources.
- Brokered, for them to be an interlocutor in lobbying US officials with respect to the extradition.

- Brokered by Harold C Brady, an attorney-at-law at the time, questioning whether his actions were on behalf of the Jamaican government or the JLP.

It was noted as being uncommon for the services of MPP to be brokered by a third party and the seemingly confusion (Luton, 2010) and mixed messaging that ensued in terms of entire transparency of the arrangement, engendered confusion. The convening and constituting of the arrangement, accountability and understanding of the parties as to the liability or lack thereof of each, in the arrangement, was shrouded. Allegations were levied against Prime Minister Golding for his allegedly protection of Mr Coke as well as trying to pervert the course of justice due to his prominence in Golding's constituency and party. The apparent confusion and non-responsiveness triggered recriminations on the part of the US Government.

However, one could surmise that Golding's decision to delay in responding to the initial US extradition request was, apart from his reticence, a pragmatic one, in the context of Government's efforts in 2009 to broker and concretize the SBA with the IMF. Given the high-risk potential or inevitability for societal disruption and violence, (which actually did materialize in 2010 in the Tivoli Incursion in efforts to apprehend Coke) if Golding had acted in 2009, there would have been a high possibility of delay or even risk of derailment of the 2009 SBA negotiations.

On 10 May 2010, and thereafter as a result of efforts made by the police and security forces to apprehend Mr Coke, a state of emergency was instated for one month from 24 May 2010. The Tivoli Incursion, which involved armed conflict between Jamaica's military and police forces in Tivoli, located in West Kingston and members of the Shower Posse drug cartel allegedly headed by Christopher Coke, which had the intent to apprehend the leader, resulted in the deaths of seventy (70) persons in Tivoli Garden's constituency with residual societal effects thereafter.

The 2010 state of emergency and societal upheaval due to the execution of the extradition request, contributed to the missing of structural benchmarks, namely, the establishment of the Central Treasury Management System (CTMS) and the development of the concept paper to combat Unlawful Financial Operations (UFOs). The overseas technical assistance mission that would have contributed to the development of and completion of the work to inform the structural benchmarks had been delayed as a result of the state of emergency.

The IMF Staff allowed the Government some flexibility in terms of time to achieve their fiscal reforms, which were deferred to September 2010, while components of the reform agenda moving from the design stage and into the implementation stage, namely:

- amendments to the Fiscal Responsibility Framework (FRF);
- Central Treasury Management System (CTMS) components;
- the Public Sector Rationalization Plan;
- various strategies to scale back tax incentives;
- divestment of public enterprises; and
- reforms in relation to tax administration.

The Government continued a gradual approach to easing monetary policy and the BOJ announced the reduction in its projections for end-year inflation from 7½–9½% to 6–8%, noting the potential to help guide and diminish inflation expectations and nominal interest rates, to which the IMF rendered their support.

Public sector salary issues and disputes in FY 2009/10, formed the basis of the Supreme Court's ruling in August 2010, that the government had a legal obligation to honour an agreement made with public sector unions for a 7% increase in public sector salaries. If fully paid, the fulfilment of this legal obligation could cost the Government up to 0.7% of GDP a year. Consequently, there were significant risks to meet the end-fiscal year targets, as well as the possibility of fiscal targets being under pressure as a result of domestic factors, amidst mounting expenditure pressures including damage from Tropical Storm Nicole, resulting in fiscal slippages and aspects the SBA 2010 commitments left in abeyance.

The Third Review revealed that the real GDP had declined by 0.5% due to the lower than projected growth outcomes with regard to increasing trade with Jamaica's trading partners. There were costs incurred with respect to the state of emergency compounded by a decline in interest income due to the JDX which actually reduces the financial sector's GDP by 2.8%. Other concerns related to inflation rising to 11.4% which had implications for food prices and the inflation targets had to be revised for fiscal year 2010/2011 from 6.1% to 7.8%. The destruction of crops as a result of Tropical storm Nicole was another factor that led to the increase in food prices and as of October 2010, preliminary estimates of damage to infrastructure and agricultural lands were US$150 million (USAID, 2011).

Efforts were made to compensate for these gaps by postponing aspects of the Palisadoes Development Project, cutting training, travel and advertising budgets as well as a 60% reduction in non-humanitarian discretionary tax waivers. With respect to alcohol products differential tax rates were applied. There was a strengthening of tax administrative efforts including an outreach campaign with respect to tax administration and a monthly reporting system implemented for expenditure commitments. New regulations to enhance degrees of accountability were also put in place.

At the end of September, the quantitative performance criteria were met however performance relating to the structural benchmarks were mixed. The primary surplus for the first half of fiscal year 2010/2011 of 1.7% of GDP were met.

However structural targets in relation to debt management benchmarks, such as the hiring of a technical advisor and the project manager for the reform programme was not met. The public sector rationalization plan was delayed and amendments to the FRF as recommended by the Fund were also delayed to January 2011. The benchmarks in relation to the central Treasury management system were met and the financial sector reforms were proceeding as scheduled.

Conclusion

The Government reiterated its commitment to the policies and objectives as established in the SBA 2010 as well as the Reviews and structural reform agenda, in the context of an unanticipated appreciation of the currency, lower inflation and the larger than expected decline in interest rates. The IMF Staff agreed to some limited flexibility in the fiscal targets which was deemed justified given the context, due to:

- weak economic activity resulting in reduced projections of the revenues from payroll taxes;
- unexpected spending on the State of Emergency;
- the need to purchase medical equipment for the two main hospitals.

The response of the Government was to request the relaxation of some of the targets equivalent to 0.4% of GDP in the primary surplus and to offset this by reducing budgeted capital spending. The debt dynamics however, only provided a limited room for flexibility which was permitted by the Fund. New structural benchmarks were established, namely;

- Draft concept paper on UFOs to be completed by 31 October 2010.
- Cost assessment of the rationalization of the wage bill over the medium term to be completed by 30 November 2010.

Given the strength of the financial sector, the Fund acknowledged the need to consider options to reallocate some of the resources in the FSSF beginning in 2011 with a view to:

- Maintaining it as part of the Gross International Reserves
- Establishing a general purpose FSSF that can be used during any period of financial sector stress
- Facilitating an early repayment to the Fund
- Deferring discussion to the next Programme Review

Of critical concern was the expenditure pressures which were jeopardizing the attainment of certain targets in the second half of the fiscal year which impacted the IMF Review process, which included:

- the unauthorized purchase of buses;
- the prolonged support of Clarendon Alumina Partners (CAP) and the divestment process;
- payments of outstanding salaries and allowances to public sector workers as opined by the courts; and
- cost overruns in relation to the highway construction projects and Central Government utility bill.

Against the backdrop of a request tendered by Government, the IMF agreed to the partial accommodation of storm-related expenditures and there were measures put in place to compensate for the gaps. However, the Fund was concerned whether these measures were 'one off' in nature as against for the long term, so the feasibility and degree of success was questionable.

The Fund emphasized the importance of trying to secure more savings over the medium term by making structural reforms a priority. There was not a unanimous agreement on the need to tighten the evaluation and monitoring of public investment projects and to keep the wage bill in line with the programme projections.

Payments were made to certain groups of workers and this raised serious concern on the part of the Fund staff with respect to the implications for the timetable for fiscal reforms in the budget and the delay that would result. As events would have it, actions were undertaken by the Government in this regard, in spite of the need for compliance with judicial decisions, surrounding public sector wage negotiations, the cumulative effects severely undermined the Programme.

For fiscal year 2011/2012 public sector rationalization and the costing of it, was a prior action which was left in abeyance, deemed incomplete. In addition, no consultant was hired to undertake the planning and implementation of the tax incentive reform and there were also delays in responding to debt management issues and the hiring of a technical advisor to ensure opportunities with respect to the Central Government external public debt were not missed.

Intensification in the efforts to divest CAP, as well as implement policies to enhance economic growth for the long term by removing constraints to private sector investment and improving the business climate indicators, were also advocated. This was additional to addressing other elements that impacted growth such as poor infrastructure and the high levels of crime.

Overall, there were key concerns with respect to the reform agenda concerning the public sector, tax incentives and debt management. There was a gap in terms of policies being implemented to enhance long-term economic growth, in contrast to the backdrop of negative growth, high unemployment and rising poverty levels. These dimensions required and reflected a demand for reforms on the productive side of the economy to be implemented simultaneously.

Cumulatively, high debt vulnerability to shocks and limited implementation capacity, presented features of a high-risk environment to the programme. Some other conclusions corollary from the reform experience that were demonstrable was the wasted social and political capital, delays in implementation which meant more stricter adjustments to be condensed over a shorter period and these would have implications for Jamaica's credibility, in terms of future budgetary support from the Fund in addition to overtures for accessing multilateral support which strengthens Programme initiatives apart from those engendered by the Fund.

References

Blake, T. (2015). *Investigating the impact of public debt on economic growth in Jamaica* (Working Paper). Bank of Jamaica. Retrieved December 10, 2018, from https://boj.org.jm/uploads/pdf/papers_pamphlets/papers_pamphlets_Investigating_the_Impact_of_Public_Debt_on_Economic_Growth_in_Jamaica.pdf.

Bullock, C. (2009, February 25) *The IMF agreement: Implications for the Jamaican economy*. PSOJ/Department of Economics Seminar. Kingston: University of the West Indies.

Esposito, R., Schone, M., and Martinez, L. (2010, May). U.S. Report: Jamaican Prime Minister Is 'Known Criminal Affiliate' of Hunted Drug Lord. *ABC News*. 24. https://abcnews.go.com/Blotter/jamaica-christopher-dudus-coke-escaped-security-forces-assault/story?id=10737428.

Foster, P. (2010, January). 760 Bauxite Workers to Lose Jobs. *The Jamaica Observer*, 7.

Government of Jamaica. (2011). *Fiscal policy paper*.

Grigorian, M. D. A., Alleyne, M. T. S. C., & Guerson, M. A. D. (2012). *Jamaica debt exchange* (No. 12–244). International Monetary Fund.

Hudson, S., & Stennett, R. (2003). *Current account sustainability in Jamaica* (Working Paper, 2[11], 1–43). Bank of Jamaica.

Inter American Development Bank. (2016). *Country strategy with Jamaica (2016–2021)*. Washington, DC: Inter-American Development Bank.

International Monetary Fund. (2010). *Jamaica: 2010 first review of the stand-by arrangement—staff report*. Washington, DC: International Monetary Fund.

Johnston, J. (2015). *Partners in austerity: Jamaica, the United States and the international monetary fund* (No. 2015–09). Center for Economic and Policy Research (CEPR).

King, D., & Richards, L. (2008). *Jamaica's debt: Exploring causes and strategies*. Caribbean Policy Research Institute.

Luton, D. (2010, May12). Flip-flop: Golding admits sanctioning contract with Manatt. *The Jamaica Gleaner*.

Reinhart, C. M., & Rogoff, K. S. (2010). Growth in a time of debt. *American Economic Review: Papers & Proceedings*, 573–578.

Schijman, A. Khadr, A., Soldano, M., Marto. R., Buitrago, P., Freeman, P., Huppi, M., Florimon, A. (2014). *Approach paper: Country programme evaluation: Jamaica (2009–2014)*. Banco Interamericano de Desarrollo.

Schmid, J. P. (2016). *Addressing debt overhang: Experiences from two debt operations in Jamaica*. Washington, DC: Inter-American Development Bank policy brief IDB-PB-259.

Schwartz, M. (2012, August). Goldings's Golden Spoon. *The New Yorker*, 3. https://www.newyorker.com/news/news-desk/jamaicas-former-p-m-opens-up-about-coke-arrest-extradition.

Spaulding, G. (2011, July). Goldings's Golden Spoon. *The Sunday Gleaner*, 17.

Summers, L. (1996). Commentary. In R. Hausmann & L. Rojas-Suarez (Eds.), *Volatile capital flows: Taming their impact on Latin America* (pp. 53–57). Inter-American Development Bank.

Thompson, K. (2007, September 4). The making of Jamaica's Eighth Prime Minister. *The Daily Observer*, p. 5.

United States Agency for International Development. (2011, October 8). Latin America and the Caribbean—Hurricane Season and Floods (2011) Fact sheet #5.

UNODC, I. (2007). *World drug report*. United Nations, New York, NY.

World Bank. (2003, December 4). *The Road to Sustained Growth* (Report No. 26088-JM). Country Economic Memorandum.

CHAPTER 2

The Second Return: The Road to the Extended Fund Facility (EFF) 2013

Introduction

On 7 October 2007 the *Jamaica Gleaner* (2007) reproduced the text of a speech made by the Opposition spokesperson on Finance in response to his claim that he had no recollection of making certain statements in his speech a year prior. The report of the speech made on 19 July 2006 indicates that the spokesperson expressed the view that the country's nurses ought to be paid a risk premium given the profile of their work and he expressed criticisms of the then Minister of Finance's approach to the plight of the nurses. The spokesperson further proposed that the overtime pay earned by nurses should be untaxed thereby providing them with additional funds on which to survive. Most importantly, he expressed his agreement with the proposal from the President of the Nurses' Association of Jamaica (NAJ) that the salary of nurses needed to be doubled as the their current wage when compared with the main migration outlets of Jamaican nurses were found to be approximately twenty per cent of the potential wage earned in comparable posts. The spokesperson gave a commitment that once he assumed office, doubling the salary of nurses would be the starting point and that he did not foresee a shortage of money to facilitate this increase.

The irony was that, this promise by the Opposition Spokesperson on Finance who later became Minister of Finance on 7 September 2007 on

C. Clarke and C. Nelson, *Jamaica's Evolving Relationship with the IMF*, https://doi.org/10.1007/978-3-030-59204-2_2

the eve of the outbreak of a food price crisis, was eventually a major stumbling block in the implementation of the 2010 SBA with the Fund. The food price crisis, instigated by the scientific community to rapidly increase the commercialisation of commodity-based renewable energy products, resulted in a rapid increase in food prices, the effects altogether threatened to upend strides made in development outcomes particularly those relating to poverty in the decade prior.

About one month prior to the installation of the Minister of Finance, a seemingly unrelated set of incidents in the global financial architecture, began to occur. This process started when the eighth largest bank in assets, BNP Paribas headquartered in Paris, prevented withdrawals from three of their hedge funds which, previously, were heavily traded. Seven days after the installation of the Minister of Finance in Jamaica, Northern Rock, became the first British Bank to have failed due to a bank run, the first such run in one hundred and fifty years. These two events now stand as important signposts in the chronology of the global economic and financial crisis that crippled international credit markets and toppled the fiscal cards of many nations including Jamaica's.

Fortuitously, the new administration had committed to re-engaging the multilateral development partners in a bid to take advantage of lower interest rates, development support, and, to avail themselves of the partnership approach taken by these entities. The domestic financial sector, although liberalized, was duly protected from the types of financial transactions that had fuelled the contagion of the global economic and financial crisis that overtook the world during 2007 and 2008. However, Jamaica's high debt-to-GDP and linkages to the major economies in the Western Hemisphere meant it would eventually have to brave a return to the International Monetary Fund. As indicated in the first volume, Jamaica's relationship with the IMF had been tumultuous and distant at best stemming from the perceived unwillingness of the IMF to provide greater room in its conditionalities to respond to the social and therefore political economy realities faced by the political leaders of economies such as Jamaica.

As the administration settled into government, two experienced trade unionists were appointed to the Ministry of Finance and the Public Service to support the thrust to reform the public sector and to simultaneously refine the pay structure. The latter issue would become a major 'sticking point' in the public sector which would lead to multiple breakdowns in not only the negotiations, but also in the hard-fought IMF

Agreement. Whilst wage negotiation in the public sector might seem straightforward, there are complexities depending on the ability of groups and sub-groups to attract the attention of the Minister of Finance and to present a case regarding the basis on which they should be treated differently. As a result, though there may be a "standard" level of wage increases across the public sector, various groups could have their own add-ons or differential treatments. In addition to the strident and dogged determination of the nurses to remind the new Minister to deliver on his aforementioned promise to double their pay and provide other benefits; the twenty-thousand strong teacher organization—the Jamaica Teacher's Association (JTA) refused to be party to the general public sector wage negotiations, as the previous administration had promised to pay them eighty per cent of what the market was paying teachers in its Heads of Agreement (HOA) with the JTA (Government of Jamaica, 2006). According to the HOA signed by the previous administration, the government had reaffirmed its commitment to completing a study that would '…bring teachers' salaries within 80% of prevailing market rates (private sector rates' (p. 7). This reclassification would emerge from the collaborative preparation of terms of reference to engage a consultant to complete the analysis and support both parties in the negotiation process with a commitment to implement on 1 April 2007.

Individually, these wage claims may appear innocuous; however, when combined with that of the armed forces and other groups, these wage claims would impact roughly sixty per cent of the total central government public sector employment and would therefore have to be funded primarily by a combination of increased taxes, increased debt or reductions in other non-wage areas of expenditure (i.e. capital expenditure). The prospects of increasing debt were slim as at this point debt-to-GDP rates of one hundred and thirty two (132) per cent for Jamaica led it to be categorized as the fourth highest indebted countries in the world (Caribbean Policy Research Institute, 2008). Reductions in capital expenditure has been a trend in Jamaica's history as a bid to contain fiscal deficits and continued structural increases in the debt; however, this has the potential to insidiously curtail the country's long-term prospects for economic growth which was so desperately needed during this period.

Despite the impinging double global crises and the reengagements of the multilaterals as well as the return to the Fund a decade or so after Jamaica had said 'ta-taa' to the latter, these two groups—the nurses and the teachers—that comprise more than fifty per cent of the total public sector employees, insisted on their promised eighty to one hundred per cent wage increases to be honoured. Both groups expressed the view throughout the negotiation period that the government had lost credibility by not honouring these commitments to them through several media modalities (*The Jamaica Gleaner*, 2008a, 2008b). Their stance was essentially due to the extensive period during which these groups had endured strictly administered wage restraint under the Public Sector Memorandum of Understanding (MOU) (Nelson, 2019) during which period the macroeconomic indicators were relatively unstable leading to erosions in purchasing power.

The new administration, faced with these internal pressures and external shocks eventually acquiesced to the demands whilst simultaneously attempting to satisfy IMF programme conditionalities that were primarily focussed on curtailing both planned and unplanned fiscal expenditure. The GOJ and the JTA concluded their negotiation for wage and fringe benefits on 27 October 2008 (Jamaica Information Service, 2008) whilst ratification of the agreement with the NAJ was not effected until 30 April 2009 after several disruptions in the negotiation process. The agreement with the teachers implied the addition of an unbudgeted J$15bn on the national budget (Jamaica Information Service, 2008) and the settlement for the NAJ of more than J$1bn (Hunter, 2010).

Of course, the Fund viewed these unbudgeted expenditures as a breach in principle of Jamaica's expressed intention to establish and entrench fiscal discipline (Government of Jamaica, 2010) despite the fact that the government was obligated to pay after both the Industrial Disputes Tribunal and the Supreme Court ruled in favour of the payments being made to public sector workers (Johnston & Montecino, 2012). The cracks in the economic programme began to emerge twenty-one days after the beginning of the 2010 fiscal year when reports were that the Prime Minister would meet with public sector workers to discuss the J$13.4bn owed to them. This was a blow to the foundation of trust on which the 2010 SBA was forged; and this was especially so in the case of Jamaica, given that only J$2bn was programmed for payments to civil servants in the economic programme that was being supported by the Fund and complemented by funding from the international development partners (IDPs) (see Chapter 6 of this volume). Ultimately, these payments ran contrary to the expressed fiscal consolidation and allied reforms expressed in the Agreement and after three of eight quarterly reviews, the tests were discontinued resulting in non-disbursements from the Inter-American Development Bank and the European Union whose programmed support was contingent upon the continuation of the IMF Agreement.

When combined with the erosion of political capital due to unfolding justice-related events, the administration found itself in the position whereby it was compelled to change its leadership at the highest level in addition to calling an early election that unsurprisingly heralded a change in administration. Nevertheless, the constant in Jamaica's equation was the need to mend and restore the relationship with the IMF because the economic situation would otherwise deteriorate with great difficulty for reversal without their renewed support. The new administration would have no honeymoon. It too had made commitments to deliver on changes that it had not delivered on during its campaign. It would need to revise the economic programme and assemble it with tighter screws to appease the IMF that, along with other development partners, had been burnt in the 2010 Agreement. This would prove to be no easy feat but would eventually yield the long sought-after macroeconomic stability.

The Road to the 2013 Extended Fund Facility

In a bid to distinguish itself as being more capable in the management of the economy, the new administration made public its commitment to successfully complete negotiations for a new agreement with the IMF whilst in its campaign as Opposition. A testament to the extensive nature of the damage to the relationship between Jamaica and the IMF was the perception that was telegraphed about the very short timeframe in which another agreement could be inked. The new Prime Minister had previously indicated her ability to secure an agreement within a short space of time; however, this did not materialize. The technical team leading the discussions for both the GOJ and the IMF engaged in several missions held in Washington and in Kingston in efforts to secure the deal. The promise of a few weeks translated into a period of extended entreaties and negotiations in multiple rounds lasting over twelve months.

It is surmised that Jamaica's abrogation of the IMF Agreement, entailed a betrayal of the faith, trust and institutional capital Jamaica had garnered from the IMF and MDPs at the start of the 2010 SBA, that was now squandered. The Multilateral Development Partners (MDPs) that supported Jamaica under the IMF Agreement had been open, accommodative and in some cases, had extended themselves beyond the norm, were also '*thrown under the bus*'. Thus making the return to the IMF and pro-development arrangements with the MDPs, a difficult one.

The collapse of the 2010 SBA, on the part of the IMF could also be interdiscursively reminiscent of modalities of the relationship between Jamaica and the IMF that were operable during the 1980s and 1990s, signalling its possible return, by Jamaica's subsequent forfeiture and inability to stay the course.

Jamaica's efforts to 'return to the Fund' were extremely arduous, reflected in the length of time and the process entailed in preparing and negotiating a programme with the Fund. Notably, despite having finally secured an Extended Fund Facility (EFF) of $2 billion, there was very little faith that Jamaica could successfully complete this agreement in the corridors of the IMF. Wigglesworth (2020) indicates that the common question uttered when the topic of Jamaica arose at the IMF during the EFF was whether or not the country had crashed yet. This question explicitly demonstrates the extent to which the fierce strictures in both the preconditions and ongoing programme requirements were expected to exert impossible pressures on not just the technical and political arms of the government but also would have resultant effects upon the people of Jamaica. There was no expectation that the population would allow the government to implement the prescribed medicine without significant social dislocation and possibly rebellion against the IMF's 'bitter medicine'.

During fiscal year 2012/2013 a comprehensive National Public Education campaign to increase awareness and understanding of the attendant pillars of the economic reform initiatives was undertaken by the government. This public education campaign, which commenced in November 2012, encompassed but was not limited to stakeholders' fora, town hall meetings and media and advertising campaigns.

The road to the EFF was preceded by a series of preconditions that were intended to ensure that the authorities were disincentivized from breaking their commitment to the signed agreement and to further entrench the push towards fundamental reforms of fiscal policy and to instigate structural changes in the regulation and management of the financial sector and by extension added support to the vulnerable through enhancements to the social safety net. Given the continued burden of the debt-to-GDP ratio despite the interest savings achieved under the Jamaica Debt Exchange (JDX)—which itself was a prior action to the 2010

SBA—the authorities were obliged to implement another debt transaction—coined the National Debt Exchange (NDX)—to further contain and control the maturity of debt instruments and interest payments that the government would have to pay in the short to medium term.

Whilst the initial debt exchange (JDX) resulted in landmark changes in the manner in which debt was acquired and administrated in Jamaica and was well subscribed by all measures, it did not reduce payments substantively, such that within a few months the debt-to-GDP ratio was again on the increase. Both the JDX and the NDX were criticized that they did not sufficiently modify the face value of the outstanding securities and still required relatively high primary surpluses for an extended period of time to avoid a renewed debt build-up. In other words, some observers argued that the debt exchanges were not deep enough and did not address the fundamental solvency problem of the country (Johnston & Montecino, 2012).

In the end, these two debt-rescheduling transactions allowed the authorities to carve out the fiscal space needed to pay down the debt whilst simultaneously making good on their new interest payment commitments. In doing so, it also signalled to market participants that the government was also intent on undertaking and implementing the complementary administrative and legislative changes that would help to support the management of central government expenditure. These changes included the implementation of a Central Treasury Management System (CTMS) that was designed to truly consolidate the proliferation of bank accounts across central government entities in order to address fluctuations and smooth cash flow challenges, previously associated with the Consolidated Fund as well as to enable the government to desist from selling instruments in the market to facilitate recurrent expenditure. In 2015, three years after the second debt exchange, the debt-to-GDP ratio hovered at around 120%—a ratio not seen since 2008.

The required fiscal and social adjustment was even adjudged as being a case study in 'macroeconomic malpractice' by Doyle (2019). Doyle (2019) contrasts the allowed nine per cent primary surplus target in the 2010 Stand-By Arrangement during the heights of the recession with the seven per cent under the EFF.

Highlights of the EFF

Jamaica officially entered a four-year Extended Fund Facility (EFF) with the IMF on 1 May 2013 after almost fifteen months of negotiations. As a prior action conditionality for the EFF, in February 2013, the Government of Jamaica undertook a National Debt Exchange (NDX) consisting of a par-on-par exchange of the Government of Jamaica (GOJ) domestic debt securities. In the NDX the face value of the securities was preserved, the average maturity of extended interest rates on fixed-rate and adjustment margins on variable-rate debt were reduced. This enabled the deferral of a critical debt repayment valued at 8% of GDP in February 2013, along with other measures that served to raise the primary balance to 7.5% of GDP, in addition to public sector wage restraint which altogether, were part of a set of game-changing, time-bound reforms to engender growth in the economy and reduce the public debt to sustainable levels in the context of an EFF with the IMF.

The NDX involved the voluntary participation of the Government of Jamaica's four main creditors (MDCs)—The Bank of Nova Scotia Jamaica Ltd, Jamaica Money Market Brokers Ltd, Sagicor Life Ltd and National Commercial Bank Jamaica Ltd—leading to a change in the terms of their respective deb t contracts and a reduction in the GOJ's debt burden. The reforms undertaken required Ministries, Departments and Agencies (MDAs) within the public sector to implement diverse activities that would enable the GOJ to meet certain quantitative and qualitative targets and various benchmarks as contained within the Memorandum of Economic and Financial Policies (MEFP) of the EFF. The activities of the MDAs would be monitored and coordinated by a Coordinating and Implementation Unit (CIU) created and established within the Ministry of Finance and Planning.

The government launched the NDX in February 2013 and successfully achieved its objective to reduce the debt stock by 8.5% by fiscal year 2019/2020 by obtaining on average, an annual reduction of seventeen billion (J$17bn) in interest costs. The successful NDX represented the achievement of another of the prior actions necessary to secure an agreement with the International Monetary Fund (IMF).

The National Debt Exchange and the implementation of measures dealing with public sector wage restraint and other expenditure containment and revenue-enhancing measures necessary to raise and maintain the Central Government primary balance at 7.5% of Gross Domestic Product

(GDP) were effected. These also contributed to the time-bound fiscal reforms to reduce the public debt to sustainable levels in the context of an Extended Fund Facility (EFF) with the International Monetary Fund (IMF).

Whilst the debt exchange supported the efforts under the EFF to stabilize the Jamaican economy, the country still remained in a vulnerable position given the high level of debt at the beginning of the programme (146% of GDP as of March 2013). Additionally, the macroeconomic framework entailed a lengthy process of fiscal consolidation—given a primary balance of 7.5% of GDP during the programme and seven per cent thereafter—leaving little space for adjustments in case of policy slippages or external shocks (Schmid & Malcolm, 2016). Supporting the second debt exchange entailed the passing of a Public Debt Law as a complementary prior action to consolidate the existing acts as well as to strengthen the institutional framework for debt management.

Understandably, of the six prior actions of the EFF, four related to the parameters that would enable further fiscal consolidation in light of the major departures from the fiscal profile anticipated under the 2010 SBA. The major of these four items attempting to ensure fiscal consolidation was on the expenditure side, that required the signing of an agreement with the major trade unions, representing at least seventy per cent of total government employees, to limit wage increases for the 2012/2013 fiscal year to zero and perfomance/merit increases to no more than 2.5%. Moreover, for the 2013/2014 and 2014/2015 fiscal years, limits would be capped at no more than five per cent for each of those fiscal years.

Prior actions involving fiscal consolidation related to the termination of the use of discretionary waivers were to be approved at the level of Cabinet under the 2013 EFF. Firstly, Cabinet was to adopt a decision regarding the granting of discretionary waivers except in the generally acceptable cases relating to charitable organizations, those already granted under existing contracts or laws, or others under a pre-approved Technical Memorandum of Understanding up to a maximum cap of J$10mn per month. Secondly, Cabinet was to cap general waivers at J$80mn per month and those for charitable purposes at J$250mn per month. Finally, Cabinet was to give up its ability to grant new or extend existing waivers or other tax incentives until the Omnibus Incentive Law was effected. These having been met, and the agreement underway, the government turned its attention to the achievement of the more than sixty benchmarks over the next four years.

The reforms under the IMF Programme required various Ministries, Departments and Agencies (MDAs) within the public sector to undertake activities that would contribute to the delivery of structural benchmarks and quantitative targets as set out in the Memorandum of Economic and Financial Policies (MEFP) agreed with the IMF. These benchmarks were spread across five main areas with Institutional Fiscal Reforms accounting for almost forty-five per cent. This was followed by structural changes to the operations of the financial sector (21.5%), tax reform (16.9%), tax administration (15.3%) and two targeting growth-enhancing types of reforms (3%).

Institutional Fiscal Reforms (IFRs)

The economic programme had to make the implementation of major reforms of several key components of the fiscal framework central to its value proposition to the Fund. This is consistent with the nickname—It's Mainly Fiscal—that is attributed to the IMF and characteristic of the root causes of the imbalances that typically push countries to negotiate for support from the institution.

The first pillar of the IFRs presented in Fig. 2.1 indicates the depth of the programmatic plans to address the weakness and gaps in the fiscal framework and advance the implementation of various tools to enhance government operations, efficiency, and, impact on the wider society. The 2010 SBA had made initial transformations in the area of the government treasury through the development of a plan to operationalize the establishment of a Central Treasury Management System (CTMS) that would consolidate the management of the cash resources across all of government that have been held in multiple bank accounts across a range of financial institutions.

The system that predated the CTMS was described as being fragmented and inefficient as total government resources were sufficient to satisfy government demands for cash, however, because of this method of holding the funds, government had to engage in borrowing to supplement the resources it could obtain through tax revenues. In the development of the CTMS, the Accountant General's Department (AGD) was designated as the account holder and the Bank of Jamaica (BOJ) was engaged as the manager of the Treasury Single Account (TSA) that would replace the several individual accounts held in the financial system. When ministries, departments and agencies (MDAs) required funds, they would

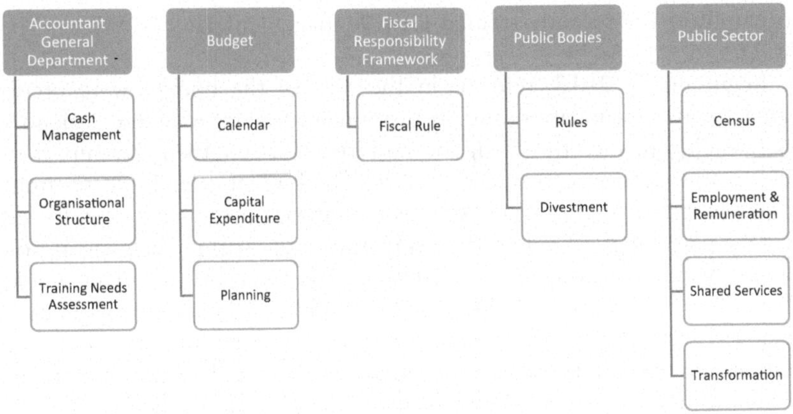

Fig. 2.1 Pillars of Institutional Fiscal Reforms under the 2013 Extended Fund Facility between the IMF and Jamaica (*Source* Author's illustration from Government of Jamaica. [2010]. *Letter of Intent*. Washington, DC: International Monetary Fund)

submit these requests through the online platform in advance and thereby obtain access to same just-in-time to complete the relevant transaction.

This service would be provided by the AGD and its centralization of the process would facilitate reductions in costs and improved efficiencies in the management of resources across all of government. The BOJ, having previously established the Real Time Gross Settlement (RTGS) and Automatic Clearing House (ACH) systems, was deemed a suitable partner to be the custodian of the TSA, whilst the daily sweeping of accounts replenishing the TSA is managed by the commercial banks.

Despite some delays in the implementation of the transition to the CTMS during the 2010 SBA, the programme received renewed emphasis during the 2013 EFF with a focus on completing the technical aspects of its implementation as well as the institutional strengthening of the AGD's office to enable it to execute the various responsibilities it would discharge in the new environment. The Fiscal Policy Management Unit that was previously implementing this function would now be able to focus purely on policy development rather than implementation of day-to-day tasks. A new organizational structure for the AGD and organizational assessment for training needs was undertaken between 2016 and 2017 in order to empower the recently formed Cash Management Unit (CMU) in the AGD.

Beginning in 2013, reforms in the area of the budget were predicated on the formulation and institutionalization of a budget calendar that would enhance the discipline required to strengthen the impact of the discretionary aspects of fiscal policy. The budget calendar institutionalizes discipline at the MDA level as prioritization of activities is forced to take place at the level of the budgeting units within each institution before being submitted to the Ministry of Finance (MOF). This would also ensure that Ministers understand that ad hoc increases in the budget that was facilitated in the past will not be tolerated and therefore line staff are forced to rationalize their proposed plans and ensure their alignment with the various development goals and objectives as well as to their mandate.

The implementation of a Budget Plan with elements and targets that were consistent with the commitments under the EFF by April 2013 was also met by the target date. Following this change, the government implemented a five-year capital budget plan in the form of a Public Sector Investment Program (PSIP). This PSIP was underpinned by institutional capacity in the form of the Public Sector Investment Management Secretariat (PIMSEC) that would facilitate various project analyses and facilitate the tracking of public sector investments over time in addition to supporting the implementation of the PSIP policy paper. Having been implemented, these projects in turn enabled the government to meet its target of presenting a budget to the Houses of Parliament that was consistent with the economic programme by April 2014.

Another significant area related to the development of a conceptual framework for the fiscal rule that would direct the fiscal authorities in the development of the fiscal framework and the limits within which it is permitted to operate as the fiscal path evolves during implementation. This was successfully completed in August 2013 and the legislation required for its adoption was revised over the course of the year that followed. This fiscal rule was used to craft the FY2014/2015 budget and signified further deepening of fiscal discipline in the macroeconomic framework.

The governance and operations of public bodies continued to be an area of emphasis and focus in the 2013 EFF carried over from the initial and historic accomplishments under the 2010 SBA. The 2013 EFF continued to advance the curtailment of the ability of historically loss-generating and debt-increasing to continue to impose unprogrammed and unbudgeted liabilities on the Jamaican population. It further advanced the cauterization of the contingent liabilities associated with the remaining major loss-making public body—Clarendon Alumina Partners (CAP)—by prohibiting its financing and that of any other public body as well as the extension of any guarantees or use of public assets as collateral for CAP apart from those owned by CAP. The government was finally to conclude the divestment or lease of CAP assets; however, this was easier said than done.

Divestment and curtailment was not sufficient to accomplish the needed fiscal consolidation over the medium term or to ensure that the operations of all public bodies would be sustainable whilst implementing the development and/or growth-enhancing mandate under which they operated. In this regard, the government developed an action plan to support public sector transformation using the reports and master plans developed by the Public Sector Transformation Division (PSTD) as part of the previous administration's thrust to reconceptualize the role of the state and to perform assessments of the relevance of all entities operating within the public sector with a view to recalibrate and reorient all organizations under the new mandates. Under the 2013 EFF the focus was on the development of an action plan that would see various aspects of the master plan being implemented. This included the implementation of shared corporate services, the reallocation, merger, abolition, divestment or privatization of departments and agencies, outsourcing of some services, strengthening of the audit and procurement functions in these entities and the realignment of remuneration with job requirements. This plan was developed and a pilot e-census was implemented to identify all government employment positions, salaries and allowances paid to public employees in the Ministries of Finance, Health, Education, Security and Education.

The e-census pilot was implemented and has since been extended to cover all MDAs. It has also enabled the government to complete its review of its terms of employment and analyse the structure and composition of its labour force in order to support the reform of its employment policy. Ultimately, the development of this database enabled the government to obtain a deeper understanding of its potential liabilities in the context of pension payments and contributed to the development of a new pension regime for the public sector.

Tax Policy Reform Agenda

The next set of reforms pertained to that of tax policy which was also comprised of five pillars. The termination of the authority of the Minister of Finance to facilitate the exemption of imports from the payment of duties at the port through the use of discretionary waivers was a major accomplishment of the 2013 EFF. In this regard, the only waivers would be provided to duly registered charities. As indicated in Fig. 2.2, the 2013 EFF further required the review of all entities to determine the extent to which they were the beneficiaries of grandfathered waivers. Although this was not met by the target of end-January 2015 the government would have already implemented broad rationalization of the incentive regime having harmonized the tax treatment for all charities in May 2013 and tabled an Omnibus Tax Incentive Act during September 2013 in the House of Representatives. The Omnibus Act established a modernized framework within which incentives offered were standardized across sectors and types of economic activities in order to reduce the extent to which tax policy and administration resulted in economic distortions and other inefficiencies in economic decision-making and business profitability.

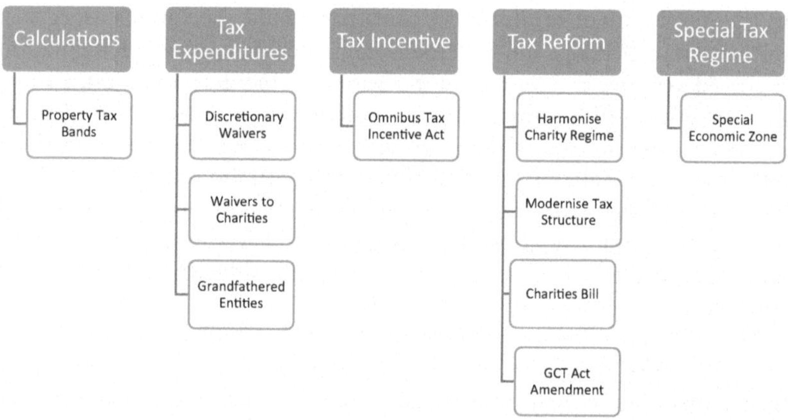

Fig. 2.2 Pillars of Tax Reform Agenda under the 2013 Extended Fund Facility between the IMF and Jamaica (*Source* Author's illustration from Government of Jamaica. [2010]. *Letter of Intent.* Washington, DC: International Monetary Fund)

Broader tax reform efforts included the modernization of multiple tax types to reduce the number of allowed exemptions as well as the applicable tax rates by March 2014. Amendments to the GCT Act were also implemented by end-June 2014 as part of this modernization thrust. The harmonization of the allowances to charities enabled the harmonization of the charity regime and facilitated the tabling of the Charities Bill that streamlined all the tax and other related provisions to support the modernization of this important sector, given Jamaica's wide diaspora. Perhaps, as part of the Ministry of Finance's attempt to support the government's intention to establish a logistics hub complemented by Special Economic Zones (SEZ), it enacted legislation to provide the economic framework and policy that would support the establishment of SEZs whilst ensuring that it also protects the substance of the tax system and prevents revenue leakage as far as is possible.

Tax Administration Reform Agenda

Leveraging the time-bound Tax Administration Reform Action Plan that was completed by the June 2010 target date, the 2013 EFF attempted to make strides in five areas. As the government collects a substantial proportion of its tax revenue at its border based on trade, two of the pillars and three of the sub-areas focussed on transforming critical aspects of the operations at the port, all of which could interface with the tax system. The Automated System for Customs Data—(ASYCUDA World)—was piloted at the Port of Kingston during December 2014 in order support the transformation of the Jamaica Customs Agency (JCA) by facilitating the digitization of all business customs information from declaration and manifesto submission to cargo release.

This digitization has reduced processing and clearance times by one-half as it has supported the use of risk-based inspections of cargo as well as the time to release cargo once payment has been received (see Fig. 2.3). As the ASYCUDA world and Port Community Systems (PCS) are increasingly integrated, efficiencies are expected to increase and support the plans to leverage the improvements of the Panama Canal. Importantly, the digitization of all this data will enable Customs to more easily collate information to support research and analysis that can be used to guide both policy and practice in trade and other areas. The other dimension of this transformation is represented by the initiation of the rewriting of

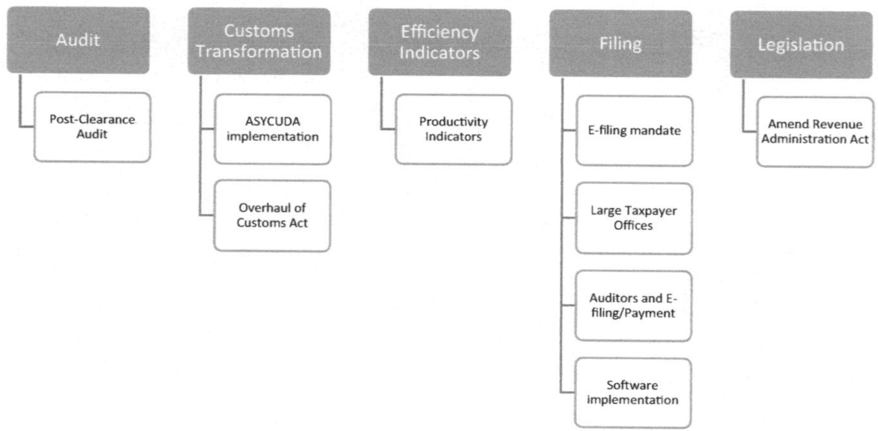

Fig. 2.3 Pillars of the Tax Administration Agenda under the 2013 Extended Fund Facility between the IMF and Jamaica (*Source* Author's illustration from Government of Jamaica. [2010]. *Letter of Intent*. Washington, DC: International Monetary Fund)

the Customs Act that would concretize the transition to a modernized customs agency as well as facilitate further modernization of the entity.

Tax Administration was also a focus area during the 2013 EFF as the government also made it mandatory for all large taxpayers to use the e-filing modality for remitting the GCT and Corporate Income Tax (CIT). These large taxpayers received prior support to adjust to the pending changes in the tax system through the establishment by the government of the Large Taxpayer Office (LTO) and which subsequently benefitted from an increase in the professional staff to support additional audits, e-filing and e-payment at the LTO. Access to and use of third-party information to support the ability of Tax Administration in managing compliance was one component of the revisions to the Revenue Administration Act during 2013. The amendments also included the empowerment of TAJ to mandate e-filing for groups of taxpayers and for various types of taxes.

Financial Sector Reforms

The main areas of focus within the financial sector was on the implementation of several financial sector legal amendments to address three key areas of the financial sector. The first is related to Unlawful Financial Operations (UFOs) and to implement a legal and regulatory framework to facilitate regulated entities that want to offer legal Collective Investment Schemes (CIS) to the investing public (see Fig. 2.4). There were also amendments to support the transition of retail repos from their historical mode of operation which was heavily based on government debt instruments—that would no longer be as prolific as they were historically—to a trust-based framework.

There was also substantive focus on the transformation of the financial sector at the macrolevel concerning the Bank of Jamaica, but from an institutional perspective (see Fig. 2.4). Under the 2013 EFF, support was extended to the government to table an Omnibus Banking Law—the Banking Services Act—that was aimed at ensuring that the BOJ would be able to efficiently deliver on its newly specified mandate—to be responsible for overall financial stability—effectively. Given the experience with the turbulence associated with the global financial and economic crisis, the BOJ also spearheaded and received support for the development of a resolution framework for the entire financial sector that detailed the entire chain of command if a resolution were necessary as well as the

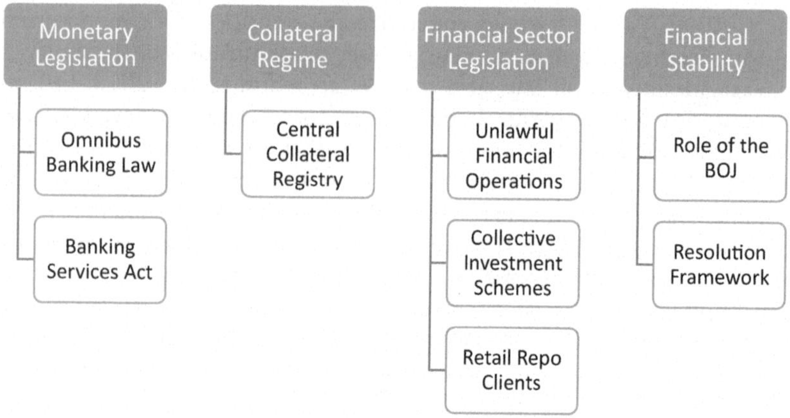

Fig. 2.4 Pillars of the Financial Sector Reforms under the 2013 Extended Fund Facility between the IMF and Jamaica (*Source* Author's illustration from Government of Jamaica. [2010]. *Letter of Intent*. Washington, DC: International Monetary Fund)

authorities, power and legal structures that could be used were a resolution effort initiated. The final area in the financial sector reform was the establishment of a Central Collateral Registry by the government to support entities with non-traditional or minimal forms of collateral to access credit and other critical services to build and maintain wealth.

Macro-Level Growth-Enhancing Reforms

The 2013 EFF also made two provisions that could be categorized as supporting growth at the macroeconomic level. The first is in the area of development tracking platforms to support investors with major infrastructure development projects to keep track of processes through the various steps in all parish councils. Development approvals have been heavily criticized in the past as being an area that was prone to corruption, low levels of accountability and transparency as well as a source of environmental degradation and pollution to the detriment of the population. The second area related to the consolidation and modernization of the laws, relating to the generation, transmission, distribution, supply and despatch of electricity and all matters associated with these areas (see Fig. 2.5).

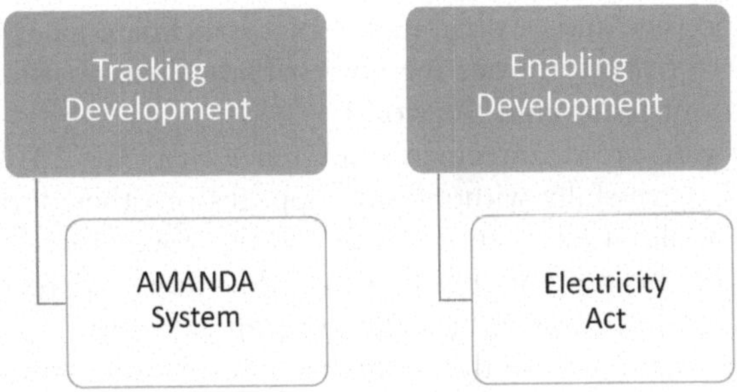

Fig. 2.5 Pillars of the Macro-level Growth-Enhancing Reforms under the 2013 Extended Fund Facility between the IMF and Jamaica (*Source* Author's illustration from Government of Jamaica. [2010]. *Letter of Intent.* Washington, DC: International Monetary Fund)

Conclusion

The 2013 EFF was designed to arrest the slippages in the policy space arising from the aborted 2010 SBA and to further deepen the reform agenda in order to solidify and extend the gains established in relation to fiscal discipline. It doubled the number of prior actions than featured in the 2010 SBA, perhaps as a means of ensuring that the government implemented these most critical interventions prior to the influx of programme support pledged by the IMF. Prior actions under the 2013 EFF required the government to implement a second debt exchange to secure the firm downward trend that was needed in the debt-to-GDP ratio and the associated debt-servicing requirements, along with four measures to deepen the efforts at fiscal consolidation. Structural benchmarks covered a far wider range of policy areas than heretofore encountered in IMF agreements. This transformation of the programme could be reflective of the evolution in the IMF system of developing more appropriate economic programmes that were more supportive of the needs of developing countries (see Chapter 8 of this volume). This process in the IMF would have emerged in the wake of several rounds of discussions about the responsiveness of the IMF and the holistic nature of the interventions needed by developing countries. These countries needed development partners who understand their situation and provide both funding and technical assistance to help them build better societies for the benefit of their populations. As the IMF and its partner institution the World Bank began to be more responsive and flexible, its internal stakeholders have moved to better resource the institutions thereby enabling them to offer enhanced support to countries around the world.

There is widespread agreement and relief that the 2013 EFF was implemented successfully without any slippages or other deviations that would cause a fallout between the IMF and the government 'a-la-2010'. The success of the programme, however, does not lead to satiation or sanguinity in and of itself. Whilst the government must be commended for this achievement with all the contextual information considered, there are fundamental questions to be answered. The primary of which is, what will be done to generate high and sustainable rates of economic growth? By when will this growth materialize as a sort of rate of return on the heavy adjustment that the entire citizenry had to endure since the onset of the 2007 food price crisis, the global economic and financial crisis, and the cost of the uncertainties due to the aborted 2010 SBA (Clarke & Nelson, 2020)? What are the necessary and what is the capacity of the government to ensure that in the transition to this growth path the poor and the vulnerable would be protected in the most efficient and effective ways possible? What are the structural changes that will have to happen on the social side—in education, health and security that would need to be effected in order that the broadest base of the population would be included in this transformation of the economy through economic growth? Chapter 5 will present an assessment of the extent to which the conditionalities of all three agreements addressed the long-standing structural challenges facing the Jamaican society and economy as presented in two successive World Bank Country Economic Memorandums and Chapter 9 will opine on the extent to which the conditionalities supported progress towards Vision 2030 Jamaica National Development Plan.

In retrospect, the 2013 EFF between Jamaica and the IMF, with additional multilateral and bilateral support from multiple development partners (see Chapter 6 of this volume) and supporters, enabled the government to accomplish far-reaching modernization and transformation in many policies and systems which presented long-standing structural constraints to economic development and growth. These issues will be explored in Chapter 5 as we explore the extent to which the IMF agreements have helped to correct long-term structural impediments and thereby facilitated advances in unlocking the Jamaica's potential for economic growth. The IMF has, however, issued several provisos for the prerequisites for growth in Jamaica. Despite the significant changes in the policy and administrative landscape in Jamaica since 2010, the first alert provided by the Fund at the concluding mission for the EFF was the need for continued fiscal discipline for continued reduction of the debt and providing sufficient space for the private sector to ramp up innovation and investment. Beyond this, a wide range of extremely intractable social problems were itemized as requiring critical attention and whose solutions were important complements to the continued efforts at fiscal discipline. These included the high cost of energy, low levels of tax compliance, infrastructure improvement and reduction of violent crime. Issues relating to the widening and deepening of the structure and operations of institutions within the financial sector to increase its competitiveness, support assessment of creditor risk and support financial inclusion were also indicated as requirements for higher rates of growth. Another major area—the source of the derailing of the 2010 SBA and a continuing battle in terms of the government's ability to meet the target of nine per cent for the public sector wage bill and, allied to it, various other metrics of public sector efficiency. The usual challenges associated with shocks and the threat of the Zika virus and the possibility that there would be a slowdown in the pace of reform and the initiation and implementation of the transformation agenda were also potential threats that could compromise the gains of the previous four years.

Despite the success of the 2013 EFF and in spite of the challenges that lay ahead of the Jamaican authorities, the IMF publicly transmitted its interest in discussing potential future engagements with the IMF. Given the emerging risks such as that associated with the de-risking activities of international bank counterparts, the authorities would ultimately strike a deal with the IMF that would be precautionary in nature in that were none of the risks and challenges to have such negative impact to require the need to use the funds, they would simply be used to shore up the foreign exchange reserves at the Bank of Jamaica. This deal was important from a signalling and credibility perspective, as some concerns were expressed that the delay or unwillingness or inability of the government to indicate decisively what were the plans post-EFF could be an indication that the government intended to relent on its commitment to fiscal discipline, further debt-reduction and a transition to the long sought-after rates of sustainable economic growth. The wider population, whilst appreciative of the achievements under the EFF, were not convinced that a four-year programme would have endowed the government with such a level of maturity that they could implement the still-remaining reforms without some form of borrowing relationship with the IMF that holds them more accountable than a simple monitoring arrangement (Thompson, 2016).

References

Caribbean Policy Research Institute. (2008). *Jamaica's debt: Exploring causes and strategies*. Kingston: Caribbean Policy Research Institute.

Clarke, C., & Nelson, C. (2020). *Contextualizing Jamaica's relationship with the IMF*. Cham: Palgrave Macmillan.

Doyle, P. (2019, January 4). *Macroeconomic malpractice in action*. Retrieved from *Financial Times*. https://ftalphaville.ft.com/2019/01/04/1546594809000/Guest-Post–Macroeconomic-malpractice-in-action/.

Government of Jamaica. (2006). *Heads of agreement*. Kingston: Ministry of Finance and the Public Service.

Government of Jamaica. (2010). *Letter of intent*. Washington, DC: International Monetary Fund.

Hunter, N. (2010, March 15). Enough Runaround. *The Jamaica Gleaner*.

Jamaica Information Service. (2008, October 29). *Gov't and JTA sign off on wage and benefits package*. Kingston, Jamaica.

Johnston, J., & Montecino, J. (2012). *Update on the Jamaican economy*. Washington, DC: Center for Economic and Policy Research.

Nelson, C. (2019). *Social partnership and governance under crises*. IGI Global.

The Jamaica Gleaner. (2007, October 7). Shaw's promise to double nurses' pay. *The Jamaica Gleaner*.

The Jamaica Gleaner. (2008a, October 14). JTA cannot guarantee normalcy. *The Jamaica Gleaner*.

The Jamaica Gleaner. (2008b, February 4). NAJ turn down third MoU. *The Jamaica Gleaner*.

Schmid, J. P. (2016). *Addressing debt overhang*. IDB.

Thompson, M. (2016, May 24). *Government should enter into another IMF programme*. Retrieved from: The Jamaica Gleaner. http://jamaica-gleaner.com/article/business/20160525/government-should-enter-another-imf-programme.

Wigglesworth, R. (2020, February 14). *Inside the IMF's outrageous, improbably successful Jamaican programme (Pt. 1)*. Retrieved from *Financial Times*. https://ftalphaville.ft.com/2019/11/04/1572874841000/Inside-the-IMF-s-outrageous–improbably-successful-Jamaican-programme–Pt–1-/.

CHAPTER 3

Lining Up and Jumping the Hurdles to Long-Term Growth (Part I)

Introduction

The Government of Jamaica had committed to implementing a programme to boost aggregate demand and increase growth by the actioning of a Growth Inducement Strategy (Planning Institute of Jamaica, 2012), as recommended by the Planning Institute of Jamaica whilst concurrently mitigating the impact of austerity measures and the reverberating impacts of the double crises—the 2007 food price crisis and the 2008/2009 global economic and financial crises—on the poor and vulnerable. Consequently, apart from addressing the macroeconomic, monetary and financial measures that were critical to providing the platform for, as well as, supportive of growth, a critical component of the EFF 2013 policy discussions, had to entail integrating within the framework of the Agreement, measures that would engender modalities of growth, simultaneously with concerns of social cohesion and social protection in the undertaking.

In this regard a number of initiatives were undertaken with the objective to further and to stimulate dimensions of economic growth, contiguous with and complementary to addressing the critical macroeconomic indicators, fiscal, monetary and financial themes and remedial concerns, required under the IMF programme interventions. These perspectives contributed to the framing of measures by the Planning Institute of Jamaica which would address growth concerns which were

C. Clarke and C. Nelson, *Jamaica's Evolving Relationship with the IMF*, https://doi.org/10.1007/978-3-030-59204-2_3

captured within the IMF EFF 2013 Agreement which would serve to enable the targets under the Vision 2030. Thereafter reducing debt and bring the economy to a healthy state would be undertaken concomitant with engendering growth creation.

Strategic Investments

It has been a never-ending critique of government, by the private sector, citizens and the overall users of government facilities and those that have had to interface with government entities, that the interface with service users and the business environment was extremely poor. There was an urgent need for a variety of interventions to transform the various points of interface with government, associated services and facilities. This would have the objective overall, to broker a more efficient and effective interface within the domestic, local economy as well as the global community in terms of furthering trade and, by extension, interface with global networks in a sustainable way to achieve comprehensive growth and development.

Broad-based growth was emphasized as a central pillar of the programme covering efforts to enhance the business environment providing access to credit and project financing for the private sector labour market interventions and reforms.

Overarchingly there would be strategic investments undertaken in logistics, shipping, tourism and businesses processing (IMF, 2013a).

Enhancing the Business Environment: Access to Credit and Private Sector Project Finance

To further a Secured Transaction Framework, a number of measures were undertaken such as the tabling of a Secured Obligations Bill in March 2013. The civil jurisdiction of the lower courts was increased from J$250,000 to J$1,000,000 to reduce the case flow burden of minor claims in the Commercial Division of the Supreme Court (see Fig. 3.1).

These were undertaken in an effort to improve the efficiency of disposing of substantial commercial disputes and their timely disposal. The Supreme Court of the Ministry of Justice had taken specific steps to process these directly, giving special attention to matters being filed in the Commercial Division. As a consequence, the judicial support was given to assignments regarding the Commercial Division of the Supreme Court and the Insolvency Act was also tabled in Parliament (IMF,

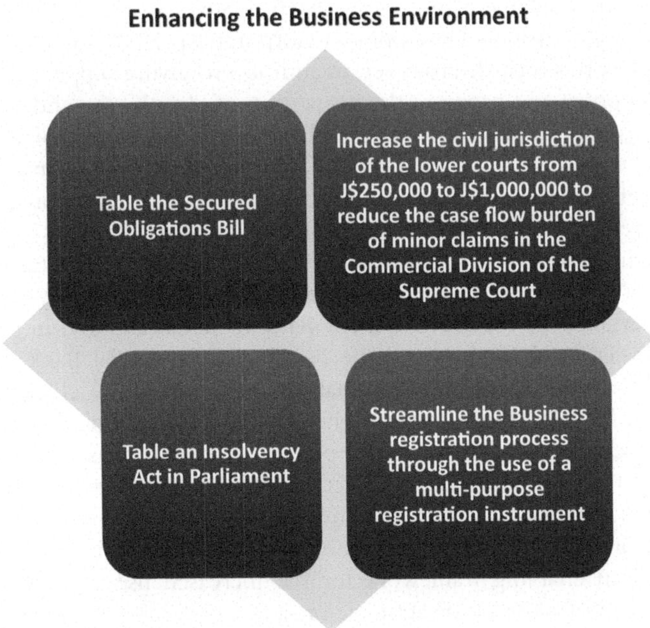

Fig. 3.1 Growth strategy—Enhancing the business environment—Extended Fund Facility (2013) (*Source* Compiled by Authors from: International Monetary Fund. [2013]. *Jamaica: Request for an Extended Arrangement Under the Extended Credit Fund Facility*. Washington, DC: International Monetary Fund)

2013b). Efforts were made to streamline the business registration process through the use of a multipurpose registration system. This also entailed the amendment of certain acts namely the Companies Act, Registration of Business Names Act, Taxpayer Registration GCT and Regulations NHT Act and Regulations, etc. The Fund supported programme sought to enhance the access to credit by firms by addressing crowding out problems with supplementary contributions in the form of legislation regarding the establishment of a central collateral registry as well as legislative requirements to enable movable property as collateral (IMF, 2013a).

Measures also entailed an increase in financing opportunities available to Micro, Small and Medium Enterprises (MSME) in terms of doubling the available resources by 2016 relative to 2013. The support of the Jamaica Business Development Corporation (JBDC) would also be increased in this regard. However, in addition to giving support to initiatives to support and promote the incubation of ideas by the end of 2014, JBDC was also supported by the establishment of a venture capital framework to be undergirded by a Venture Capital Fund to provide financing to high potential Small and Medium Enterprises (SMEs). This would necessitate a review of the market environment and legislation, as well as a strategic implementation plan which would be informed by a stakeholder workshop and a venture capital conference. A Mobile Money initiative was undertaken by the Development Bank of Jamaica (DBJ) in partnership with Transcel Limited and the National Commercial Bank (NCB). The DBJ would be required to analyze and identify the challenges of deploying Mobile Money services whereby the findings would contribute to the development of the necessary policies. Preparatory aspects involved testing of the Mobile Money product towards their eventual approval for implementation within a year, subsequent upon the review and analysis of the pilot phases (IMF, 2013a). A Public Private Partnership (PPP) Policy served as an enabling framework for the increased use of PPPs in the construction of some of the strategic projects concerning port expansion, agro-processing, health and health tourism, information and technology, logistics and transportation, as well as schools and town development or re development (see Fig. 3.2).

Under the **Third Review**, other actions for improving the business climate and enhancing reforms to engender growth entailed the implementation of software that would allow the government to track the approval of construction permits across parish councils with the system to be implemented throughout all the parishes by the end of 2014 called the Application Management And Data Automated System (AMANDA). Initiatives involving land titling were to be expanded under the Land Administration and Management Programme (LAMP) whereby around 3000 new titles were issued between 2011 and 2013. Legislation to create a Secured Interest in Personal Property (SIPP) was undertaken to prepare for the establishing of a central collateral registry. Training with respect to the financial sector stakeholders had commenced in addition to public relations and educational campaigns to support its use. Preparatory actions had been taken towards the passage of an Insolvency Act in

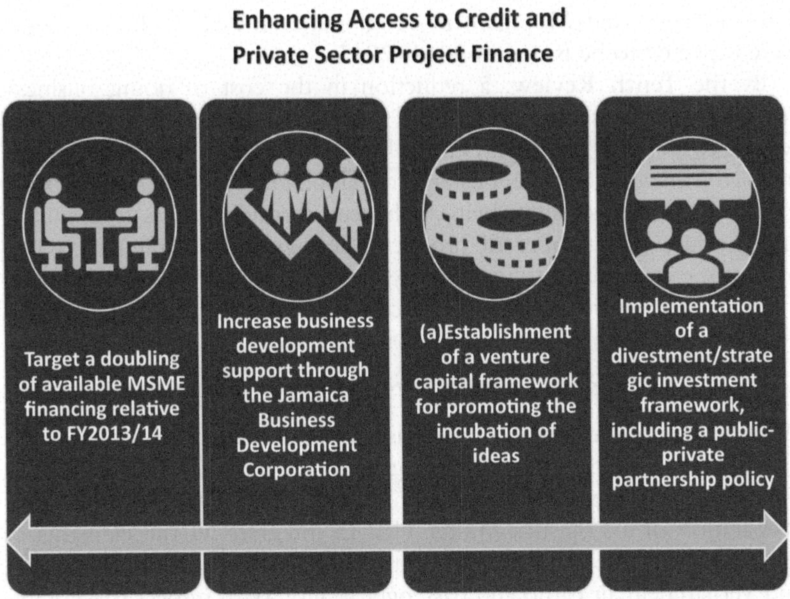

Fig. 3.2 Growth strategy: Public sector reform: Pension policy—Extended Fund Facility (2013) (*Source* Compiled by Authors from: International Monetary Fund. [2013]. *Jamaica: Request for an Extended Arrangement Under the Extended Credit Fund Facility*. Washington, DC: International Monetary Fund)

addition to the associated enabling regulations. Preparations for streamlining the business registration process which required a multipurpose registration instrument were already underway.

At the **Fifth and Sixth Reviews**, the AMANDA system had commenced operations in nine parishes as well as in four agencies of government namely, the National Works Agency, Mines and Geology Division, Agricultural Land Management Division (ALMD) and The Environmental Health Unit in Kingston. With respect to the Development Applications Process (DAP) which involves fast tracking the lower risk and smaller projects, a joint technical team was responsible for the review, assessment and monitoring of development applications furthered by an MOU Agreement between the local planning authorities and the National Environment and Planning Agency (NEPA). Under the Land

Administration and Management Programme (LAMP) 1000 new titles were expected to be issued in 2014/2015.

By the **Tenth Review**, a reduction in the cost of doing business, accessing private sector credit and the lowering electricity costs with respect to some of the interventions had materialised. These efforts were likely to encourage more business development, as well as encourage greater financial inclusion, being enhanced through efforts to stimulate and increase the number of product offerings such as regular savings products, etc., targeted to low income households and SMESs, along with microinsurance as modalities, of agricultural financial products.

Strategic Investments and Logistics Hub

With the vision to establish Jamaica as a logistics hub, necessary measures included the expansion of port, cargo and maritime facilities as well as the creation of Special Economic Zones (SEZs) by 2015 (see Fig. 3.3). Preparation of a Logistics Master Plan to integrate all the elements of the project include the establishment of a Commodity Port, Dry Dock, and Vernamfield air cargo and passenger facility. With respect to Vernamfield development, the Greenfield Development Strategy, was considered whereby the developer would complete the primary infrastructure components initially and thereafter involve various operators to provide specific products and services within an established framework.

Work was proceeding on a Special Zones Act as well at the development of the Caymanas Special Economic Zone (SEZ) being developed under the auspices of the Ministry of Industry Investment and Commerce (MIIC) and Factories Corporation of Jamaica (FCJ). Land divestment processes had begun and development was subject to the National Environment Planning Agency (NEPA) undertaking an assessment and giving an approval for the sewage connection to Soapberry. The creation of the SEZ Act was to be passed by June 2015 based on preliminary discussions concerning the White Paper and that all measures proposed were compatible with World Trade Organization (WTO) requirements, but this was delayed (IMF, 2013a). Additionally, a transhipment port, as well as industrial and commercial zones, were to be built in the Portland Bight area by China Harbour engineering company (CHEC) under a non-binding framework agreement which included several phases, which required Cabinet's approval.

Environmental impact assessments would subsequently be undertaken by CHEC in consultation with the national environmental planning

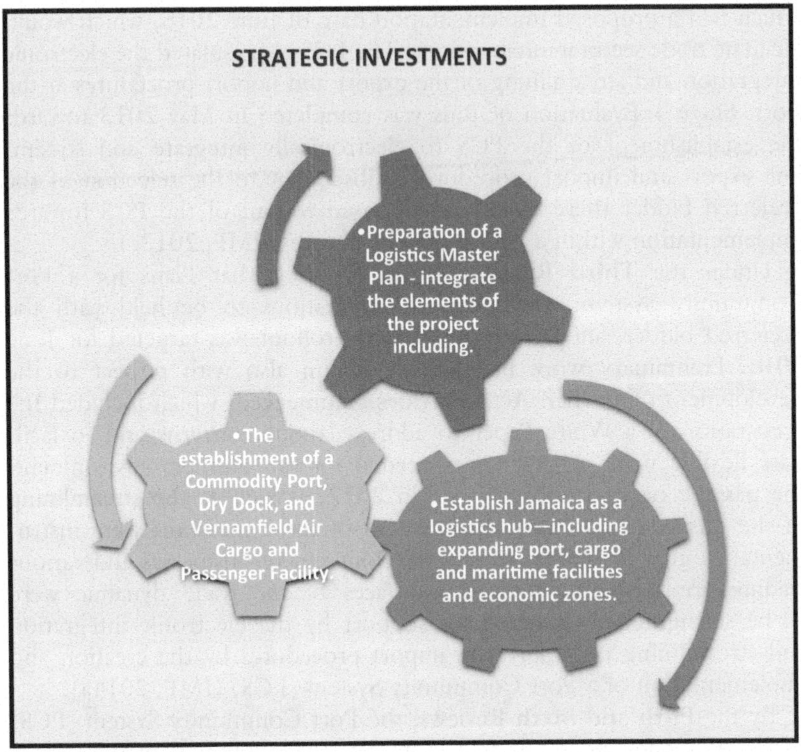

Fig. 3.3 Strategic investments & logistics hub (*Source* Compiled by Authors from: International Monetary Fund. [2013]. *Jamaica: Request for an Extended Arrangement Under the Extended Credit Fund Facility*. Washington, DC: International Monetary Fund)

agency with respect to the prerequisite terms of reference as well as furthering the completion of a technical feasibility study. Strategic investments which were critical to position Jamaica as a logistics hub entailed several initiatives such as, the privatization of the Norman Manley International Airport (NMIA) and the Kingston Container Terminal (KCT) and their upgrading.

As part of the **Second Review**, growth-enhancing reforms with the imperative to promote growth and the overall transformation of the business climate included plans to create a Port Community System (PCS) which had a proposed implementation date of June 2016, which would facilitate trade sectoral interventions. The PCS encapsulated the electronic integration and streamlining of the export and import procedures at the Port. Stage 1 Evaluation of Bids was completed in May 2013 towards the establishment of the PCS to electronically integrate and streamline export and import procedures. Subsequent to the selection of the preferred bidder there would be a phased rollout of the PCS towards implementation within a period of a 24 months (IMF, 2013c).

Under the **Third Review**, it was reported that Plans for a Port Community System now involved negotiations to be held with the preferred bidder, and a projected phased rollout was targeted for June 2014. Preliminary work had already begun also with respect to the development of an SEZ Act. Activities commenced, which included the preparation of a White Paper to address labour concerns and to facilitate flexible work arrangements needed for the business environment, the passage of an Insolvency Act in 2013, as well as the streamlining of the business registration process. All of these measures were instrumental to growth facilitation and development of businesses and various trading arrangements. Various interfaces of the trade dynamic were to be strengthened, targeted for support by the electronic integration and streamlining of export and import procedures by the creation and implementation of a Port Community System (PCS) (IMF, 2014a).

By the **Fifth and Sixth** Reviews, the Port Community System (PCS) were progressing, to facilitate a more effective alignment of the system capabilities with the competitive needs of the country. The tender for the feasibility study, in January 2015, was coupled with the Jamaica custom's acquisition of ASYCUDA, World Customs Management System. An independent assessment of both the PCS and ASYCUDA was undertaken, which would determine the next steps. The Special Economic Zone (SEZ) Act, passed in October 2015, sought to ensure that there was a level of compatibility with WTO requirements informed by both preliminary documents such as a Green Paper and a White Paper and the discussions thereunder.

Overall, the strategic investments required to establish Jamaica as a logistics hub were assuredly underway, evidenced by work proceeding on the privatization of the Norman Manley International Airport (NMIA) and the Kingston Container Terminal (KCT). With respect to the NMIA's rate review, this would be completed by September 2014 and the RFP by January 2015, and thereafter, it was anticipated that the selection of a preferred bidder could be determined by May 2015. Comparatively, the awarding of the KCT contract was scheduled by November 2014. The development of the trans-shipment port and industrial and commercial zones in the Portland Bight area to be undertaken by China Harbour Engineering Company (CHEC) was at the stage where a final framework agreement was signed in August 2014. CHEC had begun work on the technical feasibility study as required under their agreement.

With respect to the **Thirteenth Review** of the programme it was recognized that the economy was experiencing a budding but subdued recovery; however, the implementation of the Programme remained strong. A number of strategic investments that had been started at the inception of the EFF were deemed, well underway. For example, a thirty-year concession agreement was signed with Kingston Freeport Terminal Limited regarding the privatization of Kingston Container Terminal (KCT) in July 2016. A new enterprise team had been appointed to reinitiate the privatization of Norman Manley International Airport (NMIA). The Caymanas SEZ, aligned with the Master Plan for the Logistics Hub Initiative, received additional support from the World Bank in terms of proceeding with various other project activities such as the feasibility study, etc. The development of a trans-shipment port as well as industrial and commercial zones in the Portland Bight area by CHEC, was also ongoing, which included instituting preparatory measures to obtain the TOR from NEPA, for the environmental impact assessment.

Looking ahead, mention was made of further actions that were required for improving the business climate which were deemed critical. A revised standardized pricing framework for development application fees, currently being reviewed was due to be completed by October 2016. Targets relating to the timeliness of the approvals process against the 90-day benchmark for development projects especially commercial ventures needed to be monitored. Other actions requiring monitoring and follow up related to reducing the time needed for entrepreneurs to receive their electricity connections and the possible automation of the work processes within the government electrical regulator are supported further by acquiring additional modules for the AMANDA software operable throughout the parishes to more effectively streamlined procedures for scheduling, inspecting, approving and certifying electrical installations. The Port Community System (PCS) that electronically integrates and streamlines export and import procedures will be supported by the ASYCUDA World customs management system to integrate processes and procedures, and, the national single window supported by a World Bank loan.

Energy Infrastructure Improvement

Other strategic investments concerned the implementation of energy sector initiatives to achieve fuel-source diversification, facilitate energy conservation and promote liberalization in delivery to achieve progressive reductions in the cost of energy (see Fig. 3.4). Energy initiatives would include the construction of a power plant which would support Jamaica's competitive advantage with respect to mitigating the very high electricity costs for manufacturing and other industrial activities.

Given the importance of the cost of electricity and the role of energy in efforts to achieve degrees of competitiveness, several projects were initiated that would achieve fuel-source diversification, facilitate energy conservation, liberalize the electricity market and to reduce the cost of energy overall. The idea included the diversification of energy sources from oil to gas based and renewable resources. The Office of Utilities Regulation (OUR) had facilitated the issuance of a Final Proposal (IFP) to selected entities to provide additional generating capacity to the national grid (IMF, 2013b).

The construction of a new 381 MW plant was slated to start in 2014 which forms a critical part of the overall medium-term energy strategy, with the objective to enable the reduction in the cost of electricity on completion in early 2016. Measures to improve the efficiency of energy use in public spaces and promote conservation within the private sector through public education, technical assistance, along with increased access to specialized credit for energy efficiency-enhancing investments, were initiated. Buildings at several agencies had been retrofitted with solar control films and cool roof solutions whilst implementation was in progress and others scheduled to commence thereafter.

Efforts to promote liberalization in delivery through continued efforts to facilitate distributed generation networks entailed consultations to develop a model and framework for 'Power Wheeling' whereby an entity which self generates its own energy can be facilitated by the Jamaica Public Service (JPS) to allow the equivalence of the excess energy to be routed to its subsidiaries for their use. Several instruments such as Self-generation licenses, Wheeling Codes, Pro-forma Wheeling Contracts, Top-up and Stand-By Agreements and Excess Energy Sale

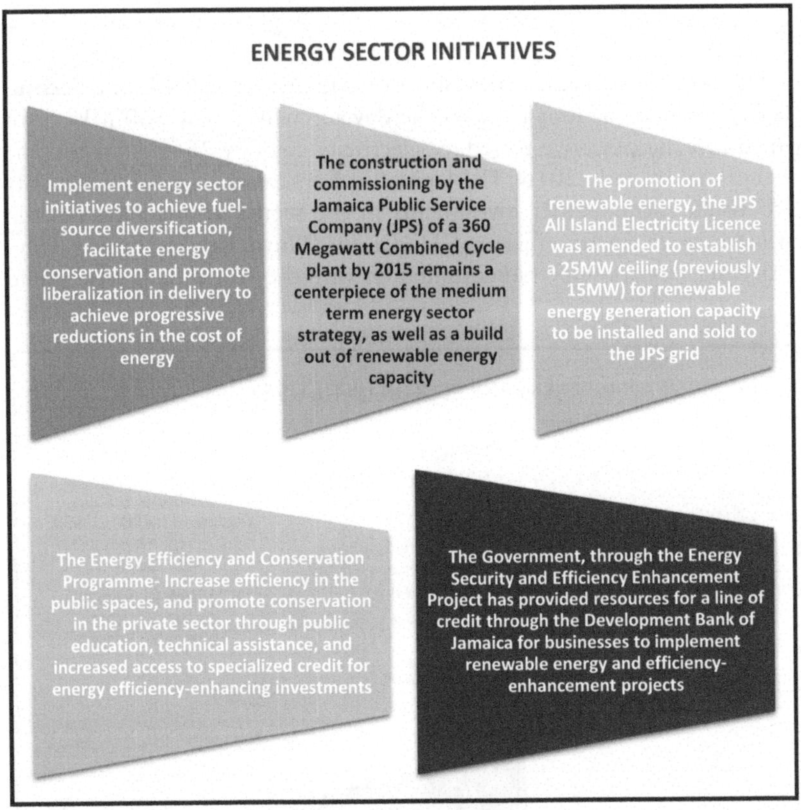

Fig. 3.4 Energy Sector Initiatives (*Source* Compiled by Authors from: International Monetary Fund. [2013]. *Jamaica: Request for an Extended Arrangement Under the Extended Credit Fund Facility*. Washington, DC: International Monetary Fund)

Contracts were created to facilitate the process. These were added to a cohort of regulatory and legislative changes implemented to improve the business environment, facilitate private sector investment in the energy sector and enhance consumer protection and safeguard standards (IMF, 2013a). Several legislative reforms were developed which included the development of an Electric Power Sector Policy, the Modernization of the Electric Lighting Act and the Development of a Natural Gas Act,

Regulations and Policy for a National Gas Regulatory Framework (see Fig. 3.5).

The Growth strategy, with respect to activities signalled in the **Second Review** entailed actions towards the development a new 360 MW plant which had the objective to reduce electricity costs by 25–40% to become operational by early 2016. The legislative framework of a new Electricity Act would allow further investments in the sector to engender overall, an increase in energy efficiency. Under the **Third Review**, a new Electricity Act was developed in consultation with the World Bank that would

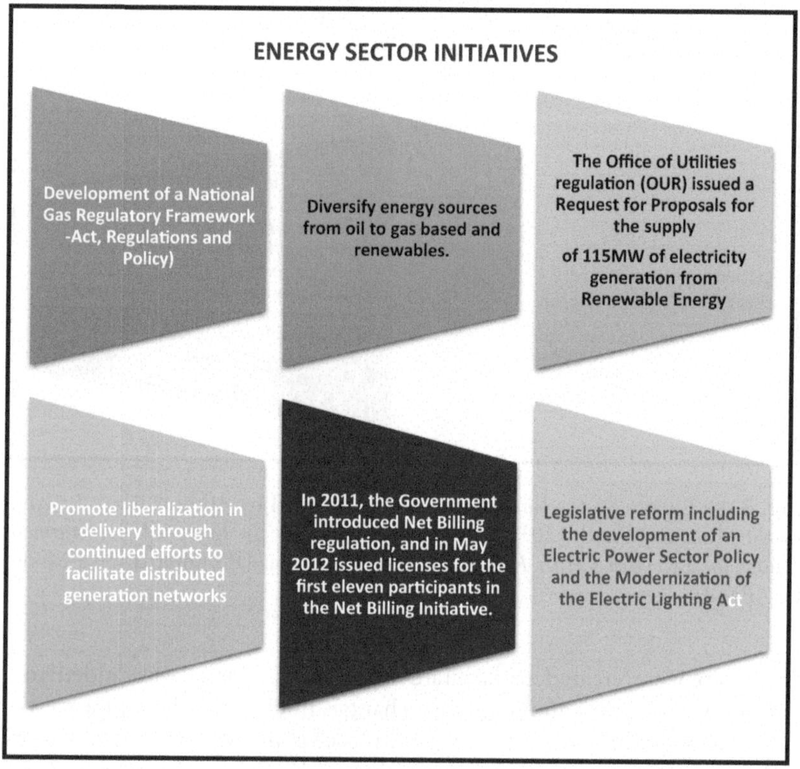

Fig. 3.5 Energy sector initiatives (*Source* Compiled by Authors from: International Monetary Fund. [2013]. *Jamaica: Request for an Extended Arrangement Under the Extended Credit Fund Facility*. Washington, DC: International Monetary Fund)

strengthen the governance in the sector and facilitate access to the grid by new power producers.

By the **Fifth and Sixth Reviews**, continuous efforts will be made to reduce the time needed for entrepreneurs to get electricity connections for business purposes which is associated with the untimeliness of the application process and delivery of electricity permits by the Government Electricity Inspectorate (GEI). The business process review conducted by the government informed this challenging process which supported efforts towards the acquisition of ICT to streamline procedures for scheduling, inspecting, improving and certifying electrical installations.

Progress had been made with respect to converting the Bogue power plant from oil to gas in addition to other projects that would serve to lower the electricity cost by the **Tenth Review** and reduce the dependency upon imported petroleum for power generation. Other exercises entailed the Development Bank of Jamaica (DBJ) expanding direct lending and partial guarantees schemes to private businesses especially SMEs. Altogether, these supply side reforms were encouraged along with a credit line to be set up in collaboration with the World Bank.

Agriculture

Other sector with growth potential also received support; an example in the form of the Agricultural Competitiveness Programme (ACP) through the Agricultural Investment Corporation (AIC) was to provide the IDB with a Master Plan for the establishment of agro-parks by June 2013. The growth of agro-parks was targeted to enable an increase in agricultural production under the whole ambit of improving competitiveness (see Fig. 3.6).

Of the nine (9) agro-parks, three were active, with the commencement of productive activity at an additional four (4) by March 2014. Myersfield (Westmoreland) awaited business plans, Ettingdon (Trelawny) required technical analyses to continue until June 2013 (IMF, 2013c). Agro-plans completed at 15 May 2013 were for New Forest/Duff House (St. Elizabeth), Hillrun (St Catherine), Yallahs (St Thomas) and Spring Plain (Clarendon) which were being reviewed (IMF, 2013c).

Efforts were made to strengthen resilience in the agricultural sector through four environmental-related projects surrounding Climate Change Adaptation and Disaster Risk Reduction. The overall objective was to assist Jamaica with its adaptation to climate change and

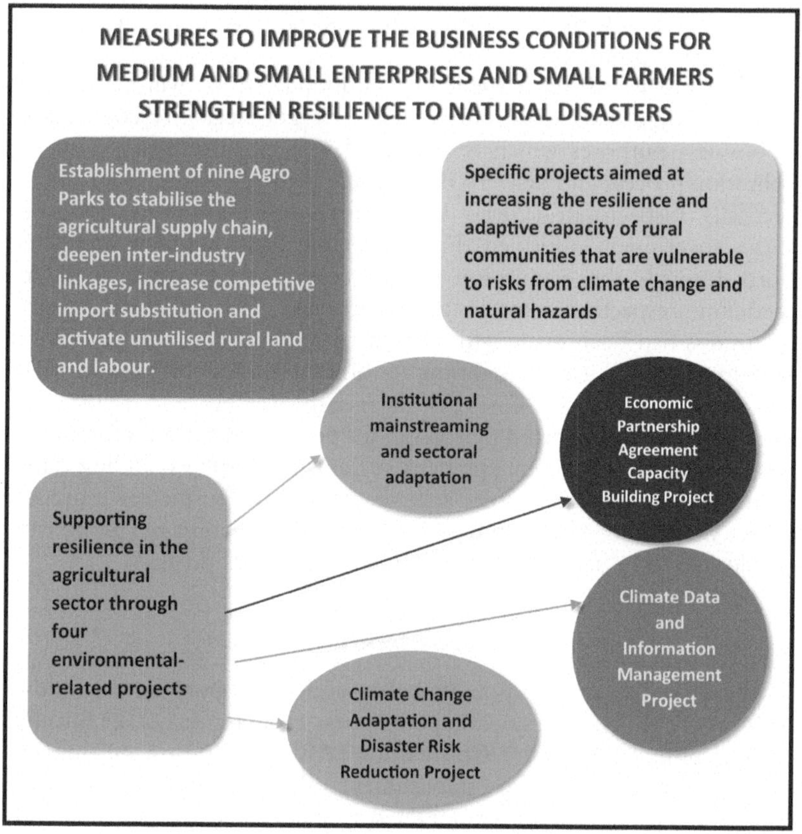

Fig. 3.6 Measures to improve the business conditions for medium and small enterprises and small farmers (*Source* Compiled by Authors from: International Monetary Fund. [2013]. *Jamaica: Request for an Extended Arrangement Under the Extended Credit Fund Facility*. Washington, DC: International Monetary Fund)

contribute to sustainable development, particularly in vulnerable communities, through increasing resilience and reducing risks associated with natural hazards.

The project has three specific objectives to firstly reduce downstream run-off and associated negative environmental and human impacts through rehabilitation and improved management of selected watersheds.

Under this component, the Forestry Department was charged with the rehabilitation of watersheds and carried out several activities. With the assistance of NEPA, the project served to increase resilience of coastal ecosystems to climate change impacts through restoration and protection of selected ecosystems, for example, to install protective infrastructure along the Negril coastline, restoring some 2000–2500 metres of the shoreline.

The Institutional, Mainstreaming and Sectoral Adaptation Project purposed the incorporation of the impact of climate change into development plans for vulnerable sections of Rio Bueno and Rio Minho river basins. Other dimensions of the project responding to the need for climate change adaptation included, water harvesting and management, sustainable land management and agriculture risk management (see Fig. 3.7).

These specific projects served to increase the resilience and adaptive capacity of rural communities that were vulnerable to risks from climate change and natural hazards. In addition, these sought to foster the renewal of community infrastructures and promote entrepreneurial development to foster self-agency and job creation (IMF, 2014a).

To improve quality climate information for effective planning and action at the local and national levels, the Climate Data and Information Management Project provided more accurate predictions and early warnings of extreme weather events and increased the capacity to interpret climate change scenarios and effect planning processes for agro-parks. Overall, the Project increased awareness of the impact of climate change and the need for the adoption of initiatives to improve resilience (IMF, 2014a). By the **Third Review** of the 2013 EFF, the established Agro-parks were contributing to an increase in agricultural production with three already in operation. Plans will being put in place to expand the number of agro-parks whilst at the same time to foster linkages between the agricultural sector and the tourism industry as a priority, which is being actively supported by the technical working group.

The Electricity Sector Enterprise Team (ESET) had created an action plan by the **Thirteenth Review** to replace oil fired generation capacity with gas and ethane- fired plants which would achieve a degree of cost savings. The conversion of the Bogue power station from oil to LNG was completed, as well as an approval being granted to the JPS, for the construction and operation of Jamaica's first natural gas-fired power plant. Several renewable energy projects serve to enable the lowering of

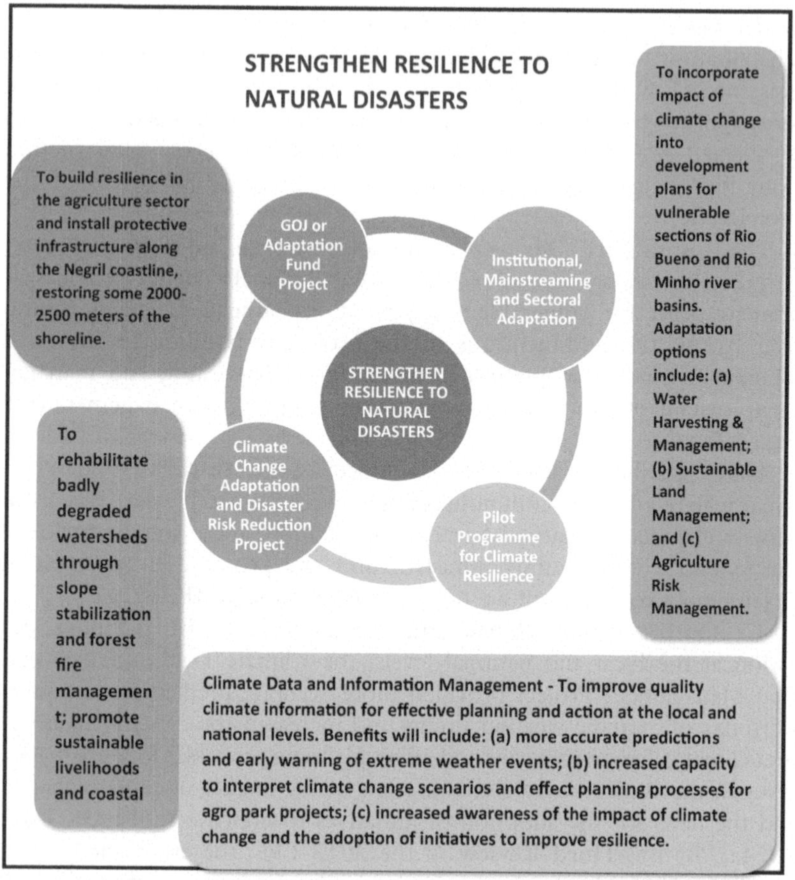

Fig. 3.7 Strengthen resilience to natural disasters (*Source* Compiled by Authors from: International Monetary Fund. [2013]. *Jamaica: Request for an Extended Arrangement Under the Extended Credit Fund Facility*. Washington, DC: International Monetary Fund)

electricity costs in addition to reducing exposure to global oil price fluctuations with cost implications, concomitant with Jamaica attaining its emissions goals with respect to climate change commitments regarding GHG emissions.

Labour Market Reform

The Government of Jamaica had infused the achievement of inclusive growth within the Programme and it would therefore require critical reform measures to enhance the business climate, access to credit reform, the labour market and to encourage and foster, strategic investments in logistics overall (see Fig. 3.8).

The labour and human resource provisioning for the multiple strategic investments and associated projects were recognized as an important contribution to the sustainability and long-term development trajectory envisaged. The lack of legislation to guide the implementation of flexible work arrangements somewhat limits businesses in its attempt to gain efficiencies through flexible deployment of human resources. As a result, labour productivity is hampered. This acts as a strain of the company's competitiveness.

The process to implement flexi work week legislation began over 15 years ago, and, since then, has endured many delays. However, in 2011, Cabinet approved the tabling in Parliament of the White Paper on the implementation of flexible work arrangements. Cabinet also approved the issuing of drafting instructions to the Chief Parliamentary Counsel to facilitate amendments being made to various pieces of legislation to facilitate the operationalizing of the flexi-work regime. Legislation was adopted on November 2014, to support flexible work arrangements in addition to a public education programme to sensitize the labour market. Against the background of the launch of the Comprehensive Labour Market Reform Agenda (CLMRA) a Commission was created which began its operations in March 2015. The CLMRA began an assessment to review existing policies and practises in the areas of education and training, productivity, technology and innovation, labour policies and legislation, social protection and industrial relations.

These included the pursuance of facilitating the use of flexible work arrangements within the labour force. Other activities to enhance the social protection framework to reduce the impact of high separation costs were explored with multilateral assistance from the Inter-American Development Bank (IADB) through a technical consultancy to examine the unemployment risks and options to support the unemployed, in 2013.

These efforts served to support Jamaica in the design of its own unemployment insurance scheme which would include covering the

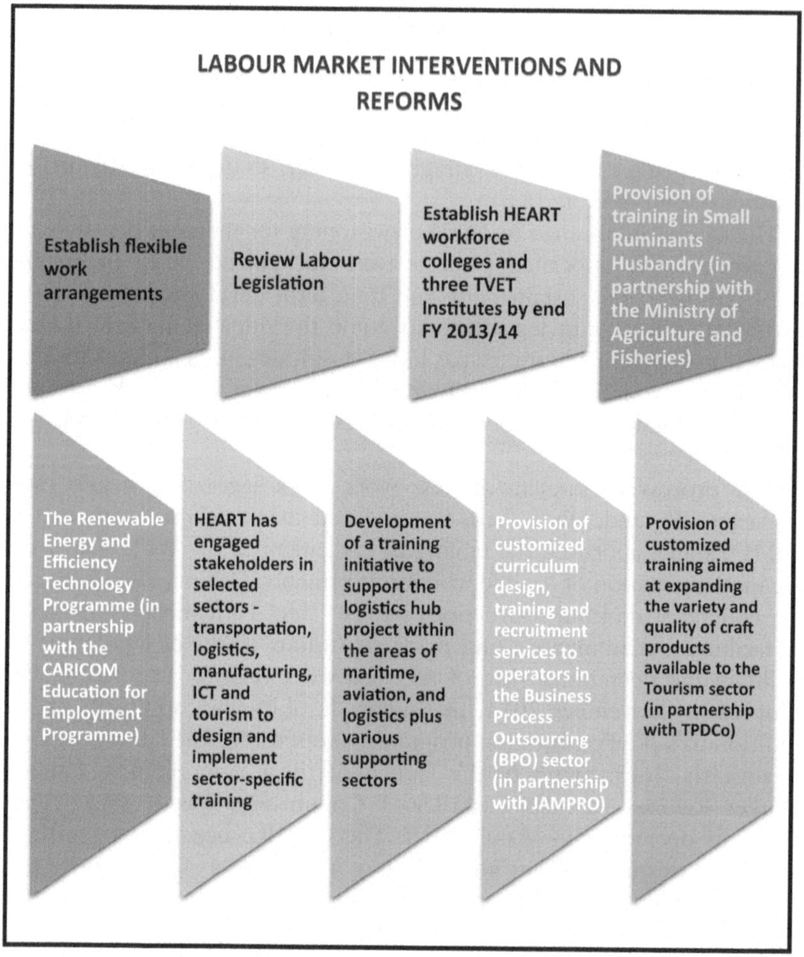

Fig. 3.8 Labour market interventions and reforms (*Source* Compiled by Authors from: International Monetary Fund. [2013]. *Jamaica: Request for an Extended Arrangement Under the Extended Credit Fund Facility*. Washington, DC: International Monetary Fund)

unemployed within it. The consultancy entailed cost analysis of the implementation of various models, using different eligibility criteria and degrees of generosity of the benefits bearing in mind the fiscal sustainability of such schemes. Measures also included a legislative review for the implementation of the different options with special attention paid to the implications for redundancy laws. A steering committee to examine the feasibility and possible implementation of an unemployment insurance scheme in Jamaica was co-chaired by the Ministry of Labour and Social Security (MLSS) and the Planning Institute of Jamaica (PIOJ) with additional membership representatives included from the private sector and the trade unions.

The growth strategy also entailed efforts to prepare the labour force to participate in the expansion of various sectors which would increase the demand for employment and also require that specific training and technical expertise be developed. Human Employment and Resource Training (HEART) workforce colleges were established as well as three technical vocational educational institutes to offer training programmes with quality assurance and accreditation for them provided by the Council of Community Colleges of Jamaica (CCCJ). Examples of such Institutes were the Falmouth and Runaway Bay Vocational Training Institutes, Cornwall Automotive Training Institute (CATI) in addition to Seaford Town Culloden and the Petersfield Institutes. These latter three represent the Western Technical Vocational Educational Training (TVET) Cluster. The vocational training colleges in Port Maria, Buff Bay and Beechamville were named the Northeast Technical Vocational Educational Training Institute (TVET) now the North East Cluster of Institutes (NECI). All of these efforts were supported by recruitment drives to fill vacancies in the TVET institutes and workforce colleges.

Additional training initiatives with respect to supporting the logistics hub project in the areas of maritime, aviation and logistics were undertaken. There was a Registered Apprenticeship Programme which was being revised as well as career advancement programmes through the Ministry of Education and other supporting agencies such as the HEART Trust/National Training Agency, the National Youth Service (NYS) and the Jamaica Foundation for Lifelong Learning (JFFL). These learning opportunities are to provide training for relevant career choices leading to the National Council on Technical and Vocational Education and Training (NCTVET) certification.

Other provisions included customizing curriculum designs with respect to the training and recruitment services required for operators in the Business Process Outsourcing (BPO) sector in partnership with JAMPRO. Efforts were also made to try to expand the variety and quality of craft products available within the tourism sector, through customized training in partnership with the Tourism Products Development Corporation (TPDCo). With respect to agricultural training, this was targeted to small ruminant husbandry in partnership with the Ministry of Agriculture and Fisheries (MOAF). Additional training was also provisioned for the energy sector with respect to renewables, through the Renewable Energy and Efficiency Technology Programme offered at HEART, in partnership with the CARICOM Education for Employment Programme for January 2014.

Labour market reform served as a critical component to support the resilience and sustainability of the supply of human resource requirements for the many strategic investments being undertaken. The Comprehensive Labour Market Reform Agenda (CLRA), had the objective to review existing policies and practices which traversed areas of labour policy legislation, social protection and industrial relations. Supplementing these efforts, the need to assess areas of training to supply the demand in the various investment projects and activities underway, but additionally, to address qualitative issues and upgrades in terms of the use of technology and innovation towards the eventual accreditation concerns, were also necessary inclusions in the exercise.

Actions taken in terms of Labour market reforms entailed the furthering of legislation to support a flexible work arrangement, which was adopted in November 2014 accompanied by a public education campaign to promote the use of flexible work arrangements.

These efforts would be accompanied by the requisite education and training as well as reviews of existing policies and practices in the use of technology innovation, etc. The purpose was to reduce the impact of high separation costs being reviewed by the Unemployment Insurance Committee (UIC). Altogether these efforts had the support of the Inter-American Development Bank in the form of consultancies on Unemployment Insurance.

Public Sector Reform

The Eleventh and Twelfth Reviews taken concurrently, showed that in the face of ongoing improvements in critical infrastructure, that Jamaica had to maintain the momentum of its efforts towards diversifying its energy resources and reducing its energy costs. Other associated concerns, related to need for the reforms to boost economic growth whereby the recognition of the role of an Economic Growth Council to advise on initiatives of government as well as ensure a level of accountability was deemed essential. Efforts to expand investments in the agro-parks and water infrastructure and to solicit large foreign investments commensurate with improved skills training to support growth and job creation were paramount.

The need to modernize the public sector and to implement certain reforms were highlighted in the context of the need to reduce the wage bill which had the effect of crowding out other forms of spending. A number of reviews within aspects of the public sector were already in progress, i.e. regarding compensation, allowances and employee verification inclusive of changes to the Human Resource Management System (HRMS). Additionally, reforms were required with respect to the public pension system upon which its sustainability was hinged. Other pending reforms in the public sector and improvements in the public financial management system overall had implications for the management of financing and monetary flows in the economy and at the interface with private capital. The persistence of deep-rooted structural issues and a history of fiscal dominance, noted for alleged inadequacies in facilitating forms of lending to the private sector, were deemed indicative of the hurdles faced towards accelerating and achieving private sector-led growth.

Unpacking the Sixteen Reviews Under the EFF

The Fourth Review reflected an explicit acknowledgement that growth was slow but increasing. The economic recovery was deemed a fragile one, although there was a contraction in the current account deficit and inflation was falling despite the latter being high in single digits. The reform agenda remained complex and challenging more so with the overall objective of trying to achieve a 7 1/2% GDP primary surplus.

Within the framework of this Review there was an emphasis on the theme 'The Path Toward Sustained Growth and Competitiveness', Creating Jobs and Addressing Social Inequalities, to encapsulate concerns around the goals of the reform agenda relating to 'Entrenching Fiscal and Debt Sustainability', 'Fortifying The Framework For Monetary Policy' and 'Institutionalizing Sound Financial Intermediation'. These themes represented mutually reinforcing outcomes namely

- Boosting private sector growth
- Putting the public debt on a sustainable downward trajectory
- Protecting social spending and fortifying the safety net
- Restoring competitiveness through productivity improvements and allowing the exchange rate to adjust as a means to reduce the reliance on imports and create jobs
- Securing necessary funding for private investment through strengthening the financial system and lessening the crowding out from government borrowing.

Whilst the IMF programme required the Jamaican government to implement some revenue-enhancing measures, the success of these in the past has been limited and revenues were actually programmed to reflect a decrease over the next few years. In the past, when revenue targets were missed, the difference was made up by further expenditure cuts, often from the important capital budget. Capital expenditure had taken a big hit in the past few years above and beyond the reduction in spending by public bodies. After averaging about four per cent of GDP over the past five years, prior to the IMF Agreement, government capital expenditure had reached a low of 1.6% of GDP in FY 2014/2015. This is less than half of what the IMF programme had initially estimated.

As a developing country plagued by low growth, strategic or other spending on infrastructure and related initiatives could play a key role in stimulating growth; unfortunately, this does not appear to be a priority going forward. Underpinning the cuts in expenditure was a three-year wage freeze that had ended whereby the government had to engage in negotiations with public sector workers over a new wage agreement.

As a result, the focus within the **Fifth and Sixth Reviews** emphasized supporting economic growth and social protection and the importance of ongoing consultation in designing reforms. The high pace of reform thus far has benefited from consultations between the authorities and domestic organizations, as well as the monthly feedback offered by the Economic Programme Monitoring Committee (EPOC), with representatives from a range of sectors. Several stakeholders noted that both the quality and the acceptance of ongoing reforms hinged on maintaining an effective partnership.

Support was reiterated for economic growth modalities to proceed along with measures of social protection. The focus was on supporting a higher level of competitiveness through the reduction of regulatory impediments and supplementary legislative support to encourage investments and business transactions. The degree of timeliness of transactions undertaken at the interface with and response from government bureaucracies was paramount.

It was noteworthy that a subcommittee of Cabinet was created with the explicit remit to coordinate key stakeholders to ensure that the implementation of strategic projects and growth reform initiatives would progress smoothly and cohesively. The sub-committee included a secretariat to undertake the follow up tracking of implementation accordingly.

The **Seventh Review** aimed to further supporting economic growth and social protection against the backdrop of an overall impetus and focus being made to adhere to the commitments and objectives. Additionally, there was also the desire to further economic confidence, against the background of a weak third quarter growth out turn. It was recognized that the social consensus achieved around the Programme was a critical component to sustaining it. Anticipating the numerous challenges ahead and the need to follow through with more difficult and painful reforms with the hope that tangible growth would be derived was acknowledged, along with the resolve to use these potentials to help preserve the social consensus and enable it in a manner that would help to create, foster and continue the momentum.

The government was urged to continue mitigating the effects of the adjustment measures and to protect social spending bearing in mind the ambitious primary surplus which was 7.5% of GDP which served to boost confidence and to further the sustainable downward trajectory of public debt. The Jamaican authorities had achieved this target by cutting expenditures by over two percentage points of GDP in 2012/2013 and 2.7% in 2013/2014.

Some authors have maintained that the Programme being undertaken by Jamaica was characterized by severe austerity with continuing low growth albeit that the objective of the comprehensive economic programme was to significantly raise the rate of real GDP and per capita growth. Johnston (2015) reiterated that the achievement of a primary surplus of 7.5% of GDP as a requirement was comparatively reflective of the context of Greece within which the IMF had an ongoing programme. Greece, a member of the European Union whose circumstances were similar to that of Jamaica, was required by the IMF, to achieve a primary surplus of only 3.0% of GDP and 4.5% thereafter, in a context which was considered politically unsustainable, hence comparatively, the notable fragility of the Jamaican situation.

It was acknowledged that the risks remained high; however, the significance and the strong commitment demonstrated by the Government of Jamaica to the implementation of the programme engendered a degree of comfort on the part of the IMF. Domestic stakeholders, such as the Economic Programme Oversight Committee (EPOC) gave support to the fundamental reforms and they played a strategic role by monitoring the Programme's implementation and the fulfilment of the targets agreed, also facilitating any minor and corrective action to be adopted.

The recognition of the potential of the completion of the Programme to enable the Jamaican economy to shift towards a new trajectory involving higher growth, improved welfare, greater job creation and moreover sustainable debt were apparent.

The Eighth Review suggested an improved business and consumer confidence against the risks to the programme, which although they were high, exhibited some recession, but still warranted a degree of care. A new Energy Stabilization and Energy Efficiency Enhancement Fund (ESEEEF) was introduced to finance a hedge against risks of sharp oil price increases, perceived as a financial buffer for the balance of payments, etc.

New regimes for special economic zones will be created to replace the existing export free zones areas ensuring compliance with WTO and CARICOM requirements. This was viewed as a means to attract new economic activities to Jamaica and support the provision of physical and human infrastructure as well as a competitive regulatory regime by exploiting the synergies created.

New legislation, with respect to the tax regimes as part of the SEZ legislative requirements, would be created to be consistent with, as well as to safeguard the tax system. The expected applications from participants from certain sectors and industries, such as tourism, telecommunications, financial services, real estate, property management and health services, etc., would be vetted in terms of eligibility as well as compatibility with the strategic objectives of the SEZ development in terms of operational access.

Although not directly related to strategic investments, the government was intent upon implementing and updating critical supporting measures, such as, revisiting public financial management practices, concerns of capital mobility, and access, the management of domestic and public financial flows, undertaking tax reforms, providing access to credit across various productive sectors, as well as lowering the costs and time taken with regard to doing business for private sector activities.

Legislative amendments and various other reforms across the board had been targeted by the government in collaboration with its development partners, to stimulate and encourage the nurturing, growth and development of the strategic investments and interventions to realize their potential in terms of impacting Jamaica's growth and wealth creation trajectory in a positive way.

The Ninth Review reflected some improvements in the macroeconomic fundamentals juxtaposed against high unemployment and fragile growth. The Petrocaribe debt buyback (Arnesen et al., 2019) afforded Jamaica some important fiscal savings in the short term however it was noted that Jamaica's wage bill was high and posed a challenge for fiscal policy. Critical reforms in the financial sector remained; however, the gaps that would impact stability were also being addressed.

The importance of the business environment and its role to boost private investment and growth was recognized through various approaches towards reducing the cost of doing business improving access to credit as well as reforms with respect to the energy sector to further the reduction in electricity costs. These were all in process. Other avenues to be explored will require time to frame and develop and also put in place, such as a comprehensive strategy to deepen the use of electronic payments as well as to establish the necessary infrastructure in rural areas. Overall mechanisms for the electronic transfer of benefits inclusive of streamlining procedures for making social payments were to be pursued.

The Tenth Review, entailed reflections on the need for a stronger financial system and to promote resilience, whereby Jamaica was encouraged to deepen aspects of the sector through a number of measures, which included prudential regulations and enhancing standards across the Deposit Taking Institutions (DTIs) in terms of a code of conduct and regulations to be implemented. This was another important appendage towards improving capital mobility, the modalities to engender the continued financial flows towards financing the strategic investments and the business environment to support growth and encourage investments. Interventions were also encouraged to improve processes concerning property registration, trade facilitation, the ease of processes for start-up businesses as well as the ease of paying taxes.

Conclusion

With respect to the pillars of the Programme (Sullivan, 2010) as well as matters of fiscal policy there remained additional structural reforms to be addressed as well as remaining policies that had to be reshaped and modified to enhance ongoing support of the growth imperatives, such as, effecting improvements and increased efficiency within the taxation system. Financial sector resilience and the strengthening of the conduct and timeliness of monetary operations were required to achieve higher growth. Continuity in strengthening the social safety net and transforming the public sector in a manner to support the growth imperatives, was critical to sustain, as well as bringing to fruition the enabling environment to provide for further movements along the growth trajectory.

References

Arnesen, A., Clancy, J., Elliott, D., & Francis, K. (2019, December 5). Venezuela, petrocaribe, and the "orgy of corruption". *Caribbean Investigative Journalism Network*. https://www.cijn.org/venezuela-petrocaribe-and-the-orgy-of-corruption/. Accessed September 7, 2020.

International Monetary Fund. (2013a). *Jamaica: Request for an Extended Arrangement under the Extended Fund Facility* (Western Hemisphere Department, No. 13/126). Washington, DC.

International Monetary Fund. (2013b). *Jamaica: First review under the Extended Arrangement under the Extended Fund Facility and request for modification of performance criteria* (Western Hemisphere Department, No. 13/304). Washington, DC.

International Monetary Fund. (2013c). *Jamaica: Second review under the Extended Arrangement under the Extended Fund Facility and request for modification of performance criteria* (Western Hemisphere Department, No. 13/378). Washington, DC.

International Monetary Fund. (2014a). *Jamaica: Third review under the Extended Arrangement under the Extended Fund Facility and request for modification of performance criteria- Staff report* (Western Hemisphere Department, No. 14/85). Washington, DC.

International Monetary Fund. (2014b). *Staff report for the 2014 Article IV consultation and fourth review under the Extended Arrangement under the Extended Fund Facility and request for modification of performance criteria* (Western Hemisphere Department, No. 14/169). Washington, DC.

International Monetary Fund. (2014c). *Jamaica: Fifth review under the Extended Fund Facility and request for modification of performance criteria—Staff report* (Western Hemisphere Department, No. 14/295). Washington, DC.

International Monetary Fund. (2014d). *Jamaica: Sixth review under the Extended Fund Facility and request for modification of performance criteria—Staff report* (Western Hemisphere Department, No. 14/359). Washington, DC.

International Monetary Fund. (2015a). *Jamaica—Seventh review under the Extended Fund Facility and request for modification of performance criteria—Staff report, press release; and statement by the executive director for Jamaica* (Western Hemisphere Department, No. 15/95). Washington, DC. http://www.imf.org/external/pubs/cat/longres.aspx?sk=42834.0.

International Monetary Fund. (2015b). *Jamaica—Eighth review under the Extended Fund Facility and request for waiver for the non-observance of performance criterion and modification of performance criteria—Press release and staff report* (Western Hemisphere Department, No. 15/150). Washington, DC.

International Monetary Fund. (2015c). *Jamaica—Ninth review under the arrangement under the Extended Fund Facility and request for modification of performance criteria- press release; staff report; and statement by the executive director for Jamaica* (Western Hemisphere Department, No. 15/270). Washington, DC.

International Monetary Fund. (2015d). *Jamaica—Tenth review under the arrangement under the Extended Fund Facility and request for modification of performance criteria—Press release; staff report; and statement by the executive director for Jamaica* (Western Hemisphere Department, No. 15/343). Washington, DC.

International Monetary Fund. (2016a). *Jamaica—Article IV consultation, eleventh and twelfth reviews under the Extended Fund Facility and request for modification of performance criteria—press release; staff report; and statement by the executive director for Jamaica* (Western Hemisphere Department, No. 16/181). Washington, DC.

International Monetary Fund. (2016b). *Jamaica—Thirteenth review under the arrangement under the Extended Fund Facility—Press release and staff report* (Western Hemisphere Department, No. 16/297). Washington, DC.

Johnston, J. (2015). *Partners in austerity: Jamaica, the United States and the international monetary fund* (No. 2015-09). Center for Economic and Policy Research (CEPR).

Planning Institute of Jamaica. (2012). *A growth-inducement strategy for Jamaica in the short and medium term* (G. Hutchinson & D. Harris, Eds.). Kingston: Planning Institute of Jamaica.

Sullivan, M. P. (2010, July). *Jamaica: Background and US relations*. Library of congress. Washington, DC: Congressional Research Service. https://apps.dtic.mil/dtic/tr/fulltext/u2/a525021.pdf.

CHAPTER 4

Lining Up and Jumping the Hurdles to Long-Term Growth II

Introduction

Jamaica is often viewed as a conundrum in discussions around economic development in small, open, developing countries. The country's status as being on par with many countries at the point of its independence in 1962 in terms of its gross domestic product (GDP) per capita can be sharply contrasted with its standing with the same countries using the same metric in 2020. The canonical comparison is between Jamaica and Singapore that had relatively similar GDP per capita in the 1960s of approximately USD430 (see Fig. 4.1). Both economies were then on the verge of initiating economic development and economic growth with Jamaica experiencing significant increases in foreign direct investment as a means of counteracting the relatively low levels of domestic financial capital and savings that could be activated to spur investment and growth. Infrastructure development would have also been nascent and required significant levels of public investment to develop critical public utilities such as bridges, sewerage, rainwater carriageways and initiation of new town developments across the island to stimulate private investment.

The divide in terms of recorded GDP per capita began to appear in the late 1970s. By 1980, Singapore's GDP per capita was almost four times larger than Jamaica's and Barbados' ratio was larger than Jamaica's by more than three times (World Bank, 2020). In 2010, the GDP per capita of Jamaica was one-tenth that of Singapore and the two countries ended

C. Clarke and C. Nelson, *Jamaica's Evolving Relationship with the IMF*,
https://doi.org/10.1007/978-3-030-59204-2_4

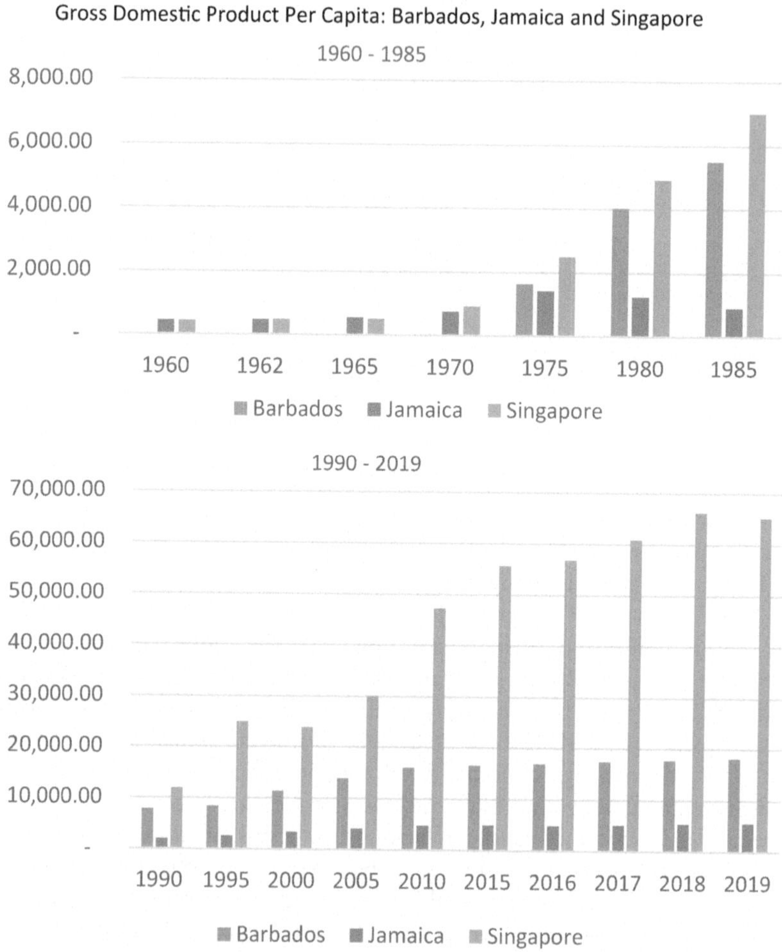

Fig. 4.1 Comparative per capita growth rates for Barbados, Jamaica and Singapore 1960–1985 and 1990–2019 (*Source* Collated by Authors from the World Bank open data portal [World Bank, 2020] Retrieved from: https://data.worldbank.org/)

2019 with the Singaporean economy generating twelve times the income per person than the amount of income per person that was generated by the Jamaican economy. Over this period, whilst Barbados' economy performed better than Jamaica's, the growth of Barbados' economy was not at the fast pace set by the Singapore economy and therefore the size of the Barbadian economy in comparison to the Jamaican economy was maintained at a factor of three.

The drive to deliver on the demands of economic development in the context of this very poor relative and absolute economic output performance, resulted in significant imbalances and challenges in the ability of successive Jamaican governments to strike a sustainable balance between meeting the needs of the poorest and most vulnerable and contending with the basic fiscal and monetary equations that determine investor confidence and broad-based private sector growth. As discussed in Clarke and Nelson (2020), the initial period within which this struggle occurred—the mid to late 1970s—was one in which the Jamaican population was agitated. More than four decades prior, the Moyne Commission, despatched to the West Indies in response to the widespread riots in the region, identified and assessed the critical areas of concern—in its broad report on the deplorable social conditions in the region—and instigated the implementation of a series of projects and interventions intended to: reverse the situation; restore order; and, empower the population to support the expanded state and private sector machinery that would be required to generate sustainable livelihoods in the twentieth-century post-Emancipation period (see Chapter 3 in Clarke and Nelson [2020]). The need to quickly and sustainably improve the socio-economic condition of a large segment of the population would be central to controlling the levels of dissent and revolt that resulted in the visit of Lord Moyne. Mechanisms to address the low levels of capital—physical, human and monetary—due to the absence of investments in these areas in the preceding century of Jamaica's development were imperative.

Nevertheless, the sentiment across the Caribbean was that whilst the efforts of the Moyne Commission and the subsequent implementation of a wide range of measures—both in individual islands and establishing multi-island interventions where the allocated amount and the logistics issues such as population size indicated it to be more efficient to do so—were commendable, they were inadequate based on the scale of the need in the majority of the islands. Many countries in the Caribbean had not had any significant improvement in the major infrastructure and systems that are required to support rapid private investment growth as well as individual empowerment. In many islands where absenteeism planters were the status quo and where the profitability of sugar had long declined, there had been little effort investment by the British Crown Government (the Crown) to maintain or provide critical public goods that were critical to the ability of ex-slaves to chart their own economic independence and thereby support the establishment of a non-plantation centred society. The Crown did not see fit to provide substantive and large numbers of educational facilities across the island; modern and broad types of health care facilities and insurance options; and, modern and non-combative security forces. The security and education systems previously installed in Jamaica were, instead, implemented largely in an effort to control the enslaved populations and to facilitate the productivity of the plantations and the export of their products to various ports in Europe. This included: shipping ports; major roads from farm areas to the ports; and, various agricultural boards to control prices, monitor production and support the protection and export of crops to Europe. As the profitability of plantation operations declined, investment in even these the barest of institutions were reduced as was their maintenance. As the prospects for Emancipation dawned and drew closer, some planters and/or their representatives exited the Caribbean and were compensated for the losses experienced due to the end of the trade in enslaved humans, the reduced profitability of their plantation in the West Indies, and, the Emancipation of the enslaved populations.

Emancipation—though a game changer in terms of the legal status of the previously enslaved population—did not bring forth the economic and social upliftment that was sorely needed (Hall, 1993). The lack of investment in both private production which was largely plantation-centric and large-scale infrastructure development by the then government, combined with the inability of the newly freed persons to produce non-sugar agricultural output on an economically efficient and profitable basis negatively impacted the optimism felt by those who were emancipated. Many were unable to eke out a subsistence for themselves and their families in the period immediately following Emancipation. With the end of the apprenticeship regime, there was an opportunity for workers to now negotiate their wages and the terms and conditions of the service rendered to their employer. This process was, however, fraught with misunderstandings and complicated by the centuries-long networks existing between the island's planter class that enabled them to collude in setting these terms. Part of their strategy was to offer workers a wage lower than that which was paid under the recently ended apprenticeship system. There were also large differences in the wages paid across parishes and the terms associated with the use of the sugar barracks also varied (Wilmot, 1993). As a result of the wage offer that was lower than the apprenticeship wage, there were a series of strikes and other actions as workers decided that their dignity was being questioned. There was also the emergence and intensification of difficult class relations which eventually manifested in resistance across the island. Planters held their line and attempted to use immigration to provide workers for their plantation, and, as a result, there were marked declines in agricultural production as it relates to sugar production. Aligned to this was the natural need for workers to secure alternative ways of generating a livelihood that now appeared to be more possible in the urban centres. The motivation for worker exodus from the plantation was therefore not only the desire to rid oneself of that environment but also the approach taken by the planter class to significantly undervalue the labour they provided (Hall, 1993). Given the pace of the development of the local economy and society vis-à-vis the size of the population that now required access to: markets for their labour, and other critical social services that each freedperson would need to provide for themselves was non-existent, and, furthermore, there was no income from which to pay for access if provided. This contributed to very negative experiences in the rural areas, and as life became more and more difficult there, the population began to migrate to the urban areas in search of better opportunities to earn an income and establish an economic base for their life.

This rural–urban drift would later be associated with overcrowding in the underprovisioned areas in urban areas. The rise of tenements and other forms of very crowded living arrangements overwhelmed the very nascent city infrastructure which did not boast indoor running water or toilet facilities, very modest dwelling, limited number of houses connected to sewerage plants, and sporadic garbage collection. In relation to eking out a living 'in town' the options for the women were in the area of domestic work whilst the men tried to get into factory and other forms of office work as the level of education that the typical rural migrant possessed was inadequate to help them obtain higher paying job opportunities. The small number of options to revisit and improve one's educational qualifications was slim and the demands and labour conditions at work became unbearable until it reached a crescendo in the 1930s when labour-related riots occurred more frequently resulting in chaos and stirring the disenchantment with not just the individual's state of affair but also with how the country was being run.

Moyne's voyage to the region appeared to open the door to the exit clause for both the Crown and Jamaica—independence. However, the disappointment did not abate despite the accomplishment of independence and national sovereignty. Despite having gained political independence from Great Britain and an expectation that self-governance of the affairs of Jamaica by Jamaicans would have resulted in the long sought-after development. Each Jamaican anticipated the expansion of the opportunities that independence would provide that would give them their own possibility of generating an income that could enable them to acquire education, better employment prospects and housing for themselves and their families.

Many of the development challenges being addressed in this modern period of Jamaica's social and economic history can be associated with the extended periods of inadequate opportunities for the population as a whole to improve themselves through their own effort, and provided room for the political machinery to step in with promises to provide for the population. The challenges of inadequate housing supply and maintenance, rural development, labour market issues and crime and violence remain topics that featured in the most recent 2020 election campaign. To do this, the emerging government needed to support the development of the economy such that its growth could provide it with sufficient derivative tax revenues that would enable it to provide the level of support required by it's citizens. Since independence, whilst there was an initial period of relatively high rates of positive growth this was dwarfed by the long stretch of consecutive decades of relatively low and negative growth. Needless to say, various governments have therefore found it difficult to resolve these issues summarily. Progress has been made in some of these areas and to some degree based on various prioritization methodologies that have helped to focus domestic and multilateral resources. Despite this, new challenges emerged thereby muting the extent to which sustained progress could be effected. Further, the informality of the economy and informal operations of even formally operating entities that have yet to be addressed makes it difficult to strengthen the social capital needed to underpin robust economic development.

Very recently issues of fiscal discipline and the need to get control of the debt burdens that had approached 150% leading up to the 2013

Extended Fund Facility (EFF) would have been part of the discussions in the public domain given the challenges encountered in the implementation of the 2010 Stand-By Agreement. The build-up in the debt was largely due to the impact of the resolution of the domestic financial sector crisis during the 1990s that prioritized the preservation of depositor Funds (Clarke & Nelson, 2020). Whilst the fiscal and debt management challenges have been dealt with quite successfully since the 2013 EFF, as indicated above, Jamaica has suffered from a series of long-standing development challenges to which its anaemic growth has been attributed. These constraints have been analysed and prioritized by the World Bank (WB) in its most recent Country Economic Memorandums (CEM) of 2004 and 2011. This chapter attempts to provide a catalogue of these binding constraints and an assessment of the extent to which the three historic IMF Agreements with Jamaica—in 2010, 2013 and 2016—have enabled Jamaica to make strides in addressing these 'binding constraints to growth'.

The Binding Constraints to Growth in Jamaica

Through its CEM the WB has consistently explored the various dimensions of the Jamaican economy and society. The emerging issues and challenges documented in the 2004 and 2011 CEMs are broadly the same despite incremental gains and they therefore continue to form part of the binding constraints to the high rates of economic growth that successive governments have attempted to achieve but which has continued to be elusive. Having emerged from a most disruptive crisis in the domestic financial sector, which arose from a combination of fiscal and monetary policy and individual and commercial risk-taking activities that resulted in an escalation of interest rates and the ballooning of unserviceable debt (Clarke & Nelson, 2020), which the government chose to resolve by absorbing the bad debt portfolio and preserving depositor savings—the 2004 WB CEM highlighted the resultant crisis in the public debt as the number one constraint to growth in Jamaica (World Bank, 2004). This is due to the fact that high rates of debt-to-GDP—which increased from 79% in FY1996/97 to almost 150% in FY2002/03 was acting to crowd out investment by the private sector as well as the ability of the government to make productive investments. Simultaneously, the way in which the governance structure of the public bodies and government entities was designed, enabled them to generate contingent liabilities that would eventually become a burden on the consolidated Fund. The other dimension of the challenge was the fact that the country's tax effort was already high at approximately 30% which was comparable to advanced economies.

In order to address these challenges the WB in 2004 recommended: an increase in the primary surplus to an excess of 10%, control the growth of the wage bill, and, constraining the other areas of public expenditure allocated to non-interest, non-capital areas, and, privatize entities that no longer needed to remain in the control of the government and sell government-held shares in entities. The report also advocated for increases in capital expenditure on infrastructure in order to provide a crowding-in effect for private sector investment. The reduction and management of existing and limitations on the growth of unbudgeted and unmonitored contingent liabilities, through increased transparency, oversight and exposure of the entities that tend to accrue these liabilities to public scrutiny were the main recommendations intended to constrain further deterioration in the fiscal accounts arising from these types of activities. The policy recommendations also included the need for an expanded tax base with specific efforts to capture the informal sector whilst simultaneously reducing the subsidies on tertiary education whilst increasing the focus on investments in the early years.

This constraint was separated into two components in the 2011 CEM. The third binding constraint of this report referenced the distortionary nature of tax policy with a focus on the role that the preferential treatment of certain industries led to an economic structure where these sectors were performing but in isolation of other sectors that, were they connected through linkages, could have yielded more robust out-turns overall, in economic growth (World Bank, 2011). The impact of the complex tax system on the business environment was borne out by the World Bank Doing Business Report in relation to the time it took to file and pay taxes and the complexity of the calculations that needed to be made to arrive at an entity's tax liability. The final strand of this constraint relates to the business environment and the challenges posed by the high concentration of economic activity in particular areas and levels within a sector; and, the combined impact of crime and violence, government bureaucracy and logistics, issues referenced in the 2004 edition and reiterated in 2011. In order to address these constraints the report proposes the initiation of a consultative process that would result in the termination of the system of tax incentives, expansion of the tax base, simplification of the policy and payment requirements, and enhancements to the business environment that would invigorate sectors and strengthen linkages between them.

The fourth binding constraint recorded in the 2011 CEM revisits the other half of the issues raised under the first constraint in the 2004 CEM. The 2011 version raises the issue of weak public financial management and public service provision that it argues contributes to the distortions created by fiscal policy and therefore constrain growth. The recommendations to address these issues in the short term included: (a) the development of budget guidelines and a complete reform of the budget process; (b) establishing a mechanism to assess and prioritize capital expenditure proposals; (c) continuation of the divestment of public bodies and control of the fiscal risks that emerge from those public bodies that would remain; (d) consolidation of the legal framework for debt management supported by a restructured organizational framework; and, (e) simplification of the operations and procedures at customs.

The 2004 CEM report lists the very high levels of crime and violence as the second most important constraint that needed to be removed to facilitate the country's ability to generate rapid rates of economic growth. The costs of crime to Jamaica's economy are well documented and have been associated with the high costs of security that have to be borne by businesses directly on security and indirectly on the limits it places on the times and physical zones within which economic activity can occur. In manufacturing, where machinery and equipment are designed to operate most efficiently when run on a twenty-four-hour shift, the costs of downtime and underutilization affect business efficiencies, productivity and production. Overall, the CEM cites estimates of crime costing approximately four per cent to the Jamaican economy inclusive of the health costs associated with violent crime (Clarke, 2017; Overseas Security Advisory Council, 2019; Jaitman, 2017). Ultimately, the costs of crime limit the economy's growth potential through various insidious means that tend to be difficult to undo. The information database to support the identification, measurement and policing of crime in ways that increase the social capital in high-crime communities. The experience of young men in the education system was also identified as another are through which reductions in crime count be effected using the school structure to teaching conflict resolution *inter alia*. It is noteworthy that by the 2011 CEM, the issue of high crime had risen to the number one position among the four identified binding constraints to growth. The report provides a series of short to medium-term solutions that could be implemented to address this issue.

The 2004 CEM ranks the poor education outcomes typical of Jamaica's education system as the third obstacle that must be overcome for the country to be able to achieve sustained growth in the medium to long term. Critical exit points from the education system into the world of work are used in this assessment of the quality of the system. The report indicated that up to the early 2000s, only thirty per cent of the students taking the Mathematics examination in Grade 11 passed the exam. When compared to peers in the US labour market—a destination which is highly popular among Jamaican migrants—Jamaicans receive the lowest returns to their education levels. Ultimately the low education outcomes reduce the level of productivity of the workforce, which, in turn, constrains the extent to which the economy can grow. A fraction of these poor outcomes can be linked to the wide variation in the quality of the education offered in many of the schools that had been built in the 1990s as part of the attempt to increase access. Coming out of this school-building drive was the emergence of a multi-tiered school system in which various types of schools with different levels of preparation of students. The most deleterious impact of this variation in quality arises from the fact that students from poor socio-economic backgrounds were disproportionately enrolled in schools that have low quality and these students were more likely to be absent, have home environments that make it difficult for them to maintain appropriate study and preparation time, and, at the time more likely to drop-out of educational pursuits. Altogether, the system and the systematic challenges experienced by poor students resulted in: low levels of education, an increase in the cadre of young persons who were at risk, and, an increased the likelihood that young males would become involved in crime. In order to address the problems the report recommended to shift subventions from tertiary education to the early years in order to improve the foundation of students entering the primary education system. Addressing the incentive structure of schools by tying subventions to enrolment and enabling the administrators to utilize Funds in more flexible ways; improving the facilities in schools that are underperforming to enhance the quality of education they provide; and, publicizing school results were the high-level suggested changes that were advanced to improve educational outcomes. Proposals akin to the voucher systems used in the United States and some Latin American countries where students who would not ordinarily be able to gain entry to high performing private schools were able to secure such places in an attempt to improve achievement as well as to incentivize private institutions to support the increase in the number of school spaces after Grade 9 was also proposed in the 2004 CEM in this regard.

The deficiencies in the country's human capital as a result of these challenges were highlighted in the 2011 CEM as the second binding constraint or obstacle to economic growth in Jamaica. Poor educational outcomes would have resulted in an inadequately trained labour force generally and those who managed to perform creditably in the system very often became migrants contributing to the phenomenon of 'brain drain'. Wenner (2016) cites calculations from research on the international mobility of skilled workers by Docquier and Marfouk (2004). Among Caribbean countries Jamaica, St. Vincent and the Grenadines, and Grenada were reported to have 85% of their tertiary trained graduates migrate to countries that are a part of the Organisation for Economic Cooperation and Development (OECD). These three Caribbean countries were only surpassed by Guyana whose rate of migration of tertiary graduates was 89%. A previous study by the Organisation of American States (OAS) explored trends in international migration had estimated that the emigration from Saint Vincent, Jamaica and the Grenadines translated to a loss equivalent to between 40 and 50% of a single-year cohort of youth ages 20–24 during the period 2005 and 2010 (Organization of American States, 2011). Guyana's loss was estimated at over 60% in the same period and the same comparator group. Immigration from Jamaica is reported to have increased from 117,795 persons in 1996 to 123,420 persons in 2006. In terms of permanent resident status for the United States, the number of Jamaicans ranged from a low of 13,347 in 2003 to a high of 24,976 during the ten-year period from the year 2000 to 2009. The migratory movement slowed during the financial crisis at lower levels however the largest migratory movements during the crisis were from Latin America to Canada and the United States (Organization of American States, 2011). In terms of the educational level of migrants, the OAS report indicated that among Jamaican migrants, 26% of men were tertiary trained, 59% had attained upper secondary education and another 16% were trained to a level equivalent to less than upper secondary. Among female migrants from Jamaica, a much larger proportion—38%—are tertiary trained; 50% were had attained education to the upper secondary level; whilst, in contrast to the males, only 12% of females had only less than upper secondary training. The report indicates that in general, it is more likely that a migrant possesses higher levels of education—that is it is the more highly skilled and educated workers who tend to migrate. The exit of these relatively highly trained and/or educated workers from the Jamaican labour market is anticipated to have negative impacts not only on the productivity of the labour force and the public and private sector's ability to renew itself and sustain high rates of economic growth, but also for the efficiency of the education and training systems that are heavily subsidized by the government.

The negative impacts on the labour market in the source countries of migrants such as Jamaica tend to be weighed against the major benefit that these migrants tend to provide in the form of remittances. Whilst Jamaica has benefitted from remittance flows that are estimated to be equivalent to 13.8% of the Jamaican economy, the OAS (2011) indicates that according to World Bank data on remittances, remittance inflows into Jamaica declined by 11.8% between 2008 and 2009 and by 7.4% during the heights of the global economic and financial crisis, 2008–2010.

The strategies proposed to address these issues in the 2011 CEM were largely centred on the development and implementation of training opportunities that would target future workers and current workers through the use of Technical and Vocational Training (TVET) type interventions that would get workers ready for employment in particular sectors. Emphasis would then be able to be placed on learning outcomes and application of knowledge to solve problems rather than only on the academic principles. On the job training opportunities would be revamped with new investment in order to upgrade the skills of workers and the infusion of modern principles in the area of standards, certification and outcome-based training that focusses on building competencies. Since then, the National Policy on International Migration and Development (NPIMD), Jamaica's migration policy framework has been developed (International Office of Migration, 2018 and Government of Jamaica, 2017). The NPIMD provides the response of the Government of Jamaica to the changing nature of migration in a manner that ensures that the goals of Vision 2030 and by extension the needs of the Jamaican population are met within the context of emigration from Jamaica and immigration into Jamaica.

Inadequate access to credit across the private sector associated with the sharp uptick in public debt-to-GDP due to the resolution regime implemented to address the domestic financial sector crisis discussed above is the fourth constraint to sustained growth identified in the 2004 CEM. The mechanism through which this impact is felt is through the heightened perception of risk associated with lending to the productive sector due to the massive defaults that led to the crisis in the late 1990s. The very conservative commercial banking system displayed even greater reticence at being willing to engaging in extensive lending to the productive sector. The constraints that this stance had on the productive engine of economic growth was most largely felt by small firms and those that were just being conceptualized and needed funding to support inception activities. The 2004 report also indicated that based on the returns to government paper that were being offered in the approach to managing the large debt stock whilst continuing to provide public services entrepreneurs may find it more financially rewarding to become *rentiers* to the government rather than enduring the risks associated with initiating and running an enterprise. In order to address these issues, the WB recommended the establishment of credit registries to strengthen the ability of lending agencies to assess potential borrowers. In addition, there needed to be an expansion in the types of collateral that was required by the financial institutions in order to enable holders of non-traditional forms of collateral to participate in the productive process using their asset holdings. The need to reduce the public sector appetite for debt through increasing the primary surplus was also flagged as an important initiative to address the poor incentives and hostile business environment that constrained economic growth.

The 2004 WB CEMs fifth and final constraint to sustainable growth in Jamaica was the range of economic conditions that compromized the competitiveness of Jamaican goods and services. The contributing factors include the appreciation of the real exchange rate throughout most of the 1990s measured with respect to the CPI as well as to wages. The report indicates that these trends contributed to the rise of production in the services sector to the detriment of tradable goods. When combined with the previous four constraints— (1) the various costs associated with and imposed by the high debt-to-GDP ratios; (2) high rates of violent crime; (3) poor educational outcomes; and, (4) the accompanying deterioration of the fiscal accounts, and the poor access to credit—the fifth constraint meant that the economy was one in which the production of goods was subject to very high costs that had implications for cash flow and other management tools that only the larger, more established firms could contend with. To address these issues, the report emphasized the need for the government to maintain credible macroeconomic policies in the context of the flexible exchange rate and to ensure that there are export enabling policies particularly in the area of wage controls and the processes to facilitate the importation of raw materials and exportation of finished goods.

Whilst each CEM could be adjudged as specifying literally a handful of constraints to growth that could lead to the belief that these issues should therefore be easily resolved, the fact that is that many of these challenges are linked to some of the systemic rules and frameworks in how many of the societal and economic structures were conceptualized and instituted for generations and in some cases centuries. These five constraints in the 2004 CEM and the four in the 2011 CEM with many common ones across both publications also find common ground with the findings in the report of the Moyne Commission. In fact, some of the proposed strategies from both CEMs are consistent with those implemented in response to the challenges pointed out by Moyne. The long-standing nature of these challenges and their seeming intractability to the solution set that is proposed by each commission, analysis, policy and project is indicative perhaps of the need for systematic structural change rather than incremental forms of change that end up being benign given the magnitude of the challenge and the realities of the difficulty of life for large proportions of the population.

The period leading up to Jamaica's return to the IMF in 2010 was fraught with public commentary on the extent to which the IMF would allow Jamaica to craft an economic programme that would allow it to also make strides to initiate the resolution of these problems rather than having the agreement be the final nail in the coffin of the viability of the Jamaican society. The next section assesses this issue partially by exploring the extent to which the agreements that Jamaica entered into with the IMF addressed any of the binding constraints raised in both CEM.

IMF Agreements with Jamaica: Solving or Worsening the Binding Constraints?

Jamaica's return to the IMF in 2009 could be viewed as historic and a turning of the tides. Having had a tumultuous relationship with the Fund during the late 1970s (Clarke & Nelson, 2020); returning to them during the 1980s; and, the termination of our borrowing relationship in the 1990s; the re-engagement of the Fund was initially viewed as the reneging of a previous disavowal of the entity by the Jamaican government if not its population. This view was quickly dispelled for the more pragmatic view of the IMF as having undergone significant internal reforms (Grabel, 2011) and the absence of any other player who could credibly support our balance of payments and help us access sufficient technical assistance to address various components of our economic reform agenda. Since the initiation of the discussions surrounding the resumption of a borrowing relationship between Jamaica and the IMF, Jamaica has entered into four arrangements—two borrowing relationships (see Clarke and Nelson [2010] for the first and Chapter 2 of this volume for the second), one precautionary (see Chapter 9 of this volume), and the other access to rapid financing (see Chapter 11 of this volume) with the Fund beginning in 2010. The aim of this subsection is to assess the extent to which the various conditionalities of the economic programme in each agreement support the reduction or removal of one or more constraint to growth identified in either of the two CEMs. In some ways, this analysis will explore whether the view that the IMF imposes conditionalities on countries in a somewhat arbitrary and unfounded manner will be indirectly explored by adjudging the authenticity of the measures implemented against long-established constraints to sustained rates of economic growth. Having successfully implementing the conditionalities, the question that follows is: to what extent has this enabled Jamaica to make progress that will unleash or propel it towards high rates of economic growth?

Table 4.1 presents a detailed breakout of the constraints in alphabetical order as outlined in both CEMs along with a brief indication of the potential impact that each constraint has had on economic growth in Jamaica and the year of the CEM that indicated the particular constraint. The remaining columns of the table present information relating to the specific IMF Agreement document or review period, the agreed timeline targeted for completion, the type of conditionality and the parameters of the reform that was implemented to address the constraint specified. Overall, reforms were implemented in the area of the debt crises and fiscal deterioration as is expected in the context of an economic reform programme supported by the IMF.

Nevertheless, it is noteworthy that the three social constraints identified in both CEMs are addressed in two of the three agreements during the period. Secondly, there are no constraints from either CEM that have not been addressed in at least one agreement or at the point of the scheduled reviews of one of the agreements.

The macroeconomic constraint identified in either of the two CEMs receiving the largest number of interventions throughout the IMF Agreements relates to the efforts related to the need to restore financial stability

Table 4.1 Alignment of constraints to growth with IMF conditionalities implemented by Jamaica 2010–2019

CEM constraints	*Impact on growth*	*CEM*	*Review/agreement*	*Completion target*	*Conditionality type*	*Direct measure implemented*
Macroeconomic constraints						
Challenging business environment	Low levels of business activity and innovation	2011	Seventh Review of 2013 EFF	1 May 2015	Structural Benchmark	Government to complete pilot testing of ASYCUDA World (covering imports and exports) in the Kingston port
			Seventh Review of 2013 EFF	30 June 2015	Structural Benchmark	Government to table in Parliament proposals for a comprehensive overhaul of the Customs Act
			Eighth Review of 2013 EFF	1 June 2015	Structural Benchmark	Comprehensive growth strategy that aimed to improve the business environment
			Tenth Review of 2013 EFF	31 March 2016	Structural Benchmark	Increase the capacity of the Post-Clearance Audit (PCA) unit in the JCA through the hiring of 15 more auditors
Complex tax system	Difficulty incentivising business formalization	2011	First Review of 2010 EFF	June 2010	Structural Benchmark	Prepare time-bound tax administration reform action plan

CEM constraints	*Impact on growth*	*CEM*	*Review/agreement*	*Completion target*	*Conditionality type*	*Direct measure implemented*
			2013 EFF	30 June 2013	Structural Benchmark	Parliament to adopt amendments to the Revenue Administration Act to (i) provide access to third-party information, to enhance compliance management, and (ii) empower the TAJ to require mandatory e-filing for groups of taxpayers and/or types of taxes
			2013 EFF	30 June 2013	Structural Benchmark	Government to increase the professional staff of Large Taxpayer Office (LTO) to 120 staff members
			Second Review of 2013 EFF	31 March 2014	Structural Benchmark	Government to make e-filing mandatory for LTO clients with respect to General Consumption Tax (GCT) and Corporate Income Tax (CIT)

(continued)

Table 4.1 (continued)

CEM constraints	*Impact on growth*	*CEM*	*Review/agreement*	*Completion target*	*Conditionality type*	*Direct measure implemented*
			Fifth review of 2013 EFF	31 March 2014	Structural Benchmark	Broader tax reform to become effective, including the modernization of taxes, with limited exemptions, and lower tax rates
			Fifth Review of 2013 EFF	30 June 2014	Structural Benchmark	Government to table in parliament amendments to the GCT as stipulated in paragraph 12 of the June 2014 MEFP
			Seventh Review of 2013 EFF	30 November 2015	Structural Benchmark	Government to introduce new productivity indicators, in consultation with Fund staff, to measure the effectiveness and efficiency of the tax system

CEM constraints	*Impact on growth*	*CEM*	*Review/agreement*	*Completion target*	*Conditionality type*	*Direct measure implemented*
			Ninth Review of 2013 EFF	31 October 2015	Structural Benchmark	Government to table legislation governing the tax regime that will be part of the SEZ legislation consistent with the criteria listed in the June 2015 MEFP par. 13 to help safeguard the integrity of the tax system and avoid tax leakage
			Thirteenth Review of 2013 EFF	31 December 2016	Structural Benchmark	Conclude all work on the calculation of new rates and bands for property taxes, consistent with the 2013 valuations, and submitting them to Cabinet for approval
			Thirteenth Review of 2013 EFF	28 February 2015	Structural Benchmark	Government to implement Phase 1 (Registration, GCT, SCT, GART, Telephone) of the GENTAX integrated tax software package

(continued)

Table 4.1 (continued)

CEM constraints	*Impact on growth*	*CEM*	*Review/agreement*	*Completion target*	*Conditionality type*	*Direct measure implemented*
			2016 SBA	31 December 2016	Structural Benchmark	The new rates and bands for property taxes using the 2013 land valuations will be completed and submitted to Cabinet
			Fifth review of 2016 PSBA	27 March 2019	Structural Benchmark	Comprehensive tax reform to broaden base and simplify the system
Debt Crisis	Crowding out of private sector Reductions in investment Limited growth in productivity	2004	2010 SBA		Prior Action	Launch and complete debt exchange operation that, in comparison to the existing securities, achieves an estimated saving of over 3% of GDP in FY2010/11 and a reduction in the amount of debt maturing during 2010–2012 by at least two-thirds
			2010 SBA		Structural Benchmarks	Debt Management Strategy
			Third Review 2010 SBA	September 2010	Structural Benchmarks	Hire a resident Technical Financial Advisor and a Project Manager for a 1–2-year period
			Third Review 2010 SBA	January 2011	Structural Benchmarks	Hire of project manager and technical advisor

CEM constraints	*Impact on growth*	*CEM*	*Review/agreement*	*Completion target*	*Conditionality type*	*Direct measure implemented*
			Second Review 2010 SBA	December 2010	Structural Benchmarks	Submit draft debt management law to Parliament
			Third Review 2010 SBA	March 2012	Structural Benchmarks	Complete restructuring of debt management functions
			Third Review 2010 SBA	September 2011	Structural Benchmarks	Make the restructured Public Debt Management Unit operational
			Third Review 2010 SBA	June 2010	Structural Benchmarks	Complete cost-risk analysis alternative debt management strategy
			2013 EFF		Prior Action	Government to complete a debt exchange for domestic government bonds consistent with a reduction in the public debt-to-GDP ratio by 2020 equivalent to at least 8.5% of GDP
			2013 EFF		Prior Action	Passage of Debt Law (November 2012)

(continued)

Table 4.1 (continued)

CEM constraints	*Impact on growth*	*CEM*	*Review/agreement*	*Completion target*	*Conditionality type*	*Direct measure implemented*
Distortionary tax policy	Distort economic decision-making with the potential to incentivize sub-optimally performing sectors	2011	2013 EFF		Prior Action	Cabinet to adopt a decision to cease granting of discretionary waivers
				30 September 2013	Structural Benchmark	Government to table Omnibus Tax Incentive Act in the House of Representatives, to eliminate ministerial discretionary powers to grant or validate any tax relief, and put in place a transparent regime for limited tax incentives
				31 December 2013	Structural Benchmark	Government to cease the granting of tax incentives under the regime prior to the Omnibus Tax Incentive Act and of any discretionary tax waivers

CEM constraints	*Impact on growth*	*CEM*	*Review/agreement*	*Completion target*	*Conditionality type*	*Direct measure implemented*
				31 December 2013	Structural Benchmark	Government to cease the granting of tax incentives under the regime prior to the Fiscal Incentives Legislation
Exchange rate appreciation	Jamaica's goods uncompetitive in the world market Transition towards non-tradable goods	2004	2016 SBA	30 September 2017 Modified to 31 October 2018	Structural Benchmark	To enhance the BoJ's governance framework, submit revisions of the BOJ Act to Parliament to improve central bank governance and independence, in line with IMF recommendations. The revisions will modernize arrangements for paying dividends, appointments to the BOJ Board, and provisions of central bank financing to the government

(continued)

Table 4.1 (continued)

CEM constraints	*Impact on growth*	*CEM*	*Review/agreement*	*Completion target*	*Conditionality type*	*Direct measure implemented*
				30 May 2017	Structural Benchmark	Instituting mechanisms to ensure full compliance with the provisions of the Securities (Retail Repurchase Agreement) Regulations that require 'retail repos' to be governed by an MRRA that is signed by both the dealer and the client
Financial Sector Instability	Loss of Investor Confidence	2004	2010 SBA	February 2010	Structural Benchmark	Freeze on issuance of new licences for securities dealers with traditional business model
			2010 SBA	March 2010	Structural Benchmark	Improve frameworks for AML/CFT
			2010 SBA	March 2010	Structural Benchmark	Review and revise, in consultation with IMF, the BOJ's concept paper for an omnibus banking law and the related legislative and regulatory framework to strengthen the oversight of the financial sector (as identified in the 2006 FSAP), (MEFP, paragraph 30)

CEM constraints	*Impact on growth*	*CEM*	*Review/agreement*	*Completion target*	*Conditionality type*	*Direct measure implemented*
			First Review of 2010 SBA	June 2010	Structural Benchmark	Prepare concept paper outlining measures to combat unregulated financial organizations (UFOs)
			2010 SBA	June 2010	Structural Benchmark	Draft a concept paper, in consultation with the IMF, on all major elements to be included in legislation and other measures to address unregulated financial organizations (MEFP, paragraph 32)
			First Review of 2010 SBA	September 2010	Structural Benchmark	Dealers requirement to register customer interest against underlying instruments in a central depository
				December 2010	Structural Benchmark	Adopt supervisory rules to take remedial measures against weak entities on a specified timetable
			2013 EFF	31 December 2013	Structural Benchmark	Government to Establish and Operate a Central Collateral Registry

(continued)

Table 4.1 (continued)

CEM constraints	*Impact on growth*	*CEM*	*Review/agreement*	*Completion target*	*Conditionality type*	*Direct measure implemented*
			2013 EFF	31 December 2013	Structural Benchmark	Government to implement a legal and regulatory framework conducive to Collective Investment Schemes (MEFP Paragraph 45) in consultation with Fund staff. (December 31, 2013)
			2013 EFF	31 March 2014	Structural Benchmark	Government to implement legislative changes regarding unlawful financial operations, consistent with Fund TA advice provided in July 2010
			2013 EFF	31 March 2014	Structural Benchmark	Government to establish a distinct treatment for retail repo client interests in the legal and regulatory framework (MEFP Paragraph 46) in consultation with Fund staff

CEM constraints	*Impact on growth*	*CEM*	*Review/agreement*	*Completion target*	*Conditionality type*	*Direct measure implemented*
			2013 EFF	31 March 2014	Structural Benchmark	Enact Omnibus Banking Law consistent with Fund Staff advice to facilitate effective supervision of the financial sector
			Sixth Review of the 2013 EFF	30 June 2015 Revised to 30 August 2015	Structural Benchmark	Government to finalize the transition of retail reponse to the trust-based framework
			Seventh Review of 2013 EFF	30 September 2015	Structural Benchmark	Government to fully implement the Banking Services Act
			Seventh Review of 2013 EFF	1 November 2015	Structural Benchmark	The BOJ to have overall responsibility for financial stability

(continued)

Table 4.1 (continued)

CEM constraints	*Impact on growth*	*CEM*	*Review/agreement*	*Completion target*	*Conditionality type*	*Direct measure implemented*
			Twelfth Review of 2013 EFF	31 October 2016	Structural Benchmark	Draft a consultation paper for the resolution framework for the entire financial sector, including proposals on (i) the scope, roles and responsibilities, and powers of institutions that would be covered by the resolution regime; and (ii) the legal structure of the regime (i.e. administrative, court-based, or a combination)
			2016 PSBA	31 December 2016	Structural Benchmark	Operationalize Financial System Stability Committee
			2016 PSBA	28 February 2017	Structural Benchmark	Issue for public comment a consultation paper for the resolution framework, developed with support from IMF TA, which describes the draft legislation

CEM constraints	*Impact on growth*	*CEM*	*Review/agreement*	*Completion target*	*Conditionality type*	*Direct measure implemented*
			2016 PSBA	30 May 2017	Structural Benchmark	Instituting mechanisms to ensure full compliance with the provisions of the Securities (Retail Repurchase Agreement) Regulations that require 'retail repos' to be governed by a MRRA that is signed by both the dealer and the client
Fiscal Deterioration	Compromized capacity of the state to deliver basic public goods and those which complement private sector investments	2004	2010 SBA		Prior Action	Tax Package of 2 of GDP
			2010 SBA	June 2010	Prior Action	Reach agreement on divestment of Air Jamaica or initiate plans to liquidate the airline
			First Review of 2010 SBA	March 2010		Lease remaining Sugar Company Factories or put on zero-deficit budget

(continued)

Table 4.1 (continued)

CEM constraints	*Impact on growth*	*CEM*	*Review/agreement*	*Completion target*	*Conditionality type*	*Direct measure implemented*
			First Review of 2010 SBA	March 2010	Structural Benchmark	Increase JUTC bus fares by 40% or more
			First Review of 2010 SBA	June 2010	Structural Benchmark	Divest or liquidate Air Jamaica
			Third Review of 2010 SBA	March 2011		Divest Clarendon Alumina Production
			Second Review of 2013 EFF	31 March 2014	Structural Benchmark	Adoption of a legally binding fiscal rule to ensure a sustainable budgetary balance, to be incorporated in the annual budgets starting with the 2014/15 budget
			First Review of 2016 PSBA	31 October 2017		The following entities will be closed: (i) Board of Supervision, (ii) Road Maintenance Fund, (iii) Kingston Waterfront Hotel Company Limited, (iv) Montego Shopping Centre Limited and (v) Portmore Commercial Development Ltd. In addition, the Children's Registry will be reintegrated into the Child Development Agency

CEM constraints	*Impact on growth*	*CEM*	*Review/agreement*	*Completion target*	*Conditionality type*	*Direct measure implemented*
			First Review of 2016 PSBA	31 October 2017		Finalize the operational merger of HEART/NTA, Jamaica Foundation for Lifelong Learning and the National Youth Service

(continued)

Table 4.1 (continued)

CEM constraints	*Impact on growth*	*CEM*	*Review/agreement*	*Completion target*	*Conditionality type*	*Direct measure implemented*
			First Review of 2016 PSBA	31 October 2017		The total stock of domestic arrears (as defined in the TMU) of the following public bodies will be capped at J$6.4 billion during the programme period: Clarendon Alumina Production (CAP), National Water Commission (NWC), Jamaica Urban Transit Company (JUTC), Housing Agency of Jamaica (HAJ), Urban Development Corporation (UDC), the National Road Operating and Constructing Company (NROCC), and the National Health Fund (NHF) and monitored on a monthly basis

CEM constraints	*Impact on growth*	*CEM*	*Review/agreement*	*Completion target*	*Conditionality type*	*Direct measure implemented*
High cost of Electricity (pKw) Unreliable power supply High dependence on imported fuel	Higher production costs	2004	Seventh Review of 2013 EFF	13 March 2015	Structural Benchmark	The Government approved the construction of a new power plant
			Thirteenth Review of 2013 EFF	31 January 2015	Structural Benchmark	Government to table in parliament the electricity Act
High public sector wage costs	Limit productive government expenditure	2011	First Review of 2010 SBA	June 2010		Conduct a government employment/compensation census and create a public sector monitoring database
			First Review of 2010 SBA	16 September 2010	Structural Benchmark	Freeze on wage and salary increases through FY 2011/12
			First Review of 2010 SBA	December 2010	Structural Benchmark	Complete time-bound public employment and compensation reform action plan (to be implemented in FY2011/12 Budget)

(continued)

Table 4.1 (continued)

CEM constraints	*Impact on growth*	*CEM*	*Review/agreement*	*Completion target*	*Conditionality type*	*Direct measure implemented*
			First Review of 2010 SBA	November 2010	Structural Benchmark	Undertake a costing exercise of the different reform options presented in the Public Sector Transformation Unit Report consistent with wage bill rationalization commitments under the SBA
			2010 SBA		Structural Benchmark	Implemented a reform that allowed for a reduction in the wage bill over the medium term from 11½ per cent of GDP to 9½ per cent of GDP
			First Review of 2010 SBA	FY2013/14	Structural Benchmark	Reduce wage bill to 9.5% of GDP

CEM constraints	*Impact on growth*	*CEM*	*Review/agreement*	*Completion target*	*Conditionality type*	*Direct measure implemented*
			2013 EFF		Prior Action	Public sector wages: Conclude a multi-year agreement with major unions (representing at least 70% of government workers) limiting nominal wage increases to zero for 2012/13 (and limiting merit increases to no more than 2.5%), and an annual average (including merit increases) of no more than 5% in the two subsequent years

(continued)

Table 4.1 (continued)

CEM constraints	*Impact on growth*	*CEM*	*Review/agreement*	*Completion target*	*Conditionality type*	*Direct measure implemented*
			2016 PSBA	March 2017		Build a comprehensive database—by occupational grouping and that includes all types of allowances paid, their amounts as well as the number of employees receiving each type of allowance in a given fiscal year—across ministries, departments and agencies to ensure adequate control and oversight over this part of the wage bill. Pilots are ongoing

CEM constraints	*Impact on growth*	*CEM*	*Review/agreement*	*Completion target*	*Conditionality type*	*Direct measure implemented*
			2016 PSBA	31 March 2017		Complete an employee verification exercise. Island-wide pilots at the Ministry of Finance and the Public Service, the civilian population of the police department, the NIS and the non-teaching personnel at the Ministry of Education are ongoing. The verification for all entities in the central government wage bill will be finalized by March 2017

(continued)

Table 4.1 (continued)

CEM constraints	*Impact on growth*	*CEM*	*Review/agreement*	*Completion target*	*Conditionality type*	*Direct measure implemented*
			2016 PSBA	31 March 2017		The creation and application of strict unambiguous rules for the decisions of the Post Operations Committee regarding all types of employment including acting. These rules are to establish a percentage reduction rate which effectively controls the rate of employment and creates a sharp downward trajectory whilst ensuring that the public sector is properly resourced
				30 April 2017		Informed by the compensation review results from end-March 2017, submit public sector wage negotiation framework to Cabinet for approval

CEM constraints	*Impact on growth*	*CEM*	*Review/agreement*	*Completion target*	*Conditionality type*	*Direct measure implemented*
				30 May 2017		Identify positions that will be affected due to the implementation of shared corporate services in human resources and quantify the implications through the development of a costed transition plan and schedule
				30 November 2017		Identify positions that will be affected due to the implementation of shared corporate services in Public Relations and Communications, and Internal Audit and quantify the implications through the development of a costed transition plan and schedule
				30 May 2017		Institute rules prohibiting the rehiring of participants in the early retirement programme into the public sector for at least 5 years unless the person returns the incentive

(continued)

Table 4.1 (continued)

CEM constraints	*Impact on growth*	*CEM*	*Review/agreement*	*Completion target*	*Conditionality type*	*Direct measure implemented*
				30 May 2017		Submit to the Governor-General through Cabinet rules and standards for the Public Service Commission for limiting the approval of continued employment after retirement age, including as contract officers
				31 July 2017		Submit to Cabinet a time-bound plan to reintegrate eligible public bodies into central government, consistent with the public financial management principles of the policy on public bodies

CEM constraints	*Impact on growth*	*CEM*	*Review/agreement*	*Completion target*	*Conditionality type*	*Direct measure implemented*
				30 September 2017		Submit to Cabinet a medium-term policy and implementation plan to revise the performance-based merit increases to make them more meaningfully related to the performance management appraisal system
				30 September 2017		Submit to Cabinet a proposal to institute clear rules for hiring, promotion and exit
			Fourth Review of 2016 PSBA	10 October 2018	Structural Benchmark	The government made a four-year—rather than the usual two-year—wage agreement with central government employees
Inadequate credit access for the private sector	Lowers productivity	2004	2013 EFF Agreement	17 April 2013	Structural Benchmark	Creation of a Secured Transactions Framework
			Third Review of 2010 SBA	28 December 2010	Structural Benchmark	The BOJ lowered the cash reserve requirement

(continued)

Table 4.1 (continued)

CEM constraints	*Impact on growth*	*CEM*	*Review/agreement*	*Completion target*	*Conditionality type*	*Direct measure implemented*
			2013 EFF Agreement		Structural Benchmark	Passage of Security Interest in Personal Property (SIPP) Act (2013)
Weak public financial management	Fiscal distortions that limit growth	2011	2010 SBA	March 2010	Structural Benchmark	Pass a fiscal responsibility framework and accompanying legislative amendments (MEFP, paragraph 26)
			First Review of 2010 SBA	June 2010	Structural Benchmark	Complete a time-bound action plan to establish a central treasury management system (CTMS) by the end of 2010
			First Review of 2010 SBA	November 2010	Structural Benchmark	Amend FRF legislation and introduce regulations
			First Review of 2010 SBA	December 2010	Structural Benchmark	CTMS system to be operational and in position to support the implementation of FY2011/12 budget
			2013 EFF	30 April 2013	Structural Benchmarks	Government to table in parliament a budget in line with programme commitments

CEM constraints	*Impact on growth*	*CEM*	*Review/agreement*	*Completion target*	*Conditionality type*	*Direct measure implemented*
			2013 EFF	31 August 2013	Structural Benchmarks	Government to present to Fund staff a conceptual proposal for the design of a fiscal rule
			2013 EFF	30 April 2014	Structural Benchmarks	Government to table in parliament a budget for 2014/15 consistent with the program
			2013 EFF	31 March 2014	Structural Benchmarks	Adoption of a legally binding fiscal rule to ensure a sustainable budgetary balance, to be incorporated in the annual budgets starting with the 2014/15 budget
			First Review of 2013 EFF	30 November 2013	Structural Benchmarks	Cabinet to approve a detailed budget calendar consistent with top-down expenditure ceilings, for the 2014/15 budget

(continued)

Table 4.1 (continued)

CEM constraints	*Impact on growth*	*CEM*	*Review/agreement*	*Completion target*	*Conditionality type*	*Direct measure implemented*
			First Review of 2013 EFF	31 March 2014	Structural Benchmarks	Revise the relevant legislation for the adoption of a fiscal rule to ensure a sustainable budgetary balance, to be incorporated in the annual budgets starting with the 2014/15 budget
			Fifth Review of 2013 EFF	30 April 2014	Structural Benchmark	4. Government to table in parliament a budget for 2014/15 consistent with the program
			First Review of 2016 PSBA	15 June 2017		Submit to parliament all necessary legislative changes to direct all earmarked revenues from the Jamaica Civil Aviation Authority, the Tourism Enhancement Fund and the CHASE Fund to the consolidated Fund

CEM constraints	*Impact on growth*	*CEM*	*Review/agreement*	*Completion target*	*Conditionality type*	*Direct measure implemented*
			First Review of 2016 PSBA	31 July 2017		Submit to Cabinet a time-bound plan to reintegrate eligible public bodies into central government, consistent with the public financial management principles of the policy on public bodies
			First Review of 2016 PSBA	31 July 2017		Submit to Cabinet a time-bound plan to reintegrate eligible public bodies into central government, consistent with the public financial management principles of the policy on public bodies
			Fourth Review of 2013 SBA	5 June 2014	Structural Benchmark	Implementation of a Fiscal Rule (FR)
			Article IV Consultation, Eleventh and Twelfth reviews of 2013 SBA	3 June 2016	Structural Benchmark	Modernisation of Accountant General's Department to manage the CTMS
Social constraints						

(continued)

Table 4.1 (continued)

CEM constraints	*Impact on growth*	*CEM*	*Review/agreement*	*Completion target*	*Conditionality type*	*Direct measure implemented*
Low-quality human capital	Reduces overall productivity	2011	First Review of 2016 PSBA	30 September 2017	Structural Benchmarks	Submit to Cabinet a proposal to institute clear rules for hiring, promotion and exit
Pervasive and high crime High rates of violent crime	Weakened business environment	2004, 2011	Thirteenth Review of 2013 EFF	January 2016	Structural Benchmarks	Put in place a full-time dedicated project management team for the implementation of the human resources software system
Poor education outcomes	Reduced productivity levels	2004	2016 PSBA	25 October 2016	Structural Benchmarks	A reform that made adjustments to the effectiveness of the police force and the administration of the court system
			2016 PSBA	31 October 2017	Structural Benchmarks	Finalize the operational merger of HEART/NTA, Jamaica Foundation for Lifelong Learning and the National Youth Service

in response to the then recent collapse of several unregistered financial organizations. These organizations attracted large sums of monies from the public in return they promised interest rates far in excess of the prevailing market interest rates. Ultimately, the payment of this interest was dependent on inflows from new investors and therefore collapse was bound to occur once new investor flows were reduced. IMF (2010) notes that the losses incurred by the bondholders who were also participants in the 2010 Jamaica Debt Exchange (JDX) had to be taken into consideration in the design of the JDX. The Fund further took into consideration the need to provide technical support through specific missions and support from the Caribbean Technical Assistance Centre (CARTAC) to the regulators and institutional stakeholders in the financial sector to improve and enhance their regulatory oversight and capacity. A review of the regulatory and legal reforms was identified and implemented in order to reduce the likelihood that schemes of this type would re-emerge in the financial sector. Under its sub-programme within the 2010 SBA to reduce systemic risks associated with the financial sector, the IMF also supported the authorities with resources to enable the development and implementation of stress testing in order to improve understanding of how risks permeate through and impact the system which would in turn empower them to develop contingency plans. The 2010 SBA also provided support to the authorities to drive re-engineering of securities dealer segment of the financial sector. These efforts continued to receive support from the Fund in the 2013 EFF with firms in the retail repo segment being treated separately and eventually they were transitioned to a trust-based framework of operations. Additional regulations implemented during the 2016 PSBA required these entities to ensure that all clients and dealers sign a Master Retail Repurchase Agreement that specifies the details of their contractual relationship.

A significant change in the structure, operation and regulation of the Jamaican financial sector is the change in the mandate of the Bank of Jamaica. The Bank of Jamaica prior to the 2010 SBA was the regulator for deposit-taking institutions. Its counterpart, the Financial Services Commission (FSC), was responsible for investment houses and other non-deposit taking entities. This meant that many forms of financial sector activity were not directly covered by the existing legislation and therefore that there was no formal mechanism of monitoring their activities on the behalf of the public. Additionally, the cracks in the financial system can often be missed by regulators who focus on mandates that are too narrow and that miss patterns of transactions that can potentially bring the financial system to its knees as occurred in the global financial crisis that had its roots in the American mortgage market. Under the 2010 SBA, the legal and regulatory framework of the BOJ and the wider financial system were reviewed to ascertain the changes that were necessary to enable the central bank to eventually assume the mandate for financial sector stability. This work continued throughout the 2013 EFF and in 2016 the Banking Services Act was passed. Through the repeals of the Banking Act and the Financial Institutions Act; amendment of sections of the Building Societies and the Bank of Jamaica Act, the BOJ is now the overarching regulator of the financial sector and along with the intelligence and efforts of the FSC has jurisdiction over unregulated financial companies through these efforts. Complementary reforms to support the strength and resilience of the financial system were implemented with the promulgation of a resolution framework for the entire financial sector. The framework detailed the authority that would preside over resolution of financial entities as well as the roles and responsibilities of the institutions covered under the resolution regime.

Another major area of focus in the three agreements between Jamaica and the IMF since 2010 is in relation to controlling the size of the public sector wage bill. Given the poor structure and coverage of government human resource information systems, the first structural benchmark in this regard under the 2010 SBA was to engage in a census to collect information on employment of workers across the public sector in order to obtain basic information to inform restructure and other efficiency generating measures (International Monetary Fund, 2010). Simultaneously, the government implemented a wage freeze on salaries and set about creating a reform agenda for public sector employment and compensation along with a costing of the reform proposals made by the Public Sector Transformation Unit as the government committed to reducing the public sector wage-to-GDP ratio from 11.5 to 9.5% over the medium term. Under the 2013 EFF, the government was mandated to secure a multi-year wage settlement with at least seventy per cent of its public sector workers who had to agree to zero per cent increases in the 2012/13 fiscal year, a 2.5% limit to merit increases, and salary increases below five per cent in the subsequent two fiscal years (International Monetary Fund, 2013).

Having concluded the census of public sector employments, the government built a comprehensive database of its workers across all ministries, departments and agencies (MDAs) inclusive of their full emolument. The verification of workers in the larger components of the public sector was piloted in order to fully calculate the total central government wage bill as of 31 March 2017 under the PSBA. In the future, the 2016 PSBA reduced the ability of MDAs to engage additional posts with the implementation of strict, unambiguous rules for deciding on additional employment of all types in the public sector (International Monetary Fund, 2016). Rules were translated into a percentage reduction rate to control the rate of employment growth. The results of the compensation review output from the comprehensive database, the parameters for the next cycle of public sector wage negotiation was developed and submitted to Cabinet for 30 April 2017. Proposals to implement shared services in the areas of human resources, public relations and communications, and internal audit were supplemented with assessments of the implications of affected employees and the development of costing of the transition arrangements. Additional benchmarks during the 2016 PSBA are related to the implementation of rules prohibiting persons participating in the early retirement scheme for public sector workers from being rehired for at least five years unless they return the incentive. Rules relating to the continued employment of public sector workers after retirement were submitted to the Governor-General for approval. The final three benchmarks implemented in relation to controlling the public sector wage bill under the 2016 PSBA were in relation to the: (a) preparation of a medium-term policy to guide the granting of merit increases that would increase the link with performance appraisal; (b) submission of rules to guide hiring, firing and promotion in the public sector to Cabinet; and, (c) negotiation of another multi-year wage agreement—this time for four years—by the government (International Monetary Fund, 2016).

Jamaica's chronically high debt-to-GDP ratio was a main area of concern to both the staff of the IMF and the Jamaican government. In order to arrest the continued secular increases in the ratio that is compounded by the deteriorating fiscal conditions necessitated the implementation of two debt exchanges as prior actions before the official signing of the agreement with the Fund. In addition, the 2013 EFF required the passage of a Debt Law as a prior action making that agreement require a total of two prior actions in contrast to the 2010 SBA (International Monetary Fund, 2013). Both debt exchanges have been assessed as being successful using the relative metrics of participation, effectiveness of the restructuring and impact on country ratings by the top agencies. There were seven structural benchmarks implemented between the first and third Reviews of the agreement. These benchmarks were designed to effect the legislative changes needed to modernize debt management operations in the debt management unit. In addition, the unit was supported in undertaking a cost-risk analysis of alternate debt management strategies to facilitate decisions making.

Various aspects of fiscal policy reform were implemented during the period. In relation to the complexity of the tax system raised in the 2011 CEM, the fifth review of the 2019 Precautionary Stand-By Arrangement (PSBA) indicates that comprehensive reform to broaden the base and simplify the tax system was to be completed by the end of FY2018/19 as a structural benchmark (International Monetary Fund, 2016). The distorting elements of the tax policy raised in 2011 CEM were addressed most substantively in the 2013 EFF that required the adoption of a decision to cease granting discretionary waivers by the Cabinet. This requirement as imposed in the form of a prior action that was completed prior to the official start of the programme. During the programme several structural benchmarks were achieved in relation to a resolution of the existing ad hoc regime with the government tabling an Omnibus Tax Incentive (OTI) Act during 2013 that would eliminate the power of the Minister of Finance to provide or support other Ministers who extend tax relief. The OTI Act further outlines the system that will be used to now determine the eligibility criteria for the limited tax incentives that will be allowed under the new Fiscal Responsibility Framework. This structural benchmark was supported by two others that legally restricted the granting of discretionary tax waivers and tax incentives by the Government.

The issue of weak public financial management was also addressed in each of the IMF Agreements since 2010. The overarching benchmark was the design and implementation of a fiscal responsibility framework with the necessary legal underpinnings that would specify the parameters within which fiscal policy is to be crafted, implemented and monitored (International Monetary Fund, 2010). A major aspect of the drive in the agreements to restore sound management of public finances was the implementation of a central treasury for the cash deposits held by all MDAs. The process began with a structural benchmark under the 2010 SBA of the creation of a time-bound plan for its establishment. It was then operationalized with the Bank of Jamaica providing administrative support and payment services through its management of the Real Time Gross Settlement payment system.

Eventually, another benchmark under the 2016 PSBA would initiate the transfer of the policy management of the CTMS to the Accountant General's department after training and modernization of that entity (International Monetary Fund, 2016). These changes were complementary to the reforms occurring in the area of the budget. The three agreements enabled the government to make significant strides to the tabling of budgets that were more predictable based on the various constraints implemented in other areas of fiscal policy and debt management. The implementation of a fiscal rule under a 2013 structural benchmark helped the authorities to constrain the expenditure profile to match the revenue intake and therefore achieve the targeted budget balance. Public bodies would also be included more fulsomely into central government budgeting in order to ensure that the budget presented the full indicators of expenditure and government intentions. This was accomplished through the submission of a plan to Cabinet during the first review of the 2016 PSBA.

Rounding off the reform efforts on the fiscal front were also efforts to address the: complex tax system (2011 CEM), distortionary tax policy (2011 CEM) and fiscal deterioration (2004 CEM). The first of the 2010 SBA structural benchmarks to address the complex tax system was the preparation of a plan to reform tax administration. There were also amendments to the Revenue Administration Act to enable the tax authorities to gain access to third-party information in order to verify compliance; empower the agency to require mandatory filing for any tax type or tax group (International Monetary Fund, 2010). Under the 2013 EFF, a large taxpayer office was established and staffed to increase the efficiency at the collectorates and these taxpayers were now legally mandated to file two main taxes electronically. Tax reform in the form of a modernization of the taxes with broader bases and reduced exemptions were part of an initial policy reform and the government implemented indicators to measure the productivity and effectiveness of the tax system. Modern legislation was promulgated to govern the tax regime that would prevail under special economic zones which were being established in order to maintain the credibility of the tax system (International Monetary Fund, 2010). After receiving new land valuations in 2013, the property tax rates were revised and submitted to Cabinet.

Tax policy elements that distorted economic incentives were dramatically reformed with the termination of the minister's ability to grant discretionary waivers and the consolidation of allowable tax incentives under one omnibus legislation using clear criteria and under very few circumstances that did not favour any economic activity were the main structural benchmarks implemented largely under the 2013 EFF. The main structural benchmarks implemented from the 2010 SBA as prior actions through to the 2016 PSBA were oriented towards the divestment and/or closure of loss-making public bodies that were important contributors to the accrual of debt through contingent liabilities that were unchecked and ungoverned. These reforms were sweeping and game-changing sparing no entity—not even the beloved Air Jamaica—that was once seen as the pride of Jamaica in the sky. Consistent with the recommendations of the PSTU, several entities were closed, merged or otherwise restructured arising from the policy position to re-engineer the operations of government.

Challenges in the business environment in the form of customs reform were addressed under the 2013 EFF in the form of the development of a new customs act, the implementation of the Automated System for Customs Data (ASYCUDA) world to facilitate smart customs operations at the port of Kingston, an increase in the use of audits to reduce customs clearance times, and the development of a comprehensive growth strategy aimed at improving the environment in which businesses operate. Efforts were also made towards the middle of the 2013 EFF to address the issue of the high cost of electricity through the passage of new legislation governing electricity production. The construction of a new power plant was also approved by the government and has since been commissioned. Many steps have also been taken to improve the underlying framework for access to credit in the private sector through the expansion of the collateral regimes of financial institutions by establishing a collateral registry and implementing a Secure Transaction Framework.

Conclusion

The cross tabulatory analysis between the binding constraints prioritized in the 2004 and 2011 CEMs and the borrowing agreements between Jamaica and the IMF reveal that the reform agenda implemented with IMF support has indeed addressed all of the macroeconomic constraints that were identified as inimical to the generation of sustained economic growth in Jamaica. Whilst both CEMs also and correctly identified Jamaica's pressing social constraint in the form of the high rates of violent crime and low levels of education and training, only one structural benchmark provided any reform support in the area of education and training and it was at the operational level to finalize the merger of the main workforce college, the institute providing lifelong learning and the national youth service. The predominant focus of the agreements was therefore on solving the macroeconomic constraints to growth. This approach is consistent with the view that in fixing these issues through deep reforms, the foundation for economic stability would be firmly established thereby providing adequate room in the economic landscape for the private sector to advance and spur growth.

Fixing the fiscal house through the major levers that generate direct and indirect liability, putting constraints and parameters on the way that the fiscal authorities are permitted to operate and controlling public sector employment and the growth of public sector wages were key components to getting control of the society and put it firmly on the road to sustained growth. Without these, the two debt exchanges would have required a few more as it is the profligacy of the expenditure side and sluggish revenue collection mechanisms that encourage avoidance and evasion that would continue to see debt build-up as the government struggles to meet its ordinary obligations. The road has been paved and the next chapters will provide an idea of the supporting cast that played invaluable contributions to the success of the initial journey and the new challenge that threaten to derail all gains and upend social cohesion in Jamaica.

References

Clarke, C., & Nelson, C. (2020). *Contextualising Jamaica's relationship with the International Monetary Fund*. Palgrave Macmillan.

Clarke, P. (2017, October 12). Crime costing Jamaica $68 billion per year. *Jamaica Gleaner*.

Docquier, F., & Marfouk, A. (2004). *Measuring the international mobility of skilled workers* (World Bank Policy Research Working Paper No. 3381). Washington, DC: World Bank.

Government of Jamaica. (2017, April 18). *White paper: National policy on international migration and development*. Retrieved from Policies & Plans: Migration Policy: https://www.pioj.gov.jm/policies/migration-policy/.

Grabel, I. (2011). Not your grandfather's IMF: Global crisis, 'productive incoherence' and developmental policy space. *Cambridge Journal of Economics*, *35*(5), 805–830.

Hall, D. (1993). The flight from the estates reconsidered: The British West Indies, 1838–1842. In H. Beckles & V. Shepherd (Eds.), *Caribbean freedom: Economy and society from emancipation to the present* (pp. 55–63). Kingston: Ian Randle Publishers.

International Monetary Fund. (2010). *Jamaica: 2010 first review of the stand-by arrangement—Staff report*. Washington, DC: International Monetary Fund.

International Monetary Fund. (2013). *Jamaica: Request for extended fund facility*. Washington, DC: International Monetary Fund.

International Monetary Fund. (2016). *Jamaica: Request for standby agreement*. Washington, DC: International Monetary Fund.

International Office of Migration. (2018). *Migration in Jamaica: A country profile 2018*. Kingston: International Organization for Migration.

Jaitman, L. (2017). *The costs of crime and violence: New evidence and insights in Latin America and the Caribbean*. Washington, DC: Inter-American Development Bank.

Organization of American States. (2011). *International migration in the Americas: First report of the continuous reporting system on international migration in the Americas (SICREMI)*. Washington, DC: Organization of American States.

Overseas Security Advisory Council. (2019, May 30). *Jamaica 2019 crime & safety report*. Retrieved from Overseas Security Advisory Council Web site: https://www.osac.gov/Country/Jamaica/Content/Detail/Report/1d98b2df-fd4b-485f-aa62-15f4aed245ef.

Wenner, M. (2016, September 28). *Inter-American Development Bank*. Retrieved from Inter-American Development Bank Web Site: https://blogs.iadb.org/caribbean-dev-trends/en/brain-drain-a-curse-of-small-states/

Wilmot, S. (1993). Emancipation in action: Workers and wage conflict in Jamaica, 1838–1840. In H. Beckles & V. Shepherd (Eds.), *Caribbean Freedom: Economy and society from emancipation to the present* (pp. 48–54). Kingston: Ian Randle Publishers.

World Bank. (2004). *The road to sustained growth in Jamaica*. Washington, DC: The World Bank.

World Bank. (2011). *Jamaica: Country economic memorandum—Unlocking growth*. Washington, DC: The World Bank.

World Bank. (2020, November 22). *World Bank open data portal*. Retrieved from World Bank Web site: https://data.worldbank.org/.

CHAPTER 5

New Governance Paradigms

Introduction

Crisis has been the catalyst for the emergence of new approaches within the practices of government and modalities of governance to treat with the potential impact. Although vested with the capacity to unravel and decay, crisis has prompted innovations, as well as diversity in governance through the modality of broadening network relations (Jessop, 1999) manifested through the creation of and forms of social partnership relations and actor networks.

At the heart of social partnership is the practice of social dialogue which has been furthered as a discourse and practice by the International Labour Organization (ILO) and is intrinsic in its discourse and formulation of global public policy. Numerous governance structures have emerged, centred upon social dialogue and partnership, institutionalized in the framework of states, through its global influence and activity (ILO, 2007). Social dialogue has been utilized in the policy process. The ILO has promulgated modalities of social partnership within the context of labour relations which has reduced the potential for industrial relations conflict (Hethy, 2001). The idea of social inclusion on the part of social partners in processes evidencing a deepening and broadening of social dialogue is deemed indispensable for increasing economic competitiveness and accomplishing social objectives' (ILO, 2001).

C. Clarke and C. Nelson, *Jamaica's Evolving Relationship with the IMF*,
https://doi.org/10.1007/978-3-030-59204-2_5

Regimes have been created within ILO's hegemonic discourse with norms, standards and conventions (Beschoner & Muller, 2007) incorporated into the legislative and policy framework of states and national policy development (Fudge (2007). Social partnerships have been examined through the lens from which they emerged and the models employed, from the perspective of ILO global discourses, classification and modalities of social dialogue. These have served to foster a global pluralist dialogue and industrial relations climate, replacing hostility with consensus (Martinez-Lucio & Stuart, 2002).

Social dialogue therefore, has been instrumental as a mechanism to further inclusive good governance and democracy, by the way in which decisions are brokered facilitating the contribution of multiple stakeholders in the decision process. However, outside of the context of labour and industrial relations discourse, social partnership can also be viewed as a strategic response and as a development strategy in reconstituting relationships under crisis or times of intense challenge requiring adjustments to treat with impending economic chaos and recovery.

Social Partnership Governance

Reflecting upon the diverse approaches taken by countries around the world in the context of crisis, social partnerships modalities have arisen repeatedly with numerous success. In the 1990s, newly independent African states, grappling with the remnants of the legacy of post-colonialism, the effects of globalization and mode of integration within the global economy, experienced deepening macroeconomic crisies and distortions within labour markets. In the pursuit of structural adjustment programmes, the conditionality of dialogue and 'good governance' became prerequisites to access international development assistance necessitating the establishment of institutions of dialogue between labour and the state. African political leaders included social partners in modalities of governance to help foster ownership of programmes pursued and as they restructured labour legislation and industry as a means to catalyze economic growth. Social partnerships have been transformative (Katz et al., 2004) as a governance mechanism in the case of undoing the legacy of apartheid (Bassett, 2004).

In Latin America, countries implementing structural adjustment programmes in the 1980s, experienced crisis through an exacerbation of economic decline impacting the standard of living and poverty with a reduction in real wages (Trebilcock, 1996). Social dialogue was critical in engendering political change towards more participatory forms of governance in the 1990s through the efforts of the labour unions and the exercise of their ability to influence public policy and relationships with the state and political parties (Cook, 1998; Levitsky & Way, 1998; Madrid, 2003).

The process of European integration led to the development of new forms of partnership at the enterprise level and nationally. Labour and capital relations were reconstructed around partnership, as well as the institutionalization of social dialogue in Europe, which became a prerequisite for acceding (Grabbe, 1999) to membership within the EU and the associated benefits. Social partnership mechanisms were used as vehicles to manage the transition of Central and Eastern European (CEE) socialist states to market economies as members of the EU.

With respect to the Caribbean, the most cited case of successful social partnership in the Caribbean is that of Barbados, where a collaborative (Kernaghan, 1993) tripartite national social partnership model emerged, in response to pending economic crisis (O'Donnell, 1996; McCartan, 2002), triggered by a downturn in the world economy. A national social partnership arrangement blossomed in response to the need to avoid the IMF's prescription of a currency devaluation in the context of an economic crisis, with the intent to restore competitiveness and increased productivity.

Social partnership as mechanisms of governance have emerged in Jamaica, in responding to contexts of crisis. Governance regimes have emerged from within a context of social partnership arrangements such as the 'Michael Manley Accord' for the Bauxite Industry signed in 2001 between the Bauxite Companies, the Government and Trade Unions. This arrangement provided among other things, a mechanism of conflict resolution and mutual benefits.

The Monitoring Committee created to aid in the governance of the Public Sector Memorandum of Understanding (MOU) in 2004, consisted of Government representatives and the Jamaica Confederation of Trade Unions (JCTU). These mechanisms of multi-partner relations, reflect deepening inclusiveness and diversity of participation in governance as state relations grow more complex to enhance sustainability in the face of crisis. There are consequently implications for the culture, discourse and practice of participating partners as each creates new or adjusts these dimensions as well as traditional structures within network relations and operations beyond those to which they have been accustomed, to broaden the diversity of societal network relations as partners multiply their relations with societal actors.

Consequently,

> social partnership becomes the outcome of adjustments made by governments, sometimes reluctantly, in power-sharing arrangements, incorporating multiple actors and stakeholders in the way societies are reorganized, to respond and treat with destabilizing forces in the struggle for self-preservation. (Nelson, 2019, p. 51)

A New Governance Paradigm—Economic Programme Oversight Committee (EPOC)

The emergence of the Economic Programme Oversight Committee (EPOC) arguably a modality of social partnership governance emerged against the backdrop of reoccurring crises warranting an extensive effort to address the persistent macroeconomic challenges plaguing the economy. Jamaica envisaged that entering into an arrangement with the International Monetary Fund (IMF) would engender the resolution of structural macroeconomic vulnerabilities and challenges that had surrounded and influenced the trajectory of its economic development over the years, such as high debt, low growth and economic resilience exacerbated by externalities of a global recession (Harris, 2010). Socio-economic and political economy challenges which arguably, bled from the past into the present, had stymied the government's ability and efforts to achieve economic growth which still remained elusive.

The Context of the Emergence of EPOC

Prior to the emergence of EPOC in 2013, the reins of the government, were held by the Jamaica Labour Party (JLP) under the Golding administration, which had been engaged in discussions with the IMF with respect to entering an SBA with them on the cusp of coming into office. Jamaica's debt was extensive at levels of 141–143% of GDP in 2003/2004 (Schmid, 2016). Debt accumulation was attributed to several factors namely, the practice for public expenditure to be supplemented by extensive foreign exchange borrowing to address external account deficits and fiscal shortfalls, debt accumulation carried over from the domestic financial crisis absorbed by the government, which was added to the fallout from the global financial crisis in the form of the reduction in foreign exchange inflows from tourism, the diaspora and the drop in the global market price of bauxite. These attributes were decisive in their effect which altogether, capped the prospects of development thereby providing the imperative to engage in negotiations with the IMF for assistance.

The extensiveness of the debt and implications for the economy's well-being and growth trajectory required a commensurate response within the IMF programme being contemplated, which would, of the necessity require an extensive debt restructuring focus as a component within the SBA being negotiated. Consequently, one of the IMF's prior actions required as a conditionality for entry into the SBA arrangement entailed the imperative of the government undertaking a debt exchange, thereafter, called The Jamaica Debt Exchange (JDX). The JDX required the cooperation, participation and expertize of the leadership with the banking sector and associated financial and monetary policy networks to be engaged around the execution of this prior action.

The 2010 SBA entered into successfully, ended, eroded by a pervasive crisis of confidence in government ideationally, by having to fulfil legal obligations which had the effect of contributing to the destabilization of the IMF Agreement, (Johnston, 2013). This relationally impacted the IMF as well as the modalities of the Programme governance networks thereunder, with development partners. This was coupled with recession, internal challenges and a crisis of confidence for the JLP itself, culminating in a change of administration soon thereafter. However, it was from within this context that the foundations of an innovative governance modality emerged.

Actor-Network Perspective

The context of social partnerships is informed by networks of relations within the domestic context which give rise to differential combinations and contribute to the character of the partnership formed. The political and cultural environment and the crisis impacting the economy and nature of societal relations precipitates representative elements which emerge and undergo 'translation' to create actor networks between themselves and other actors, composed of 'human and non-human' Callon, 1986 actors, whereby 'things, as well as humans, can have agency' (De Maeyer, 2016, p. 462.

These various stakeholders or actors within the economy convene around the Obligatory Passage Point (OPP) of the Ministry of Finance/Government the need to enter into an agreement with the IMF to treat with aspects of the crisis in the drive to find amicable solutions and the achievement of a level of stability. Sometimes the status quo is maintained, or a new one is created involving multiple stakeholders than before. Jamaica has had numerous conditions of crisis over the years of its development and emergence as an independent state where crisis has been a feature of the landscape.

In the case of EPOC, the macroeconomic imperatives and the need for the Government of the day, to undertake a debt exchange as a prior action to enter into the 2010 SBA Agreement, brought the related and relevant parties within the commercial, financial and banking sectors together with government to implement the process. From this exercise the parties each had to forgo a degree of benefit, in order to enable the system within which they operated to be maintained as well as attain a greater level of stability and a renewal of the growth and development prospects by acting together based upon the mutual coincidence of need.

The immediate circumstances and economic context of the country added to the degree of complexity within the various sectors, in this case the banking and financial sector has implications for the modalities of style of governance between the parties and the capacity for managing policy and the relations between the participants required.

The stakeholders of EPOC, represented diverse multi-sectoral interests—the private, financial and business sectors, along with civil society, trade unions and NGOs along with the public sector, each representing the interests of their constituency within the context of an IMF programme and its implications. The EPOC Network of relations, entailed the networks and their social relations within the context of the operations of the network but also externally towards their clients, which included the government network and its related connectivity into the wider domestic economy, and even beyond into external relations.

i. To monitor the compliance and progress of the MDAs in achieving the aforementioned structural benchmarks and targets and to request and receive reports from the CIU and the Core Committee in that regard;
ii. To monitor the implementation of tax reform and public sector pension reform;

iii. To monitor the implementation of the Public Sector Transformation Plan;
iv. To request meetings with the Minister at which the Chairman will present any concerns EPOC may have regarding the Government's progress in meeting programme objectives;
v. To receive from the Planning Institute of Jamaica within six months of the signing of this MOU, a four-year growth plan (the finalized Medium-Term Socio-economic Policy Framework) and at minimum, quarterly updates on its progress;
vi. Other responsibilities and authority within the committee's scope and responsibilities or which may be agreed with the Minister from time to time.
vii. The Non-Government members would make quarterly reports to the public commenting on the status of the structural benchmarks and quantitative targets and setting out any major areas of concern, such reports being subject to confidentiality requirements on specific information.

The Economic Programme Oversight Committee (EPOC) would continue over the life of the EFF, with the role to receive, review and analyse information from the GOJ on the progress of the Programme and the implementation of the financial and economic policies set out in the IMF Memorandum of Economic and Financial Policies (MEFP) document. EPOC, was to provide an avenue for the Partners and civil society, to monitor the progress of the implementation of the Enhanced Fund Facility (EFF) Agreement and to assist in ensuring that the agreed targets in the Memorandum of Economic and Financial Policies (MEFP) were achieved.

EPOC members received a copy of the agreement and within a framework of agreed obligations of confidentiality, information would be disclosed by the Government to assist them to carry out their functions. EPOC was required to evaluate and advise the public of the progress of the Programme and as necessary, any concerns they had with that progress. Information divulged by the Government for the monitoring, evaluation and review was solely for the purposes of evaluating and participating in the EPOC review and furtherance of the Programme and not for any other purpose.

EPOC members had to establish confidentiality protocols, procedures and measures to ensure that the confidential information divulged was not disclosed to members' employees and advisors inclusive of its subsidiaries and affiliates, who would likewise be connected to the provision of advice to subsidiaries or customers.

The members of EPOC consisted of

a. Four (4) representatives appointed by the Main Domestic Creditors (MDCs) representing the banking and financial institutions which participated in the Debt Exchange exercises of 2010 and 2013;
b. Governor of the Bank of Jamaica;
c. Financial Secretary;
d. Two (2) representatives of the non-financial private sector
e. Two (2) representatives of the trade unions
f. Two (2) representatives of civil society; and
g. Head of the Coordination Implementation Unit (CIU).

It was agreed by the Parties that EPOC would be co-chaired by the Governor of the Bank of Jamaica and a representative of the MDCs, selected in consultation with the Minister of Finance and Planning. Consideration was made to adopt the mechanism of using a communiqué to respond the public calls for updates regarding the implementation of the Programme.

The EPOC would operate over the duration of life of the EFF and meetings would be held on a quarterly basis or as agreed by Committee members, with the first meeting date being Wednesday 15 May 2013.

Draft Communique

Communications were made monthly in the newspapers providing the public with information about the progress of programme, identified challenges, signaled their concerns and advised the public of issues to note. There was an exchange of views around the Draft Communiqué as it was agreed that a regular communiqué had value and would be:

- An avenue through which the non-government members of EPOC could regulate the release of consistent and clear information, treating with public demands for status reports;

- The framework to interface with the media and would be issued after every meeting of EPOC;
- Seen as part of the protocols being put in place that would be durable and last beyond changes in the persona or membership of the EPOC.

Concerns were aired about EPOC members who represented different constituencies and therefore needed to distinguish, in the public arena, between their personal or professional information sources as against the information that they garnered by been a member of EPOC. Members were advised that the integrity of the EPOC had to be preserved and that members had to be responsible in their communications in public so as not to compromise EPOC and the programme. Some of the initial expectations of EPOC surrounded their obtaining access to information with respect to relevant public sector entities that would enable them to make their assessments. EPOC therefore, requested and received;

- reports from the Coordination Implementation Unit (CIU) in relation to the compliance and progress of the MDAs in achieving the aforementioned structural benchmarks and targets; The CIU managed and tracked the coordination and implementation of MEFP related activities across all ministries, departments and agencies (MDAs), geared towards achieving the agreed prior actions/commitments under the EFF.
- follow up reports (including corrective action) specific to related MDAs on their activities and to their attainment of the targets under the EFF.
- an audience with the Minister, other Cabinet-level officials and Permanent Secretaries to discuss concerns regarding the progress of MDAs in meeting programme objectives;
- from the government, by a date consistent with the requirements of the MEFP, draft fiscal rules that were suitably binding and that would incentivize prudent fiscal behaviour and long-term economic growth and to provide feedback to the Minister;
- the Public Sector Transformation Plan from the government by a date consistent with the requirements of the MEFP but in any event by no later than six months from the execution of this MOU and to monitor the implementation;

- regular reports to EPOC as to their findings and concerns, if any. Key technical persons to support and inform the discussions attended the meetings at intervals as required, to make their respective contributions.

Context of Emergence

Also included, is the perceived heightened transparency, whereby an independent body, with the power to influence, has now become privy to information and contexts that inform government decision-making, especially within the context of successive Jamaica IMF programme relations. One could argue that one of the core impetus for the involvement of members of the banking sector as part of the Committee stemmed from their direct involvement and sacrifice of their constituents in their participation in the two debt exchange programmes (JDX and NDX) which were direct contributories to Jamaica's acceptance to successive IMF programmes, namely, the Stand-By Arrangement (SBA) 2010, followed by the Enhanced Funding Facility (EFF) in 2013.

Rationale for a Fiscal Council

The prevalence of budgetary deficits and the inability of the Government of Jamaica to maintain macroeconomic stability and maintain fiscal policies leading to sustained growth suggests that there have been factors perpetuating a continuous revolution over the years of asymmetric procyclicality. Within the context of political economy, several considerations arise to explain pro-cyclicality biases in fiscal policy.

Nordhaus (1975) alludes that the relationship between budgetary practices and political motivation has been one of the influences determining degrees of deficit bias which is outside the mere consideration of economic factors. Consequently, there is a degree of short-sightedness by policymakers who become captive to modalities of public spending which are influenced by the political cycles which are swayed towards increasing the potential for re-election (Alesina & Tabellini, 1990). Uncertainty, vested in the fear of election loss and to boost re-election possibilities, casts aside concerns about the implications of future fiscal measures such as tax increases and expenditure ceilings, leaning towards benefits engendering 'politically- motivated, deficit-increasing favours' (Rogoff,

1990), reflected in deficit augmenting spending and possibly tax-cutting programmes.

Other outcomes include the reduction in the concern for the implications for tax increases and expenditure cuts for the future which serves to make dubious some of the economic assumptions that undergird budgetary financing in the present.

This can engender common pool problems whereby chances of reelection are enhanced by maximizing the marginal benefits of public goods and services, i.e. the provision of tax breaks, without the internalizing of the full marginal costs of the commitment. This results in indiscipline with respect to fiscal policy hence there is an eclipse on the impact of the aggregate fiscal position due to the decentralized entities that partake in freerider behaviour (Beetsma & Bovenberg, 1999). Issues in relation to time also arise whereby successive governments become responsible for larger debt burdens and limited fiscal space inherited from their predecessors, putting the programmes and policies to be implemented or to engender real growth and development held captive to past legacies (Alesina & Tabellini, 1990).

Within these contexts, there is an ingrained fear retained and passed on by successive governments, that public debt will approach a tipping point with costs registered by the degree of risk that becomes apparent to the stability of the economy, having the potential to unravel the very social fabric. These present adverse effects with respect to government and governance for the future, to achieve economic growth and development which becomes more elusive. Successive and increasing deficits suggest a heightened risk for potential investors, for the stability of the financial markets that view the circumstances as unsustainable, in the context of the alarm bells of monetized risk, inflation expectations and fluctuating interest rates which obtain.

The utility of institutions, legislated instruments and rules become of increased importance to decision-making and to give support to mechanisms that would enhance consistency of fiscal policy as well as buttress macroeconomic stability.

Over the years, mechanisms have been developed that would ensure that fiscal commitments are clearly articulated and transparent and placed within a medium-term fiscal framework with the required processes and requirements even more so in the context of our fiscal responsibility law (Bullock, 2010).

The use of fiscal rules which engender fiscal discipline have grown in increasing popularity and value in enhancing the management of public resources and the quality of public finances especially in the context where political will maybe reticent, as well as capping degrees of creative accounting and off-budget operations which would seek to undermine the transparency of the fiscal and budgetary process. The period following the financial crisis of 2008 precipitated an outburst in the number of countries adopting independent fiscal councils juxtaposed with stringent fiscal reform measures and efforts of financial reform.

Within challenging context like these, a fiscal council or an apolitical body has the potential to influence governments in an independent capacity that can provide a valuable counterweight in decision-making. Empirical evidence has shown that fiscal councils, especially in the OECD countries, who led in the implementation of councils post World War Two, have evidenced clear contributions to improved fiscal performance (Hagemann, 2011) limiting the biases that can emerge in macroeconomic forecasts which are used to prepare national budgets as well as enhancing transparency and de-politicizing of decision-making surrounding fiscal policy.

In some countries have delegated such roles outside of government altogether. In the case of Ireland, the Fiscal Advisory Council was been created to assess the soundness and appropriateness of the projections put forward by government and which also forms part of the reformed public financial management architecture of the country (Jonung et al., 2016). Belgium has also taken a similar approach whereby the government is required to use the macroeconomic projections of the Federal Planning Bureau (Lebrun, 2006).

> ...independent forecasts of key budgetary variables that can be prone to politically-motivated bias, such as overly optimistic revenue projections (which create fiscal "space" to boost unfunded spending) and under-projection of long-run costs of legislative initiatives'. (Hagemann, 2011, p. 94)

In the 2019 Budget Debate in the House of Representatives, Dr. Clarke the Minister of Finance & Planning, expounded upon the government's intention to draft legislation in April 2020, that would support economic policy by the furtherance of institutions such as a Fiscal Council, that would, 'entrench durable accountability of fiscal policy and address gaps'.

The remit of the Fiscal Council would include being an arbiter of Jamaica's Fiscal Rules, that predicate a debt-reduction target of 60% of gross domestic product (GDP) by the financial year 2025/2026. The Council would also ensure that government's policies are consistent with the Fiscal Responsibility Law as well as reviewing the Fiscal Policy Paper (FPP) when tabled and commented on budgetary outcomes in June and December.

The legislative framework would permit the Council to have access to information and data sources from the Government and MDAs with the obligation to comment independently on the FPP and Interim Paper, Budget and medium-term profile and projections. Further, the Council would in effect, enhance the transparency of the process by being required to make public statements about Jamaica's fiscal trajectory and the extent to which whether government policies are broadly consistent with those objectives. This reflects part of the remit of EPOC.

The remit of a Fiscal Council would supersede that of the EPOC, whereby influence would have to be deepened and strengthened as well as being provided for within a legislative framework with bipartisan agreement. Another consideration which could be contentious, relates to the criteria, the selection process and transparency of the nominations to the Committee with respect to its composition. One could argue that in the context of small island developing states with limited human resource capabilities and capacity, that to attain the benefits as envisaged, will be linked to the degree of independence and continuity beyond political cycles and the degree of insulation from political and government influence achieved, which will altogether present challenges.

The clarity of the mandate, objectives and deliverables, umbilically linked to the legal institutions Fiscal Rules and FRF would need to be complemented with sufficient financial, technical and human resources to facilitate independent, additionality as well as effective service, engendering the long-term benefits envisaged, beyond political cycles. The ability of a Council to function 'independently' will have a direct relationship to its legally constituted context and access to resources—human, financial, technological as well as information, enabling and defining deliverables concerning implementation and performance. The necessary technical systems capacity, within a context of membership that is insulated, (Mooney et al., 2018) unbiased or without affiliation to political parties or personnel responsible for budgetary and fiscal management for the government, will be difficult to attain. The clarity of the mandate, objectives and deliverables, umbilically linked to the legal institutions Fiscal Rules and FRF would be complemented with sufficient financial, technical and human resources to facilitate independent, additionality as well as effective service, engendering the long-term benefits envisaged, beyond political cycles.

Dimensions captured to a degree in EPOC, which may be lost in a standard Fiscal Council Model relates to the communication or perception of furthering transparency and accountability and being a modality to inform regularly, 'ordinary Jamaicans', sector and societal interest groups of the 'state of play' with respect to the governments implementation, this time around, of its home-grown commitments, meticulously as was undertaken within the context of the implementation of IMF programme components.

Similarly, the government's position with regard to the visibility of achieving their own goals and accountability for the variances and outcomes. This dimension, although a possible public good, may be deemed unnecessary outside of the context of an IMF programme, but could have resonance if maintained, given the fluidity of the political economy environment which could warrant future social partnership modalities to effect independent solutions and engender the 'buy-in' this time to government agreed initiatives beyond the political divide, contiguous with the imperatives of development under Vision 2030.

What one could surmise, as the differential that surfaced, especially at the signing of the IMF EFF (2013) was the degree to which the government of the day perceived and experienced past contexts, the history and nature of Jamaica IMF relations and the recognition of how critical it was to not renege on the fulfillment of the obligations of the Programme entered into this time around, under the EFF (2013). The government notably effected clear and visible change in the modalities used and measures implemented, structurally effecting a change in the approach and the manner in which the Programme was executed.

The meticulous division of labour with respect to the achieving of the benchmarks and associated tasks, along with an explicit structure of direct accountability for the execution and completion of elements of the Programme was put into effect. Clear lines of management responsibility, for programme execution, critical multi-level governance regimes with respect to the Programme components were essential. There was support from newly created Coordination and Implementation Unit (CIU) with the responsibility for monitoring, evaluating and tracking implementation of Programme benchmarks as well as growth components under the aegis of the EFF (2013). There was the explicit reallocation and deployment of public sector human resources, endowed with the requisite capability and capacity, to ensure the attentiveness to the fulfilment of the commitments under their purview, despite overall discomfort, which were also monitored by the CIU.

Institutionalization of CIU

The Coordination Implementation Unit (CIU) created to serve a strategic purpose with respect to the oversight and the governance framework surrounding monitoring the implementation of the Memorandum of Economic and Financial Policies (MEFP). IMF conditionalities required shared sacrifice across society, implying shared responsibility for the success or failure of the programme;

- Government's resolve to foster transparency;
- Future deliberations to be conducted in a spirit of trust and cooperation;
- Be led by a spirit of cooperation and exercise transparency with respect to information flow within the EPOC.
- Become engaged and participate in the decision-making of the Committee, bearing in mind what was at stake for the country.

The Coordination Implementation Unit (CIU) was created to provide cross-sector coordination, implementation guidance and advocacy with MDAs directed at monitoring progress and achieving the agreed IMF targets. This was synchronous with the implementation of a system of tracking and monitoring of performance targets, the achievement of commitments under the key components within the MEFP, included the triggering of corrective action as required to ensure commitments were met satisfactorily.

Consequently, there was weekly tracking of the progress of MDAs in relation to their individual undertaking of programme activities, inclusive of receiving reports and preparation of the necessary reports within the CIU. This was inclusive of flagging issues and recommending strategies to ensure that the specified conditions and commitments related to the respective economic reform programmes targets would be met.

Several analyses and relevant reports on the performance of the MDAs and the progress of prior actions or key component targets undertaken involved collaborating and networking with key stakeholders across Government MDAs to optimize project coordination and management and to ensure accountability re deliverables. Consequently, the monitoring of the progress or developments under the various activities were communicated to the FS/Minister re the status of implementation of commitments by MDAs.

The CIU also had responsibility for all the administrative functions with respect to the Economic Programme Oversight Committee (EPOC) which consisted of the private sector, government and civil society representatives tasked to independently oversee progress and developments surrounding the implementation of the agreement.

> Strategies for change requires discourse and narratives to be operationalized and enacted and subscribed has new ways of being and identity's to be materialized in new ways in space and time. (Fairclough, 2005)

Within the public sector network there are power relations, established hierarchies and traditional discourses and practices networked together within the ministries departments and agencies (MDAs). Each has it's own mandate and seeks to implement designated aspects of the Programme for which they are responsible as a requirement. In the 'black box' of network interaction at the interface between the CIU and the various MDA networks, discourse reveals the nature of the interface between the parties. Within the domains of traditional public sector discourse and practice, the change in power relations and the accountability the CIU was empowered to exercise, revealed contests in seeking to ascertain compliance. Most MDAs demonstrated compliance through their immediate response, without being prodded whilst others were motivated by fear of being held responsible for the targets not being met by their lack of compliance.

Overall, the interface with MDA actors demonstrated ownership for the aspects of the Programme under their purview and clear resolve to accomplish the tasks assigned.

Conclusion

Survival of the state led to compromises in power relations with external and internal stakeholders reflected in new modalities of power-sharing and governance. The crisis in relation to managing high debt levels was faced by each political party. Each of them, on forming the government, had to grapple with the issue of debt on being elected into office. Each implemented a 'debt exchange' traversing the periods, as the JLP undertook the JDX on the cusp of entering an IMF SBA in 2010 and the PNP followed the pattern in 2013, also with the NDX, to engage with an IMF EFF in 2013.

The 'tipping points' which arguably surrounded high debt issues and it's corollary effects, engendered public and private actors with diverse perspectives, ideas and competencies, to become networked together and through their interaction, institutionalized and empowered within the EPOC. The role of collaborative networks was demonstrated, engendering innovation and problem-solving in public policy through the diffusion of ideas, framing of the problems and in the process of innovative decision-making, serving to break policy deadlocks in new thinking and applications.

Collaborative problem-solving involves access to information and the widening of the knowledge base to craft innovative solutions to 'wicked' problems and raises the question of the untapped potential and value of public policy solutions derived through collaboration for the public sector. Beneficial outcomes from the construct and institutionalization of EPOC supported a momentum for the coalescing of public and private interests through collaborative processes that minimized the risk of loss on all sides, yielding mutual benefits.

Despite Jamaica being labelled a low trust society with a social capital deficit (Brown, 2002: Brewster, 2007) and fledgling social partnership developments overall, EPOC represented a typology of social partnership, representative of a 'collaborative innovation' and a 'self-organizing and interorganizational network' (Rhodes, 1997, p. 53). As a monitoring mechanism created under the auspices of the 2013 Extended Fund Facility, EPOC received commendations from Mme Christine Lagarde, Managing Director of the IMF, in relation to its contribution to the success of Jamaica's Programme, which she indicated was a model that could be emulated by other countries. Namely EPOC also taking ownership, applying private sector methods in following up the rolling out and implementation of the IMF programme, as well as enhancing accountability processes and transparency in collaborating with the public sector (*Sunday Gleaner*, 2014).

It is noteworthy that another small island developing state in the Caribbean, Grenada was commended for its progress under their 2014 IMF Extended Credit Facility arrangement whereby a similar 'EPOC' social partnership typology was used, customized to the Grenadian context. On Grenada's successful completion of its arrangement with the IMF and moving to surveillance only the relationship in 2017, one of the attributes highlighted by Nicole Laframboise, IMF Mission Chief for Grenada, contributing to Grenada's success and progress, compared to previous fund-supported programmes was the.

> broad ownership and consultation across the country on the Government's reform programme. Grenada's Committee of Social Partners and the Home Grown Monitoring Committee—representing trade unions, private companies, the Council of Churches, and nongovernment development organizations—were consulted regularly and involved in monitoring performance. They provided grassroots feedback to policymakers about how the program was affecting people in the country.' (IMF Country Focus, 2017)

EPOC provided a forum for a plurality of perspectives and interests—public, private and civil society—in supporting the resolution and mitigation of 'wicked' macroeconomic problems and their effects. The institution served as a constructive modality that also demonstrated accountability to the public and its constituents, by helping to disseminate even to the broad Jamaican society, the Governments' ongoing targeted implementation, compliance and fulfillment of objectives under the IMF Agreement and the mediation of certain challenges.

References

Alesina, A., & Tabellini, G. (1990). A positive theory of fiscal deficits and government debt. *Review of Economic Studies, 57*, 403–414.

Bassett, Carolyn. (2004). The demise of the social contract in South Africa. *Canadian Journal of African Studies, 38*(3), 543–557.

Beetsma, R. M., & Bovenberg, A. L. (1999). Does monetary unification lead to excessive debt accumulation? *Journal of Public Economics, 74*(3), 299–325.

Beschorner, T., & Müller, M. (2007). Social standards: Toward an active ethical involvement of businesses in developing countries. *Journal of Business Ethics, 73*(1), 11–20.

Bullock, C. F. (2010, June 13). On the trail of fiscal responsibility. *Sunday Gleaner*.

Brewster, H. (2007). *Understanding development challenges of the Caribbean*. Prepared for World Bank Forum for parliamentarians on 'Shaping a Trade Agenda to Promote Regional Integration and Competitiveness for CARICOM,' St. Lucia.

Brown, D. (2002). The private sector as a social partner: The Barbados model. In S. Ryan & A. Marie Bissessar (Eds.), *Governance in the Caribbean*. St Augustine: SALISES, University of the West Indies.

Callon, M. (1986). Some elements of a sociology of translation: Domestication of the scallops and the fishermen of St Brieuc Bay. In J. Law (Ed.), *Power, action and belief: A new sociology of knowledge?* (pp. 196–223). London: Routledge.

Caribbean Policy Research Institute (CaPRI). (2009). *A new social partnership for Jamaica*. Kingston, Jamaica: Author.

Colebatch, H. K. (2009). Governance as a conceptual development in the analysis of policy. *Critical Policy Studies, 3*(1), 58–67.

Cook, M. L. (1998). Toward flexible industrial relations? Neo-liberalism, democracy, and labor reform in Latin America. *Industrial Relations, 37*(3), 311–336. https://doi.org/10.1111/0019-8676.00090.

De Maeyer, J. (2016). Adopting a 'material sensibility' in journalism studies. In *The SAGE handbook of digital journalism* (pp. 460–476). London: Sage.

Fairclough, N. (2005). Critical discourse analysis in transdisciplinary research. In *A new agenda in (critical) discourse analysis* (pp. 53–70).

Fudge, J. (2007). The new discourse of labour rights: From social to fundamental rights? *Comparative Labor Law and Policy Journal, 29*(1), 2007.

Grabbe, H. (1999). *A partnership for accession: the implications of EU conditionality for the Central and East European applicants*. Robert Schuman Centre: European University Institute.

Hagemann, R. (2011). How can fiscal councils strengthen fiscal performance? *OECD Journal: Economic Studies, 2011*(1), 1–24.

Harris, D. J. (2010). *Jamaica's debt propelled economy: A failed economic strategy and its aftermath* (SALISES Working Paper, 1). Mona, Jamaica: University of the West Indies.

Héthy, L. (2001). *Social dialogue and expanding world*. New Internationalist.

International Labour Organization. (2001). *The ILO in the Caribbean: Its objectives and activities: Strengthening tripartism and social dialogue*. Retrieved from http://www.ilocarib.org.tt/Promalco_tool/productivity-tools/introilopro.htm.

International Labour Organisation. (2007). *Report of the meeting on the project "history of ILO ideas and their impact"*. Geneva: International Labour Organisation.

International Monetary Fund Country Focus. (2017, May 23). *Grenada set stage for sustainable growth* (IMF Country Focus). https://www.imf.org/en/News/Articles/2017/05/23/NA230517-Grenada-Sets-Stage-for-Sustainable-Growth.

Jessop, B. (1999). *The dynamics of partnership and governance failure: The new politics of local governance in Britain* (pp. 11–32). Basingstoke: Macmillan.

Johnston, J. (2013). *The multilateral debt trap in Jamaica*. Washington, DC: Center for Economic and Policy Research. Retrieved from http://www.cepr.net/documents/publications/jamaica-debt-2013-06.pdf.

Jonung, L., Begg, I., & Tutty, M. G. (2016). *How is the Irish fiscal advisory council performing? An independent evaluation of the first years of IFAC* (Working Paper 3). Department of Economics, School of Economics and Management, Lund University.

Katz, H., Wonduck, L., & Joohee, L. (2004). *The new structure of labor relations: tripartism and decentralization*. Ithaca, NY: Cornell University Press.

Kernaghan, K. (1993). Partnership and public administration: Conceptual and practical considerations. *Canadian Public Administration, 36*(1), 57–76. https://doi.org/10.1111/j.1754-7121.1993.tb02166.x.

Lebrun, I. (2006). Fiscal councils, independent forecasts, and the budgetary process: Lessons from the Belgian case. In J. Ayuso-i-Casals et al. (Eds.), *Policy instruments for sound fiscal policy*. Palgrave Macmillan.

Levitsky, S., & Way, L. A. (1998). Between a shock and a hard place: The dynamics of labour-backed adjustment in Poland and Argentina. *Comparative Politics, 30*(2), 171–192. https://doi.org/10.2307/422286.

Madrid, R. L. (2003). Labouring against neoliberalism: Unions and patterns of reform in Latin America. *Journal of Latin American Studies, 35*(1), 53–88. https://doi.org/10.1017/S0022216X0200665X.

Martinez-Lucio, M., & Stuart, M. (2002). Social partnership and mutual gains organization and remaking involvement and trust at the British workplace. *Economic and Industrial Democracy, 23*(2), 177–200. https://doi.org/10.1177/0143831X02232003.

McCartan, P. (2002). Towards social partnership-or co-operative industrial relations? *Irish Journal of Management, 23*(1), 53.

Mooney, H., Wright, A., & Grenade, K. (2018). *Fiscal councils: Evidence, common features and lessons for the Caribbean*.

Nelson, C. (2019). *Social partnership and governance under crises*. IGI Global.

O'Donnell, R. (1996). Ireland's experiment in social partnership, 1987–96. *Social Pacts in Europe* (pp. 79–95). Brussels: ETUI.

Osei, P. D. (2004). Tripartite social partnerships in small states: Barbados and Jamaica in comparative perspective. *Globalization and Governance: Essays on the Challenges for Small States, 9*, 34.

Rhodes, R. A. W. (1997). *Understanding governance: Policy networks, governance, reflexivity and accountability*. Buckingham, UK: Open University Press.

Rogoff, K. (1990). Equilibrium political budget cycles. *American Economic Review, 80*, 21–36.

Schmid, J. P. (2016). *Addressing debt overhang*. IDB

Sunday Gleaner. (2014, June 29). EPOC masterstroke—Jamaica praised for public-private sector team monitoring IMF agreement.

Trebilcock, A. (1996). Structural adjustment and tripartite consultation. *International Journal of Public Sector Management, 9*(1), 5–16. https://doi.org/10.1108/09513559610693233.

CHAPTER 6

Leaving No One Behind: ODA and Development in Jamaica 2010–2019

Introduction

Jamaica has a unique institutional structure that it utilizes to manage and advance its development agenda and, thereby, its interface with international development partners (IDPs)—bilateral and multilateral entities—who make wide and varied contributions to the improvement of various elements of the Jamaican economy and society. Some interventions are time bound and are implemented over a short to medium term period, however, the majority of the interventions that are made by the IDPs are the product of close collaboration between an established consular or other diplomatic arrangement on-island in the case of the bilateral engagements, or established offices in the case of the multilateral organizations, with the Planning Institute of Jamaica (PIOJ). Jamaica has had a long relationship and sometimes visible image in the international community where it has been a signatory to many critical international conventions meant to drive and motivate harmony across countries and development and economic growth in its own territory and for its own citizens. It is also supported in reporting on its adherence to many of these by United Nations organisations such as the United Nations Development Programme (UNDP) both of which have a physical presence on the island. Jamaica has strived to initiate and maintain diplomatic relationships pragmatically with emphasis on states with which it has a large portion of its diaspora, those that it believes had been downtrodden, as

C. Clarke and C. Nelson, *Jamaica's Evolving Relationship with the IMF*, https://doi.org/10.1007/978-3-030-59204-2_6

well as those that stood with it as it attempted to establish its philosophy regarding the New International Economic Order under the aegis of the Non-Aligned Movement.

As indicated by Clarke and Nelson (2020) Jamaica has had a long history of struggle as its citizens attempted to conquer the challenges presented during the long sought after Emancipation was realized. Unfortunately, the challenges could not and were not fully addressed leading to intermittent and sometimes widespread riots as workers and those who supported them opposed the social and economic systems that ought to have implemented livelihood enhancing mechanisms actually used divide and conquer tactics to reduce wages and alter the security of tenure parameters in a situation where markets were not properly established and where the ability of freed persons to participate in any such markets were slim. As indicated in Clarke and Nelson (2020) the Moyne Commission rendered the death knell on this arrangement and though the resulting Committee attempted to address the challenges reported by Lord Moyne, it was insufficient to correct the century-long neglect of all aspects of the Jamaican society and economy particularly in relation to the physical infrastructure and the advancement of the education system to cater to the entire population rather than only to the son of Englishmen who could not educate their sons in the motherland. Overall, this situation exemplified the impact of low levels of the various forms of capital that are required for a society to be sustainable and to generate economic activity that can engage and improve the human capital of a large portion of the population, thereby sustaining improvements with each generation. Because of the association of this prevailing social and economic situation with the waning interest of the British in their responsibilities to certain aspects of the Empire, and the view that self-government would necessarily provide significant improvements in the life of the average Jamaican, moves were initiated and eventually consummated that would end with Jamaica achieving political independence from Britain.

Whilst during the initial period of independence there was visible capital improvements associated with a range of Independence projects such as the National Stadium, and an influx of capital investment that established some manufacturing, bauxite and tourism ventures, the euphoria was short-lived due to the fact that the average Jamaican was still unable to participate in the benefits that these activities generated. The low levels of education, poor transportation and road infrastructure network, and, the low levels of income and wealth endowments meant that the then largely rurally based populations would need to seek engagements in the more urbanized areas where these activities took place in order for them to provide labour—largely in terms of domestic duties—to those who were able to secure formal employment in the emerging industries. At this point, it was clear to the Jamaican authorities that resources needed to be dedicated to the planning function and capacity of the government. Although Jamaica is not a vast country in terms of hectares, there were simply not enough resources broadly defined to effect the required changes and support the large proportions of the population who had high expectations of the independence period and beyond. The role of the state during this period was expectedly wide and deep given the nascence of the private sector and the low levels of financial capital that it had to put at risk in commerce and manufacture. The state therefore saw itself as needing to be intimately active in driving economic activity whilst simultaneously needing to catalogue and understand the developmental concerns, challenges and needs of the population and the nuances that were applicable in the various parishes and regions of the island. Spatial distribution—particularly given the mountainous retreat that many Jamaicans preferred to seek their tenure (Rainford, 2006)—had serious implications as it related the location of the population and the relevant efficiency ratios that typically drive investment decisions. Once poverty and other measurements of human development started to be systematically collected, collated and analysed, it would become apparent that the spatial dimension told a starker and more imperative story and that this intelligence must be used in the context of limited resources and the extensive and intensive needs of the population. Rainford (2006) reports that according to the late M. G. Smith, almost one-half but not less than one-third of Jamaica's population lived in rural communities in 1956 and that these communities were characterized with the very low levels of social services to which they had access. Rainford (2006) pointed out, that this low level of access to services would come to characterize many other communities not classified as rural by Smith, thereby increasing the scope and intensity of the work that would be faced by any governing body of Jamaica.

It would have been evident that the state in all its dimensions would have to embark upon a sustained, systematic and data-driven assault on the multiple immediate needs for life whilst preparing for the medium to long-term needs. The capacity for this kind of analytical, programmatic and research driven work in Jamaica was built along two tracks: at the still nascent University College of the West Indies founded at Mona in 1948 and, at the Central Planning Unit established by Premier Norman Manley. Rainford (2006) reports that Manley was thought to have been obsessed with planning and the need for massive resource mobilization in order to address the needs of the population. Rainford (2006) indicates that Manley sought assistance from the United Nations to establish this planning function within the government during the same week that he won elections in 1955 after having declared his intention to establish a Planning Department answerable to the Minister of Production. Based on Rainford's (2006) account, Manley had very specific requirements for the roles and responsibilities of the department and the person who ought to be at the helm of the institution inclusive of having contacts in the United Nations system and demonstrative of an understanding that the government had to take a major role in countries such as Jamaica. The responsibility for planning was to be predicated on a clear understanding of Jamaica's vital statistics and ensuring that other government departments whose operations impact the planning function submit their reports on time. Rainford (2006) reported that Premier Manley went even further to specify the number of jobs that were to be created over a five-year period and the levels of public and private sector expenditure that would be required to support these goals and he was clear that the welfare needs were contingent on the creation of wealth and therefore production. Mr. George Cadbury was recommended by the United Nations and assumed office of the Central Planning Unit (CPU) which reported directly to the Chief Minister and Minister of Development who was none other than Manley himself.

The CPU was established to be of service to the entire public sector despite it being under the jurisdiction of the Chief Minister and later Premier. It had a seat at the Economic and Financial Committee of the country's Executive Council and was expected to give broad advice to the state. Unlike other departments it was not envisioned that the CPU would simply implement instructions or an agenda provided to it by Ministries, Departments and Agencies (MDAs). Instead, the CPU was expected to operate proactively and develop its own research agenda in the social and economic areas in order to support the efforts of government to solve these issues. The small staff in the CPU prepared three national development plans over a 10-year period—the 1957 to 1967 Ten Year National Development Plan, the 1963–1968 Five-Year Independence Plan and the 1970–1975sFive-Year Plan in 1967 (Rainford, 2006).

Due to the efforts required, additional advisory work was not embarked upon to the extent originally envisaged by Manley. Since then, the CPU has transitioned to the National Planning Agency in 1972 as part of the new government's intention to enable the organization to support its policy agenda by expanding its staff and increasing the social sector focus of the organization with emphasis on critical issues including the establishment of a function to support the government's management of its interface with the IDPs. An advisory board also accompanied the transition of the institution that would support the identification of potential projects. The NPA itself would transition to become the Planning Institute of Jamaica (PIOJ) in May 1984 which was endowed with a legal identity, supported by an Act of Parliament and therefore benefitting from a far improved level of standing and autonomy. Rainford (2006) indicates that these transitions were often linked to efforts at redefinition and clarification of its mission. During this period, the Minister to which the PIOJ reported has changed—more frequently during some political administrations than in others—ranging from the Prime Minister, Ministers of Finance and Ministers with responsibility for Planning and/or Development. The corporate governance structure was developed through the appointment of a Board of Directors and an Annual Report was delivered in its first year of operation. The PIOJ Act clearly transmitted the expectation of the government that the institute would lead the planning efforts across government, develop comprehensive development plans and monitor their implementation by MDAs in order to ensure their success, and improve the impact of each plan through the engagement of the private sector as a key stakeholder.

Jamaica's Development Agenda and the United Nations System

Jamaica has been open to the broad work of the UN and the strength and openness of the relationship between the two parties could be inferred from multiple UN entities that are present in Jamaica and these entities often times are leveraged by UN headquarters to provide cover over other Caribbean countries. The UN has a history of working closely with the government through the PIOJ, having played a key role in the establishment of its predecessor twice removed. Through the PIOJ, the UN has also supported the development of several indicator systems such as the Multiple Indicator Cluster Survey (MICS) that focussed on the experiences of women and children through this instrument which was implemented by the Statistical Institute of Jamaica. It was to play a role in helping to track progress in relation to the associated Millennium Development Goals (MDGs), a World Fit for Children and a range of other targets that Jamaica had committed to achieving. As the name of the MICS indicates, a wide range of indicators were included for tracking, including: nutrition (breastfeeding and low birth weight); child health (immunization, oral rehydration treatment and care seeking and antibiotic treatment of pneumonia); environment (water and sanitation); reproductive health (antenatal care); child development (birth registration, child labour, child discipline, early marriage, domestic violence, child disability); education (pre-school attendance and school readiness, primary and secondary school participation, distance from household to primary and secondary school and adult literacy); and, HIV/AIDS, Sexual Behaviour, and Orphaned and Vulnerable Children (knowledge of HIV Transmission and Condom Use, Orphans and Vulnerable Children). Another key indicator system supported by the UN is the JamStats portal that was intended to be a comprehensive database containing information of all important development indicators in order to support tracking. The UN supported the training of key staff, the establishment of a secretariat and the dissemination of information regarding the indicator system through various training opportunities. The JamStats system enables and supports data collection, harmonization and dissemination as it is integrated with Microsoft Office enabling the user to generate customized presentations with supporting illustrations from the system. This database could be seen as a nascent form of the Results Based Management system that the PIOJ and Jamaica would adopt as it transitioned to develop the country's first long-term national development plan.The UNDP continues to support the government in the implementation of various platforms that are developed to support the tracking of various development needs such as monitoring of the implementation of Vision 2030 Jamaica and the receipt of international flows in response to disasters (See Chapter 11).

The UN Resident Coordinator began to play a more visible role among the IDPs in 1995 when it convened the IDP Annual Retreat at first as a closed meeting. The attendance at this retreat was subsequently expanded to include government officials in recognition of the fact that the IDPs were working to support the government achievement development outcomes, consistent with the emerging global trend towards improving the effectiveness of aid globally. The donor focussed nature of the thematic working groups that were being used by the IDPs to address issues relating to the area of work was transformed in 2003 to include the PIOJ and into a collaboration between the IDPs and the Government of Jamaica (GOJ) with an emphasis on improving the extent to which policy formulation was impactful. The result of this process was the development or utilization of several methodologies that were intended to support improved aid effectiveness. Among UN entities, the United Nations Development Programme (UNDP) has emerged as a major partner for Jamaica in terms of helping to coordinate a systematic approach to the programmes entered into with government and civil society through the development of a five-year programming horizon and it has supported the coordination both within the UN System and across the other IDPs. The UNDP stands as the largest and most expansive multilateral technical assistance agency globally and therefore can bring to bear technical expertise on almost any topic to support areas that the government is interested in exploring and/or pursuing. The UNDP has provided coordination and management services to the government in its first structural adjustment loan obtained from the World Bank through the contracting and supervision of experts in the programme. The UNDP has supported projects with high development value dating back to the 1960s that identified important water resources for the agriculture sector across the island including the Queen of Spain Valley, Milk River, Rio Minho and Rio Cobre Basin, Discovery Bay, and, Negril and Bull Savannah Basins (Clarke, 2013).

In the early 2000s the Director General of the PIOJ engaged the UNDP to support the development and production of a video series presenting four potential scenarios that Jamaica could potentially experience depending on the choices that it makes. The domestic sector crisis had impacted the dynamism of the local private sector and despite declines in poverty, rates of violent crime appeared to skyrocket with Jamaica eventually being ranked as among the murder capitals of the world, the educational outcomes used as an indicator of the human capital available for the initiation of economic growth were disappointing. Without serious, determined and deliberate efforts to chart the way forward, it was feared that the worst of the four scenarios would prevail and Jamaica's development trajectory would be seriously and deleteriously altered for the coming decades. This video series was used to spark extensive discussions and the need to develop a long-term national development plan emerged as a means to arrest this potential decline. The Plan—Vision 2030 Jamaica National Development Plan provided an important impetus and alignment signpost for all IDPs to develop their programmes around as it was developed in order to address all the deficiencies identified with the previous seven short-term plans—(i) a narrow siloed focus on specific sectors; (ii) absence of clear bipartisan involvement and support; (iii) absence of long-term goals and the limitation of the plans to the five-year electoral cycle; (iv) the absence of a national consensus on the content and focus of the plan; and, (v) an inadequate focus on strategy (Rainford, 2006).

Overview of Official Development Assistance in Jamaica: 2010–2019

Jamaica has had long-standing relationships with its multilateral and bilateral partners since its Independence in 1962. Beginning with its membership in the United Nations on 18 September 1962 and the International Monetary Fund in February 1963, Jamaica has benefitted from several programmes, projects, small grants and technical assistance arrangements with its partners. On the bilateral side, Jamaica has been engaged with several partners including the European Union with whom it has partnered officially since 1975 with the signing of the Lome Convention and the Cotonou Partnership Agreements. Jamaica's development partners have supported the country through various crises and difficulties. This chapter provides an assessment of the scope and scale of the support received from the wide range of development partners in Jamaica's efforts to achieve its targets under both Vision 2030 Jamaica and the three agreements it had with the International Monetary Fund between 2010 and 2019.

Hurricane disaster damage, impending changes to trade agreements that provided preferential treatment for Jamaica's major exports of sugar and banana, addressing the country's rising rates of violent crime, drives to improve the nation's education system and health care infrastructure are some of the many areas in which the network of development partners have supported various items on the Jamaican government's agenda. Looking at the period 2010 to 2019, these partners provided more than US$4.8bn in support of the various elements of the development agenda (see Planning Institute of Jamaica [2010, 2011, 2012, 2014, 2015, 2016a] and [Planning Institute of Jamaica, 2013, 2017a,

2018, 2019]). Overall, during the period 2010 to 2019, Jamaica's bilateral partners provided just under 30% of total funds disbursed; the MFIs provided an additional 67.42%; and the MTCAs another 2.11%. This financing flow is a reflection of the development cooperation framework that has been employed between the PIOJ on behalf of the government and each particular IDP. The framework is also influenced by the development perspective of each multilateral or bilateral partner. For the multilaterals, they are often guided by particular focus areas that are specified by their executive board and ultimately their shareholders and financiers, with wealthier and more influential donors emphasizing areas that are consistent with their own interests. The focus areas in Jamaica are reflective of the broad global thematic concerns such as: various dimensions of poverty including child and food poverty; sustainable development; human development; gender; climate change; renewable energy; entrepreneurship, innovation, fiscal policy management, private sector development and, more recently, digitalization and the COVID-19 response, recovery and rebuilding. Responses to these themes have varied over time and across IDP depending on the ideology of the particular IDP; the resources each IDP makes available to Jamaica; and, the predominance of a particular IDP in the thematic area. At the core of the programmatic interventions there has been a deliberate change in orientation towards people-centred development and increased attempts to make interventions at the community and individual level in order to increase the felt-impact of development.

More than three quarters of this total amount of ODA during the period was extended in the form of development and policy-based loans. According to Table 6.1, these loans are granted overwhelmingly by the multilateral financial institutions (MFI)—75% of total loans—with the Inter-American Bank (IDB) followed by the World Bank (WB) being responsible for a combined 97% of the loans extended in this category of development partners over this period. The Caribbean Development Bank (CDB) and the European Union are the other two partners in this category with the CDB accounting for the remaining 3% of loans in the MFI category. Just under one quarter of loan funds were disbursed by bilateral partners with eighteen of the 24% being provided by the People's Republic of China (PRC). Loans from the PRC were provided in three of the twenty years—2010, 2013 and 2017—in the review period increasing from USD 71.2 to 311 and 326.4 million, respectively. The focus of the loan funds from the PRC was in the area of road infrastructure under the

Table 6.1 Official development assistance by type of partner: 2010–2019 (% of total)

IDP	*Grant*	*Loan*	*Grand total*
Bilateral Partners	**49.13**	**24.17**	**29.69**
Australia	0.04	1.86	1.46
Belgium	0.23	2.38	1.90
Brazil	0.41	0.00	0.09
Canada	3.59	0.00	0.79
Chile	0.01	0.00	0.00
Cuba	0.14	0.00	0.03
Czech Republic	0.06	0.00	0.01
Germany	0.10	0.00	0.02
India	0.24	0.00	0.05
Japan	3.89	0.40	1.17
Mexico	0.17	0.00	0.04
Morocco	0.03	0.00	0.01
New Zealand	0.07	0.00	0.01
Nigeria	0.00	0.00	0.00
People's Republic of China	12.47	18.86	17.45
Scholarships	1.89	0.00	0.42
South Korea	0.60	0.00	0.13
Spain	0.09	0.00	0.02
United Kingdom	12.81	0.00	2.83
United States of America	11.89	0.00	2.63
Venezuela	0.37	0.67	0.60
Environment & Climate Change Funds	**2.35**	**0.27**	**0.73**
Climate Investment Funds	1.84	0.27	0.61
GEF	0.52	0.00	0.11
Multi-Donor Funds	**0.28**	**0.00**	**0.06**
Multi-Donor Funds	0.26	0.00	0.06
Tropical Storm Nicole	0.02	0.00	0.00
Multilateral Financial Institution	**38.72**	**75.57**	**67.42**
Caribbean Development Bank	2.18	2.53	2.45
European Union	33.20	0.00	7.34
Inter-American Development Bank	2.61	44.50	35.24
World Bank	0.74	28.53	22.39
Multilateral Technical Cooperation Agencies	**9.53**	**0.00**	**2.11**
Commonwealth Fund for Technical Cooperation	0.28	0.00	0.06
Commonwealth Secretariat	0.00	0.00	0.00

(continued)

Table 6.1 (continued)

IDP	*Grant*	*Loan*	*Grand total*
FAO	0.36	0.00	0.08
GEF SGP	0.50	0.00	0.11
Global Fund	3.52	0.00	0.78
IAEA	0.53	0.00	0.12
OAS	0.62	0.00	0.14
PAHO	0.42	0.00	0.09
Scholarships	0.15	0.00	0.03
UN Women	0.02	0.00	0.00
UNAIDS	0.14	0.00	0.03
UNDP	1.08	0.00	0.24
UNEP	0.24	0.00	0.05
UNESCO	0.23	0.00	0.05
UNFPA	0.18	0.00	0.04
UNICEF	1.15	0.00	0.26
United Nations	0.11	0.00	0.02
Grand Total	**100**	**100**	**100**

Source Collated by Authors from the *Economic and Social Survey of Jamaica* Planning Institute of Jamaica (2010–2019)

Major Infrastructure Development Programme (MIDP) aligned to the Economic Infrastructure sector. In 2017, the Southern Coastal Highway Improvement Project was signed to support the rehabilitation of the road between St. Andrew and Portland—a total of 110 kilometres. This project is now taking shape in 2021 as part of the thrust for economic recovery (See Chapter 11). Given the technical nature of the Multilateral Technical Cooperation Agencies (MTCA), no loans are expected under this line item.

On the grant side, Table 6.1 indicates that the bilateral partners provided the largest share at just over 49% over the twenty-year period. The PRC with 12.47% of grants were just exceeded by the United Kingdom at 12.81%, and the United States provided 11.89% of the grant flows into the country (Planning Institute of Jamaica, 2010–2019). The Government of Canada and the Government of Japan provided 3.59 and 3.89%, respectively. Among the MFIs, the European Union has the single largest portfolio of grants, contributing 33.2% of this category overall and approximately 86% of the grants extended by the MFIs as their contribution to the development agenda in Jamaica is concentrated in the provision of grants rather than in the form of loans. The region's development bank, the Caribbean Development Bank provided 2.18%, whilst the IDB and WB provided 2.61 and 0.74%, respectively. The seventeen MTCAs inclusive of all the UN entities and scholarships, combined to provide 9.53% of the total grants available to the government of Jamaica. The Global Fund to Fight AIDS, Tuberculosis and Malaria provided 3.52 percentage points of the MTCA-originating grants followed by the United Nations Children's Fund (UNICEF) and the United Nations Development Programme (UNDP) with 1.15 and 1.08% respectively.

Whilst the dollar value of this technical cooperation portfolio pales in comparison with the overall portfolio the technical knowledge and expertise that is brought to bear through these allocations have provided important, policy relevant information on which grant and loan funds can be mobilized for project information in the future. Additionally, they are used to provide additional public goods such as physical expansion of schools, the provision of ambulances to the Heart Institute, expanded and/or improved community infrastructure, scholarships, and, improvements to various health facilities.

ODA and Jamaica's Vision 2030 Targets

During the period 2010 to 2019, the Jamaican authorities had the unenviable task of attempting to navigate the impact of the worst economic crisis in the history of the nation—the global financial and economic crisis. The events leading up to the crisis and resulting impact of the crisis on the financial sector had a negative impact on investor and business confidence in many markets worldwide due to its widespread contagion associated with the crisis and the constrained capital markets that would normally support sovereign borrowing for development purposes. In the three years prior to the start of the decade, the Jamaican government had fortuitously decided to re-engage the multilateral community into a renewed level of engagement based on the high rates of interest being charged in the international community versus the concessional rates being offered by the multilaterals.

Figure 6.1 reflects the sharp increase in loan funding from both the IDB and WB that occurred in response to the reengagement of the Washington-based MFIs. The figure indicates that the IDB developed

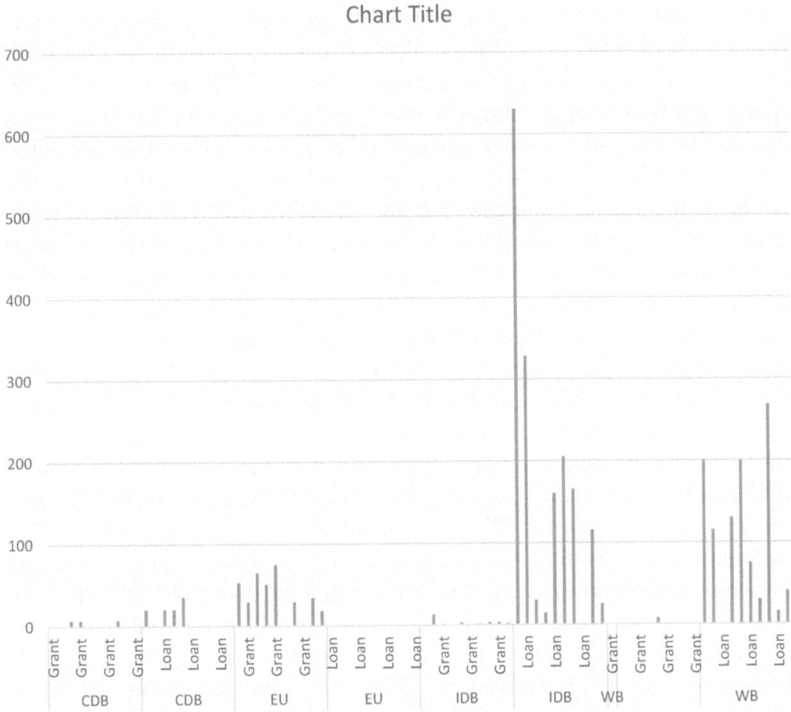

Fig. 6.1 Trends in annual grant and loan funding from the Multilateral Financial Institutions (MFI) (in US millions: 2010–2019) (*Source* Collated by Authors from the *Economic and Social Survey of Jamaica* Planning Institute of Jamaica [2010–2019])

a historic multi-million dollar cooperation programme in very visible support for the government's intended reform agenda, supported by the IMF and was valued at three times that of the WB in the year 2010. The constrained international credit market occurring at the same time also forced the authorities to approach the IMF, an option not considered in Jamaica for almost 20 years. This section will review the relative contribution of the various partners who have played a role in supporting Jamaica's efforts to achieve its various objectives in the context of scarce resources.

The 2010 Standby Agreement with the IMF was heavily front-loaded with development flows reflected in these funds from the IDB. Grant funding from the EU and loans from the CDB were also used to support the social capital dimensions of the society as well as the crucial macroeconomic and financial sector stability agenda. Given that the 2010 SBA was derailed due to fiscal slippages, there was a sharp decline in the loan flows to Jamaica from the IDB and the WB whilst EU grant funding continued to support fiscal policy reforms. When the 2013 Extended Fund Facility (see Chapter 3) was secured, loan funding from the IDB and WB resumed with a peak in 2015 for the IDB loan flows and a peak in 2017 for the WB loan flows. Though the 2016 SBA was precautionary and the funds went untouched by the authorities there were a few loans from both the IDB and WB during its implementation. This second re-engagement also occurred simultaneously with the launch of Vision 2030 Jamaica the country's first long-term national development plan in 2009 designed to make *Jamaica, the place of choice to live, work, raise families, and do business* (Planning Institute of Jamaica, 2009b). This development plan is understandably ambitious as it had to address all the long-term macroeconomic and social constraints that had bedevilled the country for more than three decades prior The Plan is organized based on a results management framework that distilled four national goals and fifteen national outcomes from the vision statement (see Table 6.2).

The goals indicate the states that would characterize the nation, its society, economy, natural environment, and, people for the vision for it to claim that the vision has been accomplished. The first goal exemplifies the transition of development planning in Jamaica from being centred on the the economy to being centered, instead on its people. When the Plan has been fully implemented, the Jamaican people would be empowered to achieve their fullest potential. Aligned to this Goal, four National Outcomes (NOs) are distilled that if achieved jointly should translate to the accomplishment of Goal 1. The NOs relate to the establishment of: (1) A Healthy and Stable Population; (2) World-class Education and Training; (3) Effective Social Protection; and, (4) Authentic and Transformational Culture.

Complementing this goal and its aligned NOs is Goal 2 which prescribes the need to ensure that The Jamaican society is safe, cohesive and just which can only be accomplished if the two NOs: (5) Security and Safety; and (6) Effective Governance are achieved. The third goal focusses on the critical elements of the economy and aspires to ensure that

Table 6.2 Four national goals and fifteen national outcomes

National Vision: Jamaica, the place of choice to live, work, raise families and do business	
National Goals	*National Outcomes*
Goal 1: Jamaicans are Empowered to Achieve their Fullest Potential	1. A Healthy and Stable Population 2. World-class Education and Training 3. Effective Social Protection 4. Authentic and Transformational Culture
Goal 2: The Jamaican society is safe, cohesive and just	5. Security and Safety 6. Effective Governance
Goal 3: Jamaica's economy is prosperous	7. A Stable Macroeconomy 8. An Enabling Business Environment 9. Strong Economic Infrastructure 10. Energy Security and Efficiency 11. A Technology-Enabled Society 12. Internationally Competitive Industry Structures
Goal 4: Jamaica has a healthy natural environment	13. Sustainable Management and Use of Environmental and Natural Resources 14. Hazard Risk Reduction and Adaptation to Climate Change 15. Sustainable Urban and Rural Development

Source Collated by Authors from *Vision 2030 Jamaica National Development Plan* Planning Institute of Jamaica (2009b)

Jamaica's economy is prosperous. To achieve this, six (6) NOs have to be in place: (7) A Stable Macroeconomy; (8) An Enabling Business Environment; (9) Strong Economic Infrastructure; (10) Energy Security and Efficiency; (11) A Technology-Enabled Society; and, (12) Internationally Competitive Industry Structures.

The final goal strengthens the sustainability dimensions of the plan. Goal 4 refers to ensuring that Jamaica has a health natural environment when the following three national outcomes are achieved: (13) Sustainable Management and Use of Environmental and Natural Resources; (14) Hazard Risk Reduction and Adaptation to Climate Change; and, (15) Sustainable Urban and Rural Development (see Chapter 10 in this volume for more on Vision 2030 Jamaica and the IMF conditionalities implemented by Jamaica).

Given the stark economic imperatives facing the government of Jamaica, it is important to explore the extent to which its IDPs supported the economic reform agenda in addition to the social and environmental dimensions of the society.

The extent to which they contributed to the achievement of all four goals would give an indication of the extent to which Jamaica was still able to maintain its focus on and achieve accomplishments in these critical aspects of its development agenda, that though important would not be the direct focus of any of the IMF agreements that it would engage in. Looking at the IDPs with the largest grant and loan cooperation programmes with the government of Jamaica reveals that in terms of total ODA allocation or commitment between 28.2% in the case of the United States to 74.8% in the case of China for the twenty-year period from 2010 to 2019 went to supporting the achievement.

The goals indicate the states that would characterize the nation, its society, economy, natural environment and people for the vision to have been achieved. The first goal exemplifies the transition of development planning in Jamaica from being centred on the economy to being centred, instead, on the people. It specifies the ideal that when the Plan is fully implemented or the success of the Plan can be measured in part by the extent to which Jamaicans have been This was followed by the IDB and WB who each contributed 64% of their allocation each to Goal Three. Approximately 60% of the allocation to Jamaica by the EU was spent in relation to Goal Three. At the lower end of the proportional contribution to the achievement of Goal 3 is the United Kingdom that split its allocation almost evenly between Goals One to Three in the proportion of 33, 34 and 30%, respectively. The United States allocated almost 50% of their funds to activities aligned with Goal 1 of Goal Three—Jamaica's Economy is Prosperous (see Fig. 6.2).

The projects implemented through the United States Agency for International Development (USAID) (see Table 6.3) covered a wide range of interventions in the areas of education, HIV/AIDS, supporting the Government's response to the outbreak of Zika, supporting the development of the social enterprise business model, and, capacity building for law enforcement offices. In the environmental area, the United States allocated 13.1% which was utilized in the areas of climate change, forestry management and conservation, an analysis of the impact of weather on the transportation sector, and, biodiversity analysis, all of which are aligned

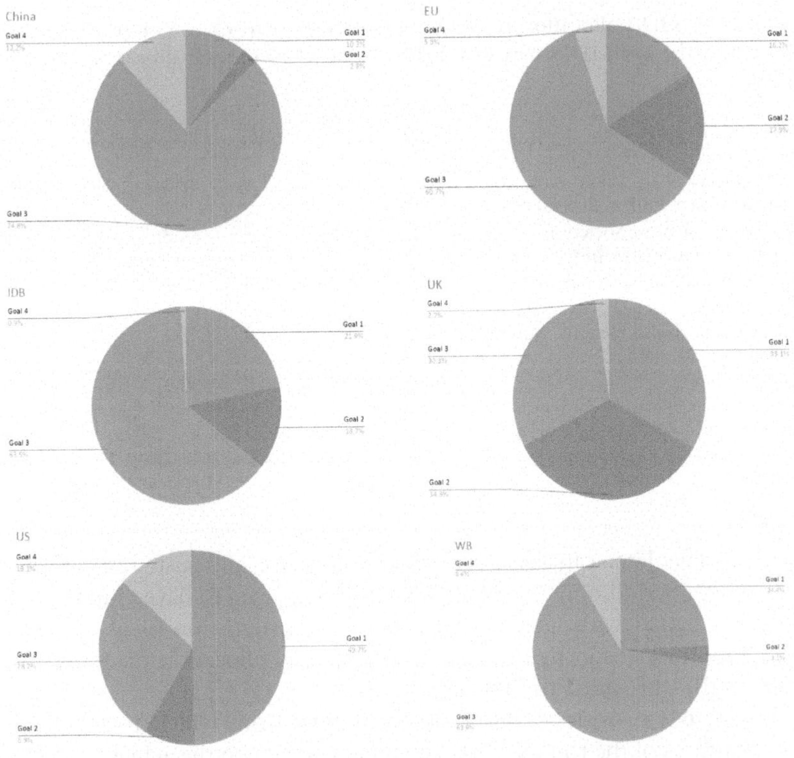

Fig. 6.2 ODA allocation or commitment aligned to each Vision 2030 goal by each of the main IDPs between 2010 and 2019 (% of total allocation by each IDP) (*Source* Collated and calculated by Authors from Planning Institute of Jamaica [2009b] *Vision 2030 Jamaica National Development Plan* and Planning Institute of Jamaica [2010–2019] *Economic and Social Survey of Jamaica*)

to Goal 4: Jamaica has a Healthy Natural Environment. The PRC allocated 12% of their respective overall allocations to supporting efforts at ensuring Jamaica has a Healthy Natural Environment through projects which include the construction of sea defences along the Palisadoes Highway which allows access to the country's major international airport during 2013 (Planning Institute of Jamaica, 2013). The EU provided 16 and 17% of its total allocation or commitment during the period on Goal 1: Jamaicans are empowered to achieve the fullest potential and on

Table 6.3 ODA allocation or commitment aligned to each Vision 2030 goal by each of the main IDPs between 2010 and 2019 (% of total allocation by each IDP)

Vision 2030 goals	*China*	*EU*	*IDB*	*UK*	*US*	*WB*
#1—Jamaicans are Empowered to Achieve Their Fullest Potential	10.3	16.2	21.9	33.1	49.8	24.4
#2—The Jamaican Society is Secure Cohesive and Just	2.8	17.9	13.7	34.3	8.9	3.1
#3—Jamaica's Economy is Prosperous	74.8	60.7	63.5	30.3	28.2	63.9
#4—Jamaica has a Healthy Natural Environment	12.2	5.3	0.9	2.2	13.1	8.6
Grand Total	100.0	100.0	100.0	100.0	100.0	100.0

Source Collated and calculated by Authors from Planning Institute of Jamaica (2009b) *Vision 2030 Jamaica National Development Plan* and Planning Institute of Jamaica (2010–2019) *Economic and Social Survey of Jamaica*

Goal 2: The Jamaican society is secure, cohesive and just, respectively. During the period only the United Kingdom appears to have emphasized projects aligned with Goal 2 in terms of the proportion of its ODA—34.3% in comparison to the proportion of total allocation made by the other IDPs—provided to Jamaica.

Figure 6.3 provides a different perspective from which to view the contributions of the top six MFIs and bilateral IDPs to the achievement of each goal under Vision 2030 Jamaica. The figure indicates that the IDB has contributed the largest financial support to Goal 1—Jamaicans are Empowered to Achieve their Fullest Potential, to the tune of 41.7% of the total allocation under their cooperation programme with the government. In terms of proportional allocations, the IDB contribution was followed by the WB and PRC with 22.5 and 13.9%, respectively. For Goals 2—The Jamaican Society is Secure, Cohesive and Just and Goal 3—Jamaica's Economy is Prosperous, the IDB also contributed the largest proportions of their programme with the government to the tune of 51.5 and 36.8% of the total allocations to these goals, respectively, to the total allocated to activities under each of the two goals. The EU was the IDP with the next largest supporting contribution with 22.7% followed by the United Kingdom with 10.4% to the government's efforts to make progress towards achieving Goal 2.

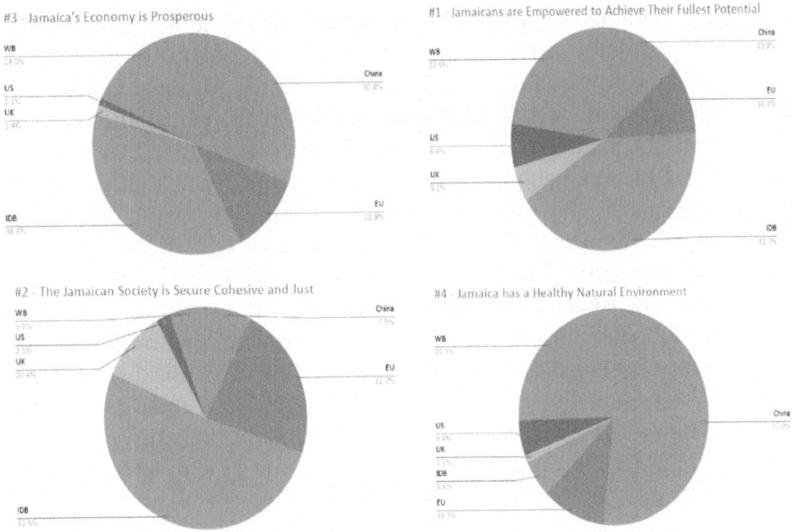

Fig. 6.3 ODA allocation or commitment aligned to each Vision 2030 goal by each of the main IDPs between 2010 and 2019 (% of allocation to each Vision 2030 Goal by each IDP) (*Source* Collated and calculated by Authors from Planning Institute of Jamaica [2009b] *Vision 2030 Jamaica National Development Plan* and Planning Institute of Jamaica [2010–2019] *Economic and Social Survey of Jamaica*)

Following on the IDBs contribution to the achievement of Goal 3, the projects supported by the PRC comprised another 30% of the total funds allocated by the top six IDPs towards establishing a prosperous economy in Jamaica. Finally, the PRC made the largest dollar value contribution to the achievement of efforts to make Jamaica's natural environment healthy with an allocation of 52% under the fourth goal—Jamaica has a Healthy Natural Environment due to the value of the investments made in building sea defences to protect the only access road to the country's major international airport. Their allocation was followed by the WB with 25.3% and the EU at 10.7%, both in relation to the overall project expenditure on Goal 4 by the selected top six IDPs.

At the level of the Goals as presented in the two previous figures, the specific focus and contribution of each IDP to the achievement of each goal may appear muted because of the high-level nature of goals and therefore it is important to look at the next tier of the strategic framework below the goal-level at the National Outcomes, progress towards which signals progress towards the accomplishment of the National Goals.

According to Fig. 6.4 that presents details on the contribution of the six selected IDPs to the fifteen National Outcomes aligned to the four Goals, the PRC cooperation programme was the most highly concentrated in terms of the focus area of the largest proportion of its total allocation or commitment. The table indicates that 61% of the total allocation/commitment of the PRC was focussed on supporting the efforts of the government to achieving Strong Economic Infrastructure—National Outcome 9, reflecting its emphasis on improving the transportation infrastructure in Jamaica. The WB was the IDP with the next highest portfolio concentration in terms of proportion of spending assigning 56.4% of its total allocation to supporting the authority's drive to establish A Stable Macroeconomy—National Outcome 7. This allocation was

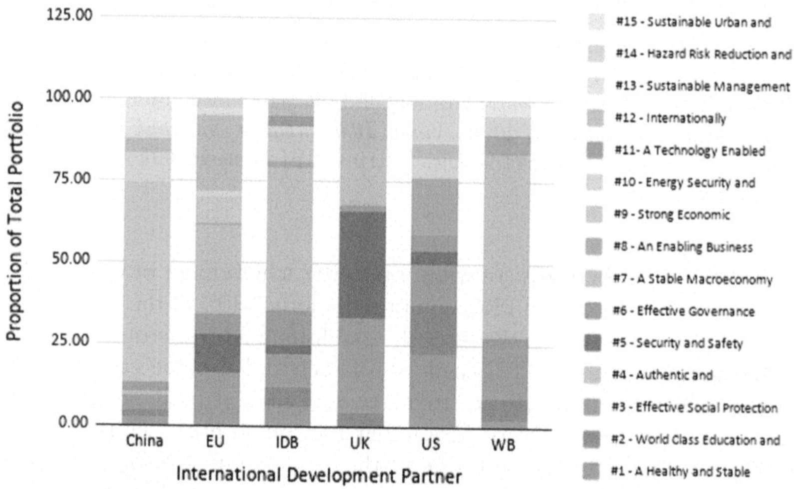

Fig. 6.4 ODA allocation or commitment aligned to each Vision 2030 National Outcome by each of the main IDPs between 2010 and 2019 (% of total allocation by each IDP) (*Source* Collated and calculated by Authors from Planning Institute of Jamaica [2009b] *Vision 2030 Jamaica National Development Plan* and Planning Institute of Jamaica [2010–2019] *Economic and Social Survey of Jamaica*)

supported by the IDB who contributed 43.5% to National Outcome 7—A Stable Macroeconomy and 10% to National Outcome 3—Effective Social Protection and National Outcome 6—Effective Governance, respectively. In relation to National Outcome 7, the IDB cooperation programme provided support to the government's economic reform agenda in the areas of the modernization of fiscal administration, the reform of the financial sector, support for the establishment of the fiscal responsibility framework, improved public financial management, and, fiscal consolidation.

The UK cooperation programme was focussed on supporting the efforts of the Jamaican government to accomplish strides in relation to National Outcome 5—Security and Safety to which it allocated 32.7% of its total portfolio (Planning Institute of Jamaica, 2010–2019). The United Kingdom allocated roughly one-fifth of its overall allocation to both National Outcome 7 and National Outcome 12—Internationally Competitive Industry Structures, respectively, and another 10.5% was allocated to National Outcome 3—Effective Social Protection. The US portfolio was most dominant in supporting National Outcome 1—A Healthy and Stable Population receiving 23% of their overall allocation, the largest concentration for the United States, and was channelled to support the Ministry of Health through various projects targeting their HIV/AIDS response and the Jamaica AIDS Support for Life (Planning Institute of Jamaica, 2010–2019).

During the period, another 17% of the US cooperation programme funds were allocated to National Outcome 8—An Enabling Business Environment and supported improvements in the administration of business processes and the provision of incubator opportunities for emerging social enterprises. The areas of World-Class Education and Training, Effective Social Protection and Hazard Risk Reduction and Adaptation to Climate Change each received between 12.5 and 14.6% individually from the US allocation.

When the allocation is explored from the perspective of each National Outcome, interesting patterns emerge (see Fig. 6.5). The PRC is the only IDP among the six selected to have made a contribution to National Outcome 4—Authentic and Transformative Culture due to its projects geared at supporting Jamaica's efforts in training coaches, and preparing athletes and coaches for the 2018 Central American and Caribbean Games, the 2019 Pan-American Games, and, the 2020 Olympic Games (Planning Institute of Jamaica, 2018, 2019). The other

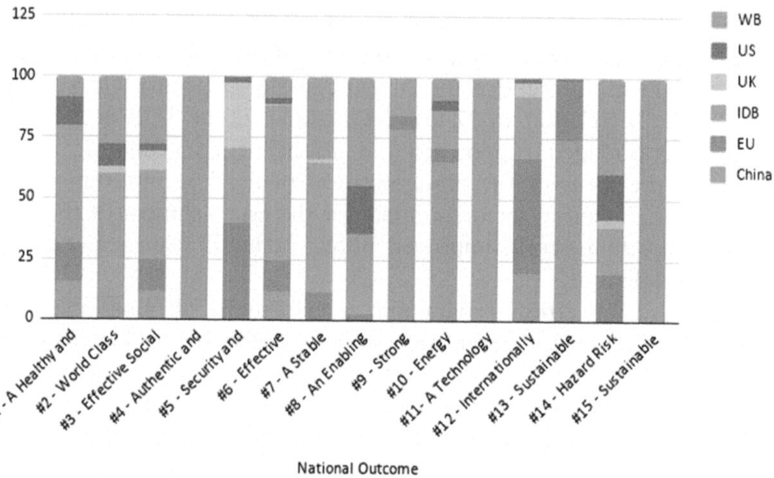

Fig. 6.5 ODA allocation or commitment aligned to each Vision 2030 National Outcome by each of the six main IDPs between 2010 and 2019 (% of allocation to each Vision 2030 National Outcome by each IDP) (*Source* Collated and calculated by Authors from Planning Institute of Jamaica [2009b] *Vision 2030 Jamaica National Development Plan* and Planning Institute of Jamaica [2010–2019] *Economic and Social Survey of Jamaica*)

project contributing to the cultural transformation envisioned in National Outcome 4 during the review period was the establishment of a Chinese Garden at the Royal Hope Botanical Gardens on 5.5 hectares of land (Planning Institute of Jamaica, 2015). The IDB was the only IDP to have made contributions to National Outcome 11—A Technology-Enabled Society during the ten-year review period. The funds allocated to this National Outcome was used to support a multi-year project of the government to establish the National Identification System premised on digital identification mechanism (Planning Institute of Jamaica, 2017b). The IDB also supported reforms of the regulations governing the ICT environment through a review of the existing model to support the implementation, oversight and monitoring of the new ICT Policy (Planning Institute of Jamaica, 2015). In 2010, the IDB had also supported the government with the implementation of online systems to facilitate all the major tax types such as the General Consumption Tax, Special

Consumption Tax and the payroll tax (Planning Institute of Jamaica, 2010).

Figure 6.5 also provides insight into the relative diversity of each IDPs cooperation programme with the Government of Jamaica. The United Kingdom supported projects across five of the fifteen National Outcomes over the review period. The US and WB had projects that spanned six and seven National Outcomes, respectively. Whilst China, the EU and, the IDB had the most broad-based contribution in terms of the number of National Outcomes to which the projects that they supported contributed to, with ten, eleven and twelve of the fifteen National Outcomes, respectively. The IDB contributions to National Outcomes 1, 2, 6 and 7 comprised 49% of the total project allocation to these Outcomes in addition to the fact that it was the only IDP supporting projects in terms of National Outcome 11 as indicated above. The PRC provided more than 50% support for National Outcomes 9, 10, 13 and 15 in addition to its 100% contribution to National Outcome 4 as discussed above.

Conclusion

The role of the IDPs in the development landscape clearly cannot be overlooked or downplayed whether from a comparative or absolute perspective. Jamaica's IDPs appear to have accomplished much of the spirit and letter of the 2005 Paris Declaration on Aid Effectiveness (PDA). The breadth of the cooperation programmes between Jamaica and this large number of IDPs, each with their own internal focus areas, and the alignment with Vision 2030 Jamaica that appears to have predicated each cooperation programme is noteworthy, remarkable and commendable given the natural human tendency to narrowly pursue own interest regardless of the interests and needs of the other party. In 2010, Jamaica participated in the Organisation for Economic Cooperation and Development (OECD) survey on the implementation of the 2005 PDA and the achievements in relation to the 2010 targets established for the twelve indicators.

Arising from the failures of many projects that were seen by IDPs as clear successes, the critical importance of country ownership in the success of projects emerged and therefore ownership of development policies and strategies was established as one of the five pillars of the PDA (Organisation for Economic Co-operation and Development, 2012). In this regard,

Jamaica had clearly met the 2010 target with the launch of Vision 2030 Jamaica in 2009 after preparations over the previous half decade.

That Vision 2030 Jamaica is so clearly and intimately aligned to the cooperation programmes is commendable and indicative of the adherence of the IDPs to the principle and spirit of the PDA fifteen years later. Vision 2030 Jamaica along with the JamStats and MICS systems also enabled Jamaica to achieve the prescription for a results-based framework through which to both focus IDP and government efforts on results as well as to simultaneously support monitoring towards the Millennium Development Goals. By 2010, all IDPs were able to utilize the 2009–2012 Medium Term Framework (MTF)—aligned to and distilled from Vision 2030 Jamaica—to design their own programmes to support the prioritized focus areas of the government.

The harmonization effort was advanced through the UNDP sponsored government-led through the PIOJ thematic Working Groups and Annual Retreat described above. The public financial management systems were strengthened through the transformation of the procurement process, the strengthening of the Contractor General and National Contracts Committee process which have recently been synthesized into an omnibus Integrity Commission.

This has improved the extent to which IDPs can utilize local procurement processes. The Public Expenditure and Financial Accountability (PEFA) conducted in 2007 helped to support this transformation and supported Jamaica's eligibility to receive wider budget support given the fiscal challenges associated with the high debt-to-GDP ratios. The PEFA would highlight several innovations such as the establishment of the Central Treasury Management System that would feature in the 2010 SBA and 2013 EFF that Jamaica entered into with the IMF (see Chapter 3 of this volume).

It is clear that these achievements could only have materialized based on the foundation provided by increased country dialogue between the government of Jamaica and the IDPs. Although in its final communication regarding progress towards achieving the MDGs Jamaica did not meet all its targets under the MDGs having lagged in: promoting gender equality, integrating the principles of sustainable development into country policies and programmes, and, in reducing biodiversity loss (Planning Institute of Jamaica, 2009a).

Jamaica was far behind in reducing child mortality by two-thirds, and, in reducing by three quarters the maternal mortality rate. Regrettably,

Jamaica also appeared to have slipped back in improving the lives of slum dwellers. Despite this, Vision 2030 Jamaica was developed with the insights gained through a wide range of development lessons having been learned—inclusive of those learned through the implementation challenges associated with the MDGs—that when the UN launched the seventeen Sustainable Development Goals (SDGs), an assessment against Vision 2030 Jamaica indicated a more than 90% alignment between the two frameworks (Government of Jamaica, 2018). In this regard, it is therefore anticipated that along with the gains from improved relationships with the IDPs, that Jamaica should make far further progress in terms of achieving the SDGs. The most recently available progress report on Vision 2030 Jamaica for 2015 to 2016 utilized 67 indicators aligned to eight of the prioritized National Outcomes selected in the MTF to determine the extent to which the combined efforts of the public sector, private sector, civil society, citizens and the IDPs have supported the achievement of the priorities delineated in the MTSEPF. The results indicated that there were improvements in 62 of the 67 indicators when compared with their value at the 2007 baseline (Planning Institute of Jamaica, 2017b).

The remainder showed no improvement or worsened in relation to the comparative figure. Overall, one quarter of the targets established for 2015 were already met with another 37% reflecting some improvement towards achieving the targets. Another indicator of the improvement of performance in the implementation of Plan targets is the fact that when the periods FY2009/10–2014/15 and FY2009/10–2015/16 there is a decline in the number of indicators whose reading was categorized as being the same as the baseline or worse whilst the categories Met or Exceeded Target, and, Improved Above Baseline but did not achieve target, both increased. Despite this, the review pointed to the need to increase efforts in the social areas relating to the goals as they displayed the poorest outturn in terms of improved indicator readings.

Regarding the achievements documented in this Chapter, the PIOJ has shone as a true interlocutor for the government with its key international development partners—an important role envisioned and provisioned for by its mastermind and founder Norman Washington Manley. Manley's journey to the United Nations with precise definitions of the focus areas and characteristics of its first leader, and the establishment of the predecessor CPU almost a decade prior to Independence is indicative of the inextricable role, burden and expectations of the PIOJ in helping to chart the course for the Jamaican society, and, in doing so to ensure that this course is charted in ways that ensure is sustainability and viability and that the path to getting to the end goal is not pyrrhic but, that with the enduring help of and partnership with the United Nations, all the IDPs and all other stakeholders, no government can claim victory in the development arena without ensuring the achievement of Leaving No One Behind as it makes *Jamaica, the place of choice to work, raise families, and do business*.

References

Clarke, C. (2013). *The United Nations and Jamaica, 1962–2012*. Kingston: Technical Report commissioned by the PIOJ and UNDP.

Clarke, C., & Nelson, C. (2020). *Contextualising Jamaica's relationship with the International Monetary Fund*. Cham: Palgrave Macmillan.

Government of Jamaica. (2018). *Jamaica: Voluntary National Review on the implementation of The 2030 Agenda for Sustainable Development*. Kingston: Planning Institute of Jamaica.

Organisation for Economic Co-operation and Development. (2012). *Aid effectiveness 2011: Progress in implementing the Paris Declaration, better aid*. Paris: OECD Publishing.

Planning Institute of Jamaica. (2009a). *National Report of Jamaica on Millennium Development Goals for the UN Economic and Social Council Annual Ministerial Review*. Kingston: Government of Jamaica.

Planning Institute of Jamaica. (2009b). *Vision 2030 Jamaica: National Development Plan*. Kingston: Planning Institute of Jamaica.

Planning Institute of Jamaica. (2010). Official development assistance. In PIOJ, *Economic and social survey of Jamaica (ESSJ)* (pp. 2.1–2.15). Kingtson: Planning Institute of Jamaica.

Planning Institute of Jamaica. (2011). Official development assistance. In PIOJ, *Economic and social survey of Jamaica (ESSJ)* (pp. 2.1–2.22). Kingston: Planning Institute of Jamaica.

Planning Institute of Jamaica. (2012). Official development assistance. In PIOJ, *Economic and social survey of Jamaica (ESSJ)* (pp. 2.1–2.14). Kingston: Planning Institute of Jamaica.

Planning Institute of Jamaica. (2013). Official development assistance. In PIOJ, *Economic and social survey of Jamaica (ESSJ)* (pp. 2.1–2.17). Kingston: Planning Institute of Jamaica.

Planning Institute of Jamaica. (2014). Official development assistance. In PIOJ, *Economic and social survey of Jamaica (ESSJ)* (pp. 2.1–2.15). Kingston: Planning Institute of Jamaica.

Planning Institute of Jamaica. (2015). Official development assistance. In PIOJ, *Economic and social survey of Jamaica (ESSJ)* (pp. 2.1–2.19). Kingston: Planning Institute of Jamaica.

Planning Institute of Jamaica. (2016a). Official development assistance. In PIOJ, *Economic and social survey of Jamaica (ESSJ)* (pp. 2.1–2.17). Kingston: Planning Institute of Jamaica.

Planning Institute of Jamaica. (2016b). Official development assistance. In PIOJ, *Economic and social survey of Jamaica (ESSJ)* (pp. 2.1–2.17). Kingston: Planning Institute of Jamaica.

Planning Institute of Jamaica. (2017a). Official development assistance. In PIOJ, *Economic and social survey of Jamaica (ESSJ)* (pp. 2.1–2.25). Kingston: Planning Institute of Jamaica.

Planning Institute of Jamaica. (2017b). *Update on vision 2030 Jamaica—National development plan and MTF 2015–2018*. Kingston: Planning Institute of Jamaica.

Planning Institute of Jamaica. (2018). Official development assistance. In PIOJ, *Economic and social survey of Jamaica (ESSJ)* (pp. 2.1–2.32). Kingston: Planning Institute of Jamaica.

Planning Institute of Jamaica. (2019). Official development assistance. In PIOJ, *Economic and social survey of Jamaica (ESSJ)* (pp. 2.1–2.28). Kingston: Planning Institute of Jamaica.

Rainford, R. (2006). The early social and economic impetus for planning in Jamaica. In R. Rainford, *Central Planning Unit to Planning Institute of Jamaica: 1955–2005. Anchoring 50 years of development planning in Jamaica* (pp. 1–14). Kingston: Planning Institute of Jamaica.

CHAPTER 7

'Leaving No One Behind'—Reflections on the Social

Introduction

The IMF is a global actor network and an institutional outgrowth of globalization with its connectivity within the space of flows of the global financial and monetary actor network. The furtherance of macroeconomic resilience and economic growth by participating countries, in which the IMF becomes engaged, facilitates their deeper integration and participation within the global political economy network.

The financial turmoil of the Sub Prime crisis of 2008, which originated within the United States which also impacted and the United Kingdom as founders of the IMF, undermined the economies of these representatives and the hallways of the advocates of economic liberalization, prompted their interventions within their own respective financial systems to further the implementation of measures to stem the fallout, inclusive of degrees of nationalization. The international environment and geopolitical events culminating in the crisis stimulated forms of introspection accompanied by advocacy and global solicitation efforts for the IMF to further re-examine modalities of lending arrangements given the prevailing criticisms that modalities of IMF programmes, on implementation, pushed fiscal austerity and paid little regard to social costs and the safety nets needed for the poor and vulnerable in the respective populations of their client countries.

C. Clarke and C. Nelson, *Jamaica's Evolving Relationship with the IMF*,
https://doi.org/10.1007/978-3-030-59204-2_7

However, the impact of a global recession and the accentuating of financial and economic crises at the domestic level of states, effervescing in terms of increased poverty, job losses and unemployment were significant, as the ripple effects of the global financial crisis of 2008 circumvented the globe. These events deepened the context and precipitated more urgent calls for the IMF to become more engaged, participatory and definitively aligned with the broader global development agenda and policy concerns.

The IMF and the Social

This apparent obfuscation and even the omission of the social parameters within the construction of IMF programmes and instruments was one of the critiques levelled at the IMF in the early years of their operations, arguably even beyond the 1990s. While not an explicit part of its core mandate, the Fund has made efforts to address or embrace social protection issues in programmatic interventions. It has done so through modalities for example, of ensuring fiscal sustainability in member countries—insofar as social protection policies or measures mostly entail public expenditures—and the need to mitigate adverse impacts, particularly on the poor, during periods of economic adjustment (not least to enhance the political sustainability of economic reforms).

Investigations by Gupta et al. (2018) have found that when considering the long run and short run impact of IMF expenditures on public spending components, it was ascertained that specific aspects of spending could actually assist in the achievement of short-term objectives under the Programme. Further, it was determined that structural conditionality delivered benefits over the longer term, when budget execution was boosted, impacting health and education inclusive of public investment expenditures. There was the recognition, however, that increasing spending may come at the expense of other expenditures, consequently, the successful implementation of conditionality can improve outcomes, especially bearing in mind the achievement of Sustainable Development Goals (SDGs) (Gupta et al., 2018).

These modalities of programmatic interventions have direct implications for poverty reduction which has garnered an increasing focus. Under the rubric of global public policy advocacy around the Sustainable Development Goals (SDGs) concerns arise with the perusal of IMF interventions and capturing the effects of policy measures and programmatic components surrounding the achievements of the macroeconomic monetary, financial and fiscally related targets and the impact upon human development and the softer, social concerns, linked to poverty reduction, education, health, labour, issues of crime and climate change. The IMF's recognition of these concerns and them being incorporated into IMF Programme interventions can be revealed in measures to address social spending by safety nets and the ceilings placed upon measures in this regard, which targets economic monetary and decisions of social sector related factors within the economy.

Jamaica and the International Monetary Fund

When reflecting upon Jamaica's historical interface with the International Monetary Fund it is apparent that the relationship between them prior to 2010–2013 has been tenuous, which reflects itself in the quality of the networked relationship which spills over, flowing through various modalities and mediums of communication to the Jamaica citizen. The 1980s into the 1990s reflected the political and ideological divide between the two political parties which was evident, shaping the nature and character of the political discourse in Jamaica engendering degrees of hostility and adversarialism. This served to present the image of the politics of Jamaica as being combative, furthering social divides and tribalism along political party lines, which effervesced in acts of violence married to the political process in selecting consecutive leaders through the electoral process in the country.

The ideological divide towards the end of the 1990s became not so apparent as both parties gradually increased their subscription to neoliberal economic development paths, with heightened adversarialism seemingly receding with the generations. Moreover, the subscription by both parties to democratic modalities of government, and the consecutive commitments to pursuing IMF Programme interventions and arrangements due to persistent macroeconomic vulnerabilities and the need for external financial support has precipitated the;

> ideological shift towards the individualistic political culture of the market and has uprooted the normative collective action image of the state as the epitome of collective interests. (Nelson, 2019, p. 5)

Consequently, the ideological divide has been somewhat diminished as evidenced by the types of policies, interventions, programmes and projects which now reflect more a similarity or continuation of the same, despite political regime change. It can be argued that the prevailing macroeconomic circumstances require structured commitment and consistency to undo and recover lost ground in order to etch out development gains, within a changing and fluid global political context, with tacit acknowledgement that Jamaica needs the assistance to navigate its own development trajectory.

Each political party on being elected into office, comes to power with their own subjectivities, purposes and creativity, associated with political and ideological thought, which albeit, eventually becomes captive to the overarching goal of envisioning and bringing into fruition a 'developed' Jamaica. Consecutive governments have become confronted with challenges and nuances subject to Jamaica's economic realities. These give way to a cognizance that converges around simple truths, that development is contingent upon the establishing of certain fundamentals, of which macroeconomic stability and debt reduction are essential precursors to economic growth, and to further development holistically, and that these are inescapable.

Consequently, the variance of the interface and modalities within the arrangement brokered between the IMF and each political party, whenever each was elected into office was complex. Notably, the influence of ideological positioning was diminutive compared to the period of the 1980s and 1990s, where the influence of Cold War geopolitical positioning between the two superpowers of the day, had engulfed the global economy dividing it according to ideological and political allegiances.

However, one could posit that the commitments designed under an IMF Programme, whichever Party was elected in office, would have retained some similar characteristics, given the decade long persistence of debt, macroeconomic fragility and the persistence of monetary difficulties that had to be mitigated against. Moreover that these would necessitate long-term commitments from either party to address them, whatever the arrangement brokered. The eventual realization of the unravelling that retrograde and policy inconsistencies can do to hard fought gains in the economy between electoral cycles, arguably has culminated in efforts, spearheaded by the Planning Institute of Jamaica (PIOJ) towards the development and realization of Jamaica's first long -term National Development Plan-Vision 2030.

This Plan involved the participation of both political parties in its development as well as broad consultation with various societal groups, private sector interests, non-governmental organizations, trade unions, civil society, business clusters as well as contributions from international development partners in its construction. The coalescing of all of these interests and the contributions made into the conceptualization, design and eventual development of the strategic interventions and policies integrated into the Plan, served to engender a degree of longevity and commitment from administrations, beyond political electoral cycles. In addition, the Plan comprehensively signalled critical attributes and the consideration that would be necessary with respect to requirements, the fiscal and budgetary requisitions and commitments needed to bring the Vision to fruition.

The IMF, in the Jamaican context, has had to engage with the nuances, characteristics and the policy and programme divergence portrayed by elected Governments, and representatives of the two (2) major political parties, as each oscillates with the other, each assuming national leadership responsibilities at intervals after various election cycles. Upon each administration being elected over time, to the helm of government and decision-making, the IMF has had to treat with, at their interface with multidimensional change, shifts in policy and the subsequent surfacing of vulnerabilities and inconsistencies, coupled with a lack of coherence and continuity between parties compared to the next, sometimes resulting in economic fallout and Programme collapse.

In navigating these political economy variances as an outcome of regime change, the IMF as an actor and upon its engagement with Jamaica, expectedly impinges upon the state's network of relations, its customary discourse, centricity and domain in decision-making, also in discoursal terms. Consequently, change is furthered and becomes manifest through the extent to which the inculcation of the IMF Programme discourse, and practice institutional, structurally and distributive are rolled out and reflected in the efficacy and effectiveness of programme interventions. The change, is distilled through commensurate networks of social practices and relations and on taking effect, there is the displacement of existing practices and modalities and reconfigurations in the discourse of government and the approaches taken by policymakers, managers and implementers of the diverse aspects of the Programmes, spilling over and exhibited in reconstructing and affecting attributes of the economy.

The degree of change manifest is revealed in the manner and degree to which the domestic execution of the programme has been inculcated and implemented IMF Programme modalities and discourse in accordance with its relative capacity and capability, giving due consideration to the constraints. From the lens of Actor Network Theory (ANT) the stability of the Programme network, the social practices and relations or its longevity, will be a function of an effective *translation* process, where IMF Jamaica programmatic interests, once negotiated, has in the implementation, resulted in mutual shaping and adaptation within the constructs of Government operations. These have now been interwoven by a common inscription reflected as the IMF Programme's discourse and practice. The outcomes, responsiveness and manifestation of incremental and critical gains are linked to degrees of compliance, which has correlated to how Jamaica was and is perceived, internally by the Programme institutionally at its origin (IMF), as well as perceived by the country with respect to the public sector and those translating Programme modalities into reality within the domestic space. This, in turn, spills over with implications for the perception of Jamaica by other development partners and bodies externally, reflected in the degree of ease of the formation of ancillary relationships and arrangements, which altogether has converged around giving support to the Programme interventions, observed and experienced by the general public. Within the context of the diversity, dynamism and fluidity within the social, domestic ecosystem of the Jamaican economy, the variants within and without, issues of social dislocation due to poverty and untethering of the realms of the social sectors,—education, health, labour and unemployment, crime and climate change—these have not been easily or directly appreciated, addressed nor captured, under the regimes of traditional IMF discourse and programme interventions which are actualized from the context of the market macroeconomics. This recognition, calls for an embrace of and appreciation for the role of other dimensions and adjuncts—history, culture and behavioural elements.

The Social: Jamaica Programme Reviews

In undertaking the commitments under the EFF 2013 and SBA 2016 Programmes, the role of the International Development Partners (IDPs) was essential and cannot be overstated. These entities supported aspects of the Programme interventions themselves, including those projects and programmes that had been agreed prior bilaterally and through country assistance programme commitments with the Government. The significant collaboration and complementarity between the IDPs and the IMF were clearly demonstrable. The European Union (EU), IDB and World Bank were the three main sources of multilateral financing for the period of the IMF Agreements providing resources to undertake projects of critical development priority, with funding mainly as budget support and project financing.

Social Objectives

The SBA of 2010 included measures that would assist to soften any negative impact on the poor and to strengthen the social safety net. The Programme included important measures to mitigate adverse economic conditions in the midst of generating significant structural changes in the Jamaican economy. The programme had been designed to ensure that the adjustment burden is effectively shared across society and economic agents. Safeguards have been included to ensure that the social safety net is not only preserved but broadened, with special attention being given to enhancing those social programmes that are well targeted and far reaching. See Fig. 7.1.

Towards the end of this SBA, there was a need to increase social assistance programming by 40% alongside attention paid towards containing the levels of spending and putting in place contingency plans in response to potential risks from revenue shortfalls. There are recent reforms to enhance effectiveness and efficiency of social spending such as the benefits under the Programme of Enhancement Through Health (PATH) as an income support programme which were increased in August 2013 by 15% implying an increase in real terms. A graduation strategy for PATH participants was also designed along with enhanced welfare to work programmes.

Within the context of the extended arrangement under the EFF 2013 social protection was deemed a priority by the included reforms, linked to the efficiency and effectiveness of social spending. One of the concerns surrounded the assurance that the available resources would assist those who were really in need through technical assessments.

Under the First Review, the reforms to enhance the efficacy of social spending were implemented in line with the Programme requirements and benefits under the PATH income support programme were increased

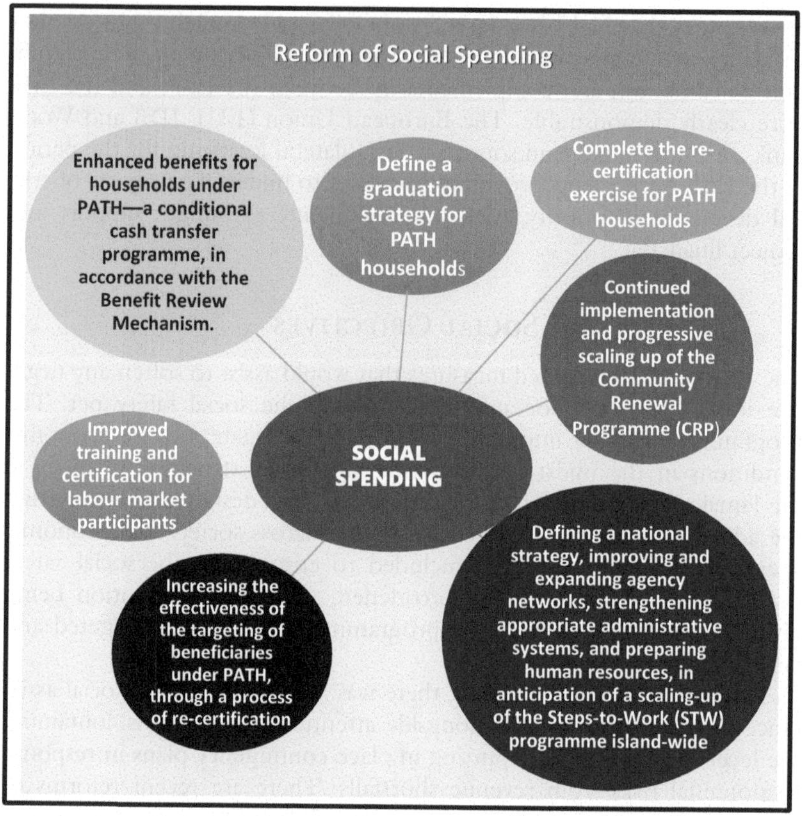

Fig. 7.1 Reform of social spending: extended fund facility (2013) (*Source* Compiled by Authors from: International Monetary Fund. 2013. "Jamaica: Request for an Extended Arrangement Under the Extended Credit Fund Facility." Washington, DC: International Monetary Fund)

by 15% overall, in real terms. A graduation strategy for PATH recipients as well as enhanced Welfare-To-Work programmes was defined by the government. The Second Review of the EFF in December 2013, explored measures to enhance the effectiveness of social protection programmes recognizing that there were possible adverse effects, due to the impact of the authorities fiscal consolidation activities on the most vulnerable. Consequently, the government increased in real terms, the transfer's to

PATH beneficiaries and ensured that social spending was consistent with the floor on social spending within the Agreement.

Other reforms sought to move PATH recipients from the Welfare-To-Work activities through intermediation and access to professional training modalities. The authorities confirmed their commitment to the social protection programme by strengthening it and adopting a graduation strategy that would move PATH recipients from the Welfare-To-Work activities through intermediation and professional training activities. Additionally, a comprehensive social protection strategy was being prepared for submission to Cabinet by March 2014. Meanwhile, the government adhered to the budgetary spending on social priorities which were maintained in accordance with the programme floor under the 2014/2015 budget. Other measures entailed the recertification of 34,000 PATH households by March 2014.

It is recognized that the social spending floor in the Programme signifies the degree of priority as well as the effort to safeguard the spending category in line with the specific social protection initiatives and programmes. The floor on social spending represented the minimum annual expenditure and was funded by the government resources only. These entailed:

- conditional cash transfers to children 0–18 years old and the elderly,
- youth employment programmes,
- the poor relief programme for indoor and outdoor individuals,
- the school feeding programme,
- the basic school subsidy,
- basic education including early childhood,
- primary and secondary education,
- the provision of assistance for persons with disabilities and
- targeted components of Primary Health care.

The graduation strategy for PATH households involved the strengthening of agency networks and broad institutional strengthening that supported The Steps -To-Work Program which is an integral part of the graduation strategy itself. Certification exercises were conducted on 34,000 PATH households which enabled targeting of the interventions. The Vision 2030 Jamaica, National Development Plan, had articulated progress towards the development of a comprehensive social protection strategy which was completed and approved by Cabinet in March 2014. These developments were consistent with the implementation of effective social protection within Vision 2030.

The 5th review of the EFF (2013) in September 2014 involved efforts to further a strategy for a more comprehensive approach to social protection which involved the streamlining of programmes engendering higher institutional coordination and greater cost-effectiveness alongside improvements in the targeting of beneficiaries. Another increase of 15% in the benefits provided under the PATH programme which involved a conditional cash transfer, was provided in September while the recertification exercise was ongoing.

Implementation of the new Social Protection Strategy commenced with the launch of it in July 2014 and steps to include a costing to institute a social protection floor. The successful execution of a Graduation Strategy in 2015 will enable the selected welfare recipients to return to the labour market. Despite the constraints in the fiscal envelope, social spending was still prioritized, amidst the increasing incidence of poverty which grew in 2010 from 17.6 to 19.9% in 2012. The authorities, nevertheless, had been consistently and progressively strengthening the social protection framework especially the conditional cash transfer programme—PATH. The creation of a National Poverty Reduction Committee to develop a new National Policy on Poverty was prefaced by the launch in July 2014 of the Social Protection Strategy. By June 2015 in the newly created National Poverty Reduction Committee had the assistance of an Intersectoral Committee which was convened to guide and monitor the progress of the development of the new National Poverty Policy as well as the new Poverty Reduction Program by the end of the fiscal year 2015/2016.

The broad implementation of the graduation strategy for PATH households was still anticipated and efforts to strengthen the social protection framework continued, along with monitoring and evaluation frameworks being developed with regard to assessing the Comprehensive Social Protection Strategy. The National Social Protection Committee convened its first meeting in November 2014.

Under the 9th Review, the National Poverty Reduction Committee (NPRC) and the Intersectoral Committee convened to guide and monitor the processes surrounding the development of the new National Policy on Poverty and a new Poverty Reduction Program. Thereby consultation processes were initiated with key stakeholders with a view for the new Policy and Program to be scheduled for approval by the end of the fiscal year 2015/2016. These would support efforts being made to strengthen the social protection framework. A comprehensive Social Protection Strategy (SPS) was launched by the government in July 2014 and overall there was an intention to improve the administrative efficiency of the social protection programmes, as well as to further the comprehensive plan for the transition of PATH and National Insurance Scheme (NIS) payments to an electronic payment modality, with the required provisioning for electronic access.

The new National Policy on Poverty as well as the Poverty Reduction Program is being guided and monitored through the development process by an Intersectoral Committee which meets on a quarterly basis and has continued to guide the process. Efforts to strengthen the social protection framework as well as the graduation strategy for PATH have begun whereby the implementation is to be reviewed by the World Bank in December 2015 with respect to the potential improvements as well as recommendations to be provided. Overall, the intention is to improve the administrative efficiency of social protection programmes in addition to determining a comprehensive plan for the transitioning of PATH as well as NIS payments to retail electronic payment products. These measures represent efforts to deepen the payment infrastructure especially in rural areas as well as streamline the procedures for collecting social payments of which the latter are being identified.

By the end of the 11th and 12th review, The World Bank had provided recommendations on potential improvements after a review of the graduation strategy for PATH households as well as measures to strengthen the social protection framework. Other plans included the rolling out of a National Identification System (NIDS) By 2020 which would improve the targeting of social spending as well as improve the administrative efficiency of social protection programs. The effecting of the transition of PATH and NIS payments to retail electronic modalities is expected by the end of June 2016 while measures to deepen payment infrastructure in rural areas and streamline the procedures for the collection of social payments are in the process of being identified.

Under the 2016 SBA, a number of priorities pursued under the EFF (2013) were continued, given that pervasive poverty in Jamaica is a critical problem that requires long-term provisioning and commitment of resources to address. The PATH school feeding programme for PATH beneficiaries as well as the cash transfer benefits have been increased about 40% in the fiscal year 2017/2018. These programmes of transfers to vulnerable populations are reviewed for efficiency and effectiveness to ensure that the children from poor households are able to pursue an education and training to enable them to attain access to opportunities for a better quality of life.

The plethora of social issues to be addressed such as crime and homicides which seek to engulf the youth and those unemployed requires that activities to mitigate or deter a subscription to these types of activities be strengthened. Expanding early childhood education, enhancing the benefits and coverage of the PATH programme, as well as provisioning for rural transportation to enable school attendance, as well as daycare centres all serve as means to enable opportunities for beneficiaries to be empowered but also by changing attitudes and through access to education.

It is anticipated that through more effective social spending, significantly increasing allocations to the main social assistance programme, PATH, with additional support from the multilateral development partners such as the World Bank, that provisioning can be expanded to include the poor and the elderly and to further expand the coverage of PATH. Associated investments could also be considered, given the potential that exists to mitigate rural poverty and improve agricultural resilience, by undertaking investments in irrigation, fortifying farm roads and providing storage facilities inclusive of expanding the network of rural linkages which could provide opportunities for tourism interests, to boost rural incomes.

Crime

The phenomenon of crime and violence, associated with Jamaica are historical, having a negative legacy enhanced by the semiotics of the media, conveying a permanent and enduring characteristic associated thereby. The challenge of crime and its long association within Jamaica society partially relates to the character, diversity and complexity of the phenomenon which can be further disaggregated, revealing increased complexity and the conundrum presented for solutions and ameliorative methodologies, traversing relations within and between the economic, sociopolitical, cultural and psychological spheres.

A cursory examination of the relationship between the dates of IMF Jamaica agreements being brokered and the trend line relating to the incidences of crime per thousand population, See Fig. 7.2, shows no direct or significant relationship. The sharp peaks in 2009, can be attributed to the 'Tivoli Incursion' at the time and the subsequent state of emergency enacted by the government. IMF programmes followed in 2010–2013 and IHS Global Insight indicate that although Jamaica still retains a relatively high-crime rate, 'there had been a reduction in violent crime' (IHS Global Insight, 22 October 2014. IMF programmes). The upward consistency in the crime trend line remains irrespective of the IMF interventions.

The acknowledged effects of IMF interventions in terms of the potential to exacerbate issues of poverty and Jamaica's efforts to mitigate these effects have been ably assisted by the IDP's through direct social interventions and supportive programming. The European Union's Poverty Reduction Programme (PRP III) contributes to the implementation of

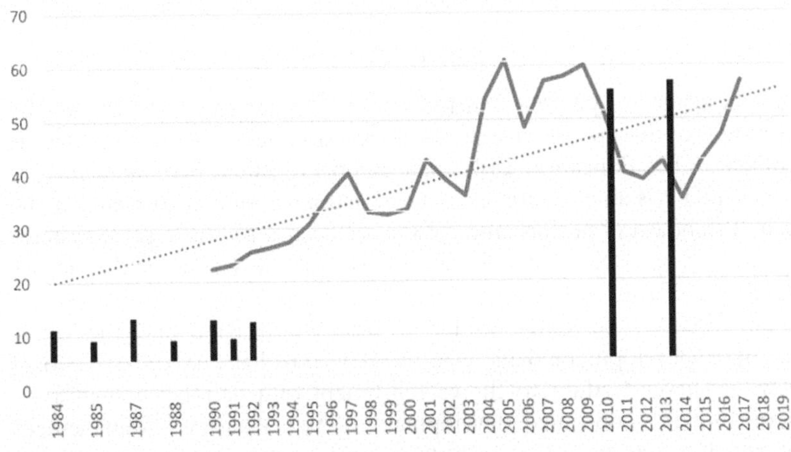

Fig. 7.2 Jamaica: IMF interventions and incidence of crime 1984–2019 (*Source* Bank of Jamaica (1991) Jamaica's Relationship with the International Monetary Fund, Research and Economic Programming Division, Bank of Jamaica, Kingston; Jamaica World Bank Statistics, https://www.macrotrends.net/countries/JAM/jamaica/crime-rate-statistics)

the Community Renewal Programme (CRP), targeting four components—Governance, Physical Transformation, Socio-economic Development and Youth Development. This should result in:

- Increased access to basic infrastructure and services through projects implemented with community support,
- Increased capacity of communities to demand for, plan implement and manage local development projects,
- Increased business and job opportunities, and
- Reduced deviant behaviour through work with unattached youths.

Activities for PRP III, included infrastructure works, strengthening of NGOs and NSAs (Non-State Actors) participation, as well as providing funding support to micro enterprises and granting of scholarships and internships. Under the Jamaica Social Investment Fund (JSIF), two infrastructure projects have been approved for Tivoli & East Downtown—CRP communities).

Education

The Education System Transformation Programme (ESTP) is the response to the assessment of the Education sector's performance as outlined in the Education Task Force Report of 2004. See Fig. 7.3.

The ESTP is an all-embracing set of actions designed to result in the desired standard of performance of the sector and to put in place systems to ensure greater accountability at all levels of the sector for the quality of delivery of education.

The ESTP is currently funded by the World Bank and the Inter-American Development Bank, (IADB). The IDB has financed a National Literacy Survey leading to the establishment of a national literacy rate, supporting the continued development of the Ministry's Management Information System (MIS) as well as funding the construction of two secondary schools to be executed by the National Education Trust (NET), the arm of the Ministry mandated to undertake capital works on its behalf. In addition, support was provided for the pilot of a National Curriculum for Grades 1–9; improvements in teacher quality and added school spaces through expansion of 4 schools at secondary level aimed at reducing the number of schools on shift.

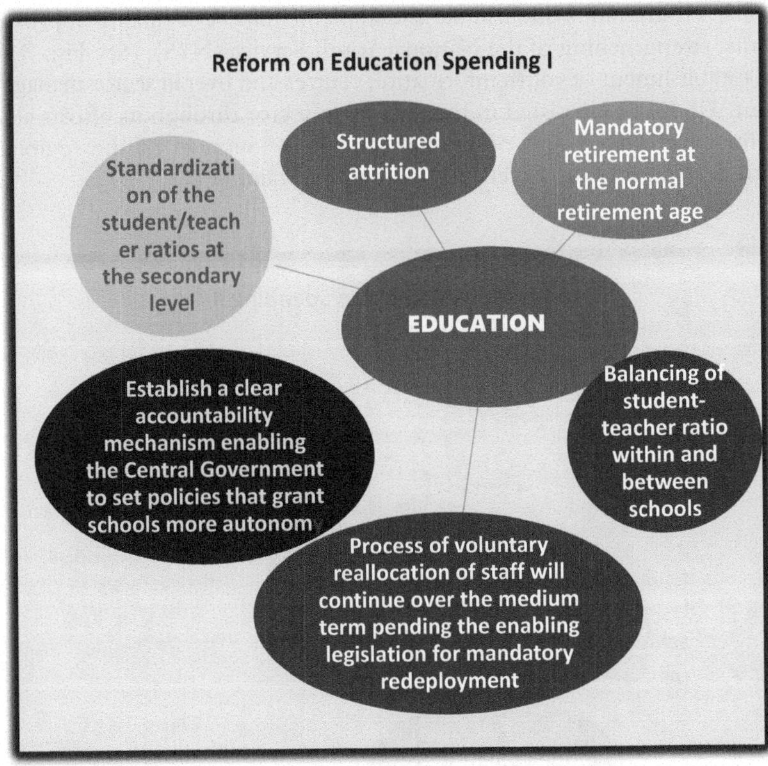

Fig. 7.3 Reform of social spending: Education-extended fund facility (2013) (*Source* Compiled by Authors from: International Monetary Fund. 2013. "Jamaica: Request for an Extended Arrangement Under the Extended Credit Fund Facility." Washington, DC: International Monetary Fund)

The World Bank provided funding to support the start-up of operations of the National Education Inspectorate (NEI), the Jamaica Teaching Council, capacity building to support the establishment and operations of the Regional Education Entities and Central Policy Ministry as well as, activities in support of the National Education Trust. To facilitate the transition of unattached youths to adulthood and the world of work through training, on the job experience, information dissemination and labour intermediation services.

The Programme will facilitate the implementation of quality improvements, strengthening of the National Youth Service (NYS), (See Fig. 7.4) the establishment of youth information centres and overall sector management. USAID has assisted in the education sector through its efforts also to improve literacy and other skills and in its support of the regional Caribbean Center for Excellence in Teacher Training (CCETT).

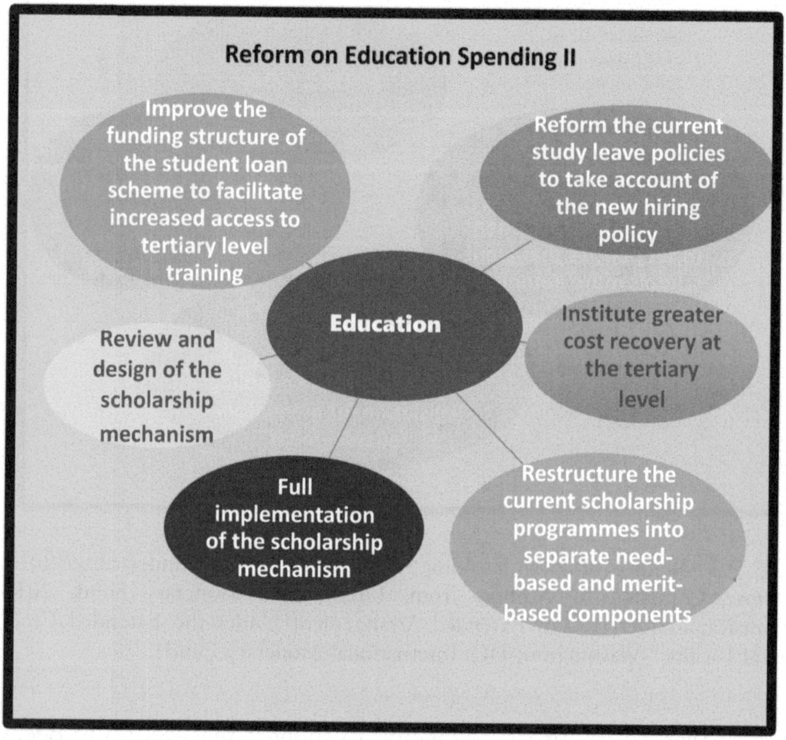

Fig. 7.4 Reform of social spending: education-extended fund facility (2013) (*Source* Compiled by Authors from: International Monetary Fund. 2013. "Jamaica: Request for an Extended Arrangement Under the Extended Credit Fund Facility." Washington, DC: International Monetary Fund)

Health

The World Bank has supported health interventions under the PATH programmes, through support of the social safety net. Poor families are assisted by health interventions, primary health care and support in the form of social assistance, employment, cash grants for children from 1 to 6 years, in addition to measures that improve early childhood health by regular clinic attendance. Efforts are also made to assist pregnant and lactating women. See Fig. 7.5.

The Caribbean Development Bank (CDB) through the Basic Needs Trust Fund (BNTF) assisted to improve infrastructure through the construction of a health centre in addition to engaging in capacity building and community development.

USAID has also assisted according to its programmatic intervention with respect to supporting HIV/AIDs activities and Child Survival and Health.

Petrocaribe Agreement

One arrangement recognized for the role it has served in supporting and facilitating the Government of Jamaica during the rigours of IMF Programme implementation, with respect to social development interventions was the Petrocaribe Agreement. As the brainchild of the late Venezuelan President, Hugo Chavez in October 2000, the Petrocaribe Agreement allowed for low-interest Venezuelan oil to be exported to Belize, Costa Rica, The Dominican Republic, Guatemala, Honduras, Haiti, El Salvador, Nicaragua, Panama and Jamaica, through the Caracas Energy Agreement (CAE). Thereafter, at the first Petrocaribe Summit in 2005, the group was formed, consisting of fourteen countries, that participated with the signing of the Petrocaribe Agreement. The Group were able to negotiate low-interest oil agreements and in return pay their debts through the provision of goods and services to Venezuela, such as beans, sugar as well as services, e.g., medical services.

Signatory states to the Agreement were required to pay 60% of their oil bill within 90 days and the remaining 40% could be held by the country as a long-term loan for about 25 years, at 1% interest, should oil prices stay above 40 dollars a barrel. More favourable terms arise when the cost of oil appreciates, as financing considers the current costs of oil, and despite each country having its own quota it is not automatic that countries receive their maximum allocation (Arnesen et al., 2019).

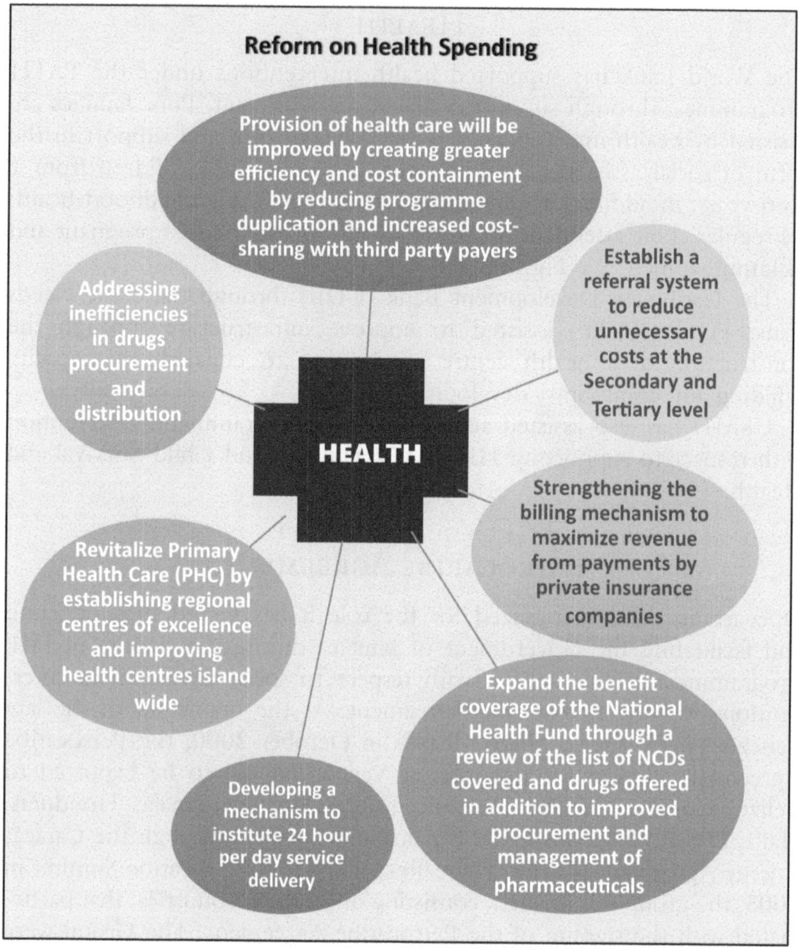

Fig. 7.5 Reform on Social Spending: Health -Extended Fund Facility (2013) (*Source* Compiled by Authors from: International Monetary Fund. 2013. "Jamaica: Request for an Extended Arrangement Under the Extended Credit Fund Facility." Washington, DC: International Monetary Fund)

With respect to Jamaica, a large percentage of the funds accruing from the Petrocaribe Agreement had been used to refinance domestic debt with respect to the IMF Programme. However, A portion of the resources had also been allocated to social development activities, supporting the poor and vulnerable. Net disbursements of 1 billion, was contributed over three years through Petrocaribe (IMF, 2015). The Petrocaribe Development Fund is financing a wind farm expansion project in the parish of Manchester (Sullivan, 2010) called 'Wigton II', addressing the long term objective of contributing to the transformation of Jamaica's energy mix and increasing the percentage of renewable energy and green energy sources used by the country. This is part of the 20% renewable energy target for 2030, as per the National Energy Policy. This is also contributory to the climate change commitments made under the Clean Development Mechanism (CDM) under the Kyoto Protocol.

EPOC

In the realm of the social, a multi-sectoral social partnership governance mechanism emerged that resonated within the societal domain, attracting and embracing a wide public constituency while additionally, providing a modality of private, public interface and communication, with respect to ongoing IMF Programme effectiveness. The communiques produced were released to the public as well as accessed by those bodies with a vested interest in the Programme. This collaborative governance mechanism which also performed functions of monitoring and evaluation, was undertaken by the Economic Programme Oversight Committee (EPOC) established in 2013 to monitor the government's implementation of the 2013 EFF with the International Monetary Fund.

Monitoring of the fiscal monetary and financial benchmarks and targets of the programme as well as economic reform measures under the Agreement were some of the responsibilities. However, EPOC served as a mechanism for fostering broad-based social relations, education and awareness of the ongoing IMF intervention. The composition and involvement of this group served to engender a degree of social capital and investment by these groups and society in the outcome of the Programme, more so that these could have direct implications for the trajectory or direction of Jamaica's development path thereafter.

EPOC served as a public good, being a mechanism to monitor the government's compliance with the commitments made under the

Programme, ensuring that the agreed targets and objectives were met, in addition to these being tracked by the CIU towards full compliance. The work of these entities was also supported by having access to various analyses by a technical subcommittee that undertook various assessments with respect to the Programme targets and objectives. The success of EPOC as fulfilling an important role in the successful implementation of the 2013 EFF, resonated even with the IMF which lauded the concept as a modality which could be used to strengthen the successful implementation of IMF programmes in other small island developing economies. Over these latter years, Jamaica has succeeded in rebuilding the credibility and confidence with respect to the manner in which it has fulfilled the requirements under programmatic interventions with the IMF and EPOC has assisted at that interface.

Jamaican Society: The Semiotics of IMF Programmes

On retrospection, from the 1970s to the 2000s the name of the International Monetary Fund or IMF has become etched within the psyche of the Jamaican society. The older generations of Jamaicans recall the ethos of the 'Manleyian' and 'Seaga' eras, whereby stark political and ideological differences were razor sharp, creating an expansive, divide along bipolar and tribal political lines.

Jamaica's successive defaults of IMF Programme interventions from the experiences of the 1970s, attributed in part to and accumulation of factors—the debt and poverty overhang, the ideological/rhetorical divide, lack of internal political and policy cohesion, thereafter juxtaposed against institutional geopolitics, ideological opposition, capitalist self-interest packaged with degrees of financial inflexibility, altogether has, overtime configured the varied perspectives and views held of the IMF. Time, has over the more contemporary and recent years resulted in a repositioning of discourse, attitude and practice on both sides.

Over the years the relationship has reflected change within the discourse and practice of implementing the IMF arrangements brokered, reflecting degrees of struggle, on the part of Jamaica being obligated to change or of necessity to adjust, accomodate or replace, or, to recognize and diverge, to the point of changing its traditional discourse and practice. This may obtain, especially with respect to its management and handling of the economic, monetary and fiscal dimensions of the economy and modalities of prioritization and decision-making. In addition, these may warrant reciprocity, whereby change has to be furthered also within multi-level cultural and social relations, to undo and unlearn elements of discourse and practice entrenched institutionally, behaviourally and ideationally, towards inculcating and accommodating a new discourse. There have been media communications portraying the 'ebb and flow' of the relationship between Jamaica and the IMF and their engagement over the years which has been translated to the Jamaican society, the ordinary citizen and recipients of the decisionmaking and outcomes through different modalities of the media. Through the years there has been a multiplicity of communications made concerning the Government and the IMF—rhetorical commentaries, aural pronouncements made, visuals of live events and photographs, media footage of interactive socio-political liaisons and significant milestones and meetings. Visual semiotics, imagery and written texts surrounding the IMF Jamaica interface have been shared with the Jamaican society, celebrating the 'good', regarding its progress and development; the 'bad,' pertaining to its failings and deficiencies and the 'ugly', with respect to regression, unravelling and falling apart as a collective.

Appeals have been made to the poor and disenfranchised, of freedom and hope. Promises have been made of change ahead and economic development on the horizon. There have been calls registering hope for a brighter future, contrasted with words and warnings of 'bitter medicine,' juxtaposed with appeals for understanding and patience on the eve of the commencement of austere policy measures and their effects. Allegations and exposures of corruption, dishonesty and misconduct on the part of those designated to lead or expected to take the moral high ground, are metered with calls for a more just, politically detribalized and 'gentler' society with human rights and justice for all. The media has distilled these diverse messages, prefaced with personal opinions, commentaries and characterizations on the part of the messenger, through communicative devices which feed and inform '*John public*' on the societal undercurrents and personal perspectives, resonating the same messages recursively upon the society from whence it came.

Perkins (2002) quoted the former Prime Minister P J Patterson which described the character of national politics at the time of being '*a fight for scarce benefits and political spoils (that has contributed to a polarized society… as hostile tribes that seems to be perpetually at war*'. Higgins (2015) also quoted the former Prime Minister P J Patterson who had also said that, '*Our politics is a stage four cancer. This is the primary reason Jamaica is the sick man of the Caribbean. We have squandered and misused billions upon billions of dollars, much of it borrowed money that needed to have been spent on developing Jamaica for Jamaicans*'.

Thereby Higgins (2015) seemingly ascribes ownership for Jamaica's demise, as a country locked into borrowing cycles of conditional lending, to the lack of political and policy accord and not to the IMF conditionalities which had to be engaged with as a result.

Jamaica's engagement with the International Monetary Fund and the historic contests between them in terms of IMF's order of discourse and practice articulating against the discourse and practice of the Jamaican government, militated against the achievement of Jamaica's 'buy-in' or *interessement* and *enrollment* into the IMF network, which has since reflected progressive change. This is mirrored in the extent to which Jamaica has committed itself and maintained convergence in the IMF network, ceding degrees of their relative power positions in light of subscribing to the IMF Agreement provisions reflected in the inculcation of agreed tenets within Government's discourse and practice.

The Jamaican society becomes a recipient of the outcomes of decisions, forged by those placed in elected leadership and government positions as the purveyors of the modalities through which public servants fulfil and implement policies and undertake tasks to execute and deliver services in the public interest. Sociopolitical issues align in a queue along the trajectory of the media society government relationship which are further mirrored in negative or positive incidences or occurrences, inclusive of those that resonate in society, which are captured within cartoon imagery with its symbolism, visual rhetoric, social commentary and hidden layers of coded meaning.

One of the most effective vehicles communicating, representing, as well as reflecting, the fluidity of societal issues within the Jamaican society has been the modality of imagery and the visual. Issues and events with sociopolitical, and economic overtones have been captured in the media and reflected through the lens of editorial cartoons, produced over the years within the two (2) major newspapers the Jamaica Gleaner Company and the Jamaica Observer Company.

These newspapers originally utilized the printed format but have broadened their networks and spheres of influence by transcending these and have additionally embraced electronic and digital means of dissemination and distribution. The creation and production of editorial cartoons by Mr. Lascelles (Las) Mays of the Jamaica Gleaner Company and Mr. Clovis (Clovis) Brown of the Jamaica Observer Company have played a creative and communicative role across society, bringing to the forefront local issues of socio-political economy, cultural significance and also ethical concern for the citizenry, inclusive of global issues, current events and controversies. Both cartoonists were initially, employed to the Jamaica Gleaner Company in their early years, after which, Mr. Clovis Brown, was engaged by the Jamaica Observer Company, rising to be a prolific creator of cartoons, reflective of current and local affairs which resonate within the society, as issues of debate or reflection over the years.

Conveying and representing opinion and controversies, ripe with semiotic content, the cartoons capture sociopolitical overtones and key moments within the effervescent environment of Jamaican society and culture. These cartoonists have positioned political, social, economic and cultural dimensions juxtaposed with salient issues, at the forefront of the visual senses, through imagery, comedy and satire and representing their perspectives over the lifetime of the emergence and growth of contemporary Jamaican society. One could argue that the semiotics of the cartoon imagery, communicates the views, opinions, perspectives and positions held by the creators.

However, corollary to this, is that the imagery may intimate, to a degree, the pulse of societal undercurrents, through the capture in imagery of views, opinions and the emotions resonating, being the common or shared sentiments that are held on the part of the ordinary citizen. The views and perspectives reflected within the cartoon imagery by the creators, resonate with society as the outcome of reciprocity between their creators and the societal concerns that they portray.

The populous, if unaware, may even become informed about an issue from these devices of imagery and from these visual representations, which are then used to begin forming their own understanding, views and perspectives as a result of it, accordingly. The citizens may relate in visual terms, with the cartoons, which reflect, sometimes in a humorous way, societal discourse, the moments, and relations of societal pain disappointment, individual decline, political and economic struggle, corruption, the demise of cultural icons, individuals publicly exposed in terms of weaknesses, strength, character, in triumph or even ridicule—which are all being brought to the forefront. These cartoons can evoke responses in the capture of symbolism, satire, humour and may even place a comical spin on issues that are completely the opposite, aiding consumption of matters otherwise indigestible, given the nature of the content.

Punctuating the newspapers with such content has become accepted and normalized over decades, being enshrined within the cultural fabric of Jamaican society and diaspora. These cartoonists have become iconic in their representation of salient and diverse issues of societal currency, positioning issues at the forefront of the Jamaican psyche, reflecting the ebb and flow of societal interaction and the multidimensional concerns that arise out of politics, economics, social, cultural and foreign relations, religion, etc. Embracing moments in the visual rings true to the adage *a picture is worth a thousand words.* One theme that has played out in society over the years, concerns the impact upon the Jamaican Dollar as a result of Jamaica committing to various IMF Agreements over the years. In 1967, 1972–1973, 1976–1977 and 1978, for example, there were incidences of devaluation within the context of IMF programme interventions in an effort to induce competitiveness for exports and maintaining markets, which had implications for the trade balance and a fall in incomes (Brown, 1981).

Consecutive Government administrations have had the choice to defend their currency or devalue it under crisis conditions. In the case of the former, they could sell foreign exchange reserves and increase short-term interest rates and in the case of the latter, devalue until the pressure of speculation subsides. The short-term consequences of devaluations are painful for the society while possessing the possibilities for benefits over the long term. However, the negative repercussions for the consumers or the voting public in terms of inflation, increased prices for imports, goods and services can translate into unpopularity and negative political consequences for the incumbent government in office.

Figure 7.6 in the *Jamaica Observer* editorial '100–1 Makes Sense?' on 12 June 2013, after Jamaica's commitment to an IMF Agreement under the EFF, depicts the scene of a crucifixion, where the Jamaican Dollar, that is connotated as being 'innocent of any sin' is being 'crucified'/devalued by the Government. The EFF was negotiated under a PNP administration, whereby the Minister of Finance, the Hon. Peter Phillips is presiding as the guard who has crucified the Jamaican Dollar

Fig. 7.6 Clovis Toon (2013) 100 to 1 makes sense? Jamaica (*The Jamaica Observer*, June 12, 2013, https://www.jamaicaobserver.com/business/100-to-1--makes-sense-_14465183&template=MobileArticle)

on the cross. The Jamaican Dollar is on the verge of giving up the ghost, committing his soul to God. The PNP had been elected into office defeating the JLP after the collapse of the 2010 SBA. The Jamaican Dollar was subject to and was required to be devalued to 100.14: 1 US Dollar, on account of it being overvalued, hence the IMF Programme dynamic of the devaluation would assist to support price competitiveness. There were cries and fears expressed by the President of the Manufacturers' Association (JMA) with respect to the inability for productivity and growth if the Jamaican Dollar declined further.

About five years later, the JLP having formed the new administration now had a Precautionary SBA arrangement with the IMF in place and decisions with respect to undertaking a devaluation resurfaced. The Minister of Finance, Dr Nigel Clarke, caricatured in this Clovis (2018) cartoon, See Fig. 7.7, supervises the Jamaican Dollar as it goes through a routine on the exercise machine to get in shape.

Fig. 7.7 Clovis Toon (2018) pains of a sliding dollar (*Jamaica Observer*, August 8, 2018, https://301-joweb.newscyclecloud.com/opinion/the-pains-of-a-sliding-dollar_140787?profile=109)

Ironically, the shape the Jamaican Dollar is in suggests that the exercise will do little to assist especially for a one legged scrawny character that looks like it would need more medical attention than the stress of exercise and can barely keep up, with the strong possibility of collapse. A similar view and concern for the Jamaican Dollar was expressed by the child with the 'big belly' in the picture, which character is used to represent the state of the Jamaican economy, who reiterates that the dollar has gone through the same exercise of devaluation by consecutive political administrations from both parties. The child vocalizes the implications of dollar devaluations that always results in negative repercussions for the poor or middle class who are disproportionately affected and feel its impact the most, through the costs of services and the price of goods.

The Minister, asserting that the dollar should '*run 'til he corrects himself*', evidences his advocacy to the principles of economic neoliberalism and a subscription to the belief that market forces should be the determinant of the exchange rate, more so under the IMF SBA 2016. This, however, does not allay the fears nor does it not hide the concerns and the realities faced by the 'economy' due to the Dollar devaluing unchecked, which from past experience has resulted in increased prices for goods and services, that the child as 'the big belly economy' has clearly recognized.

About 13 months later, on the week of 10 November 2019, the US dollar was sold for $142.23 and on Thursday, 14 November 2019, Scotiabank was selling the US dollar at $141.81 the Prime Minister reiterated that it was in relation to a new economic model being implemented to manage the foreign exchange rate and reassured the public that the inflation rate and level of price increases was under control (*Jamaica Observer* 2019). Other reasons for the slide were attributed to the increase in demand for foreign currency due to the restocking by retailers in preparation for the Christmas season in addition to extraordinary demand relating to portfolio transactions. (See Fig. 7.8) On 27 November 2019, The Bank of Jamaica Governor, Mr. Richard Byles indicated that US$ 20 million would be pumped into the exchange market for businesses to shore up the Jamaican Dollar that had experienced a slide in its value due to a number of multi-million US Dollar transactions over the 2018–2019 period that placed pressure upon the local currency.

The Jamaican Dollar recovered from the slide, regaining upwards of 139.0: I US which was reassuring. The cartoon 'Jamaica Dollar', depicted the Jamaican Dollar as a patient in hospital receiving a blood transfusion, but relaxed and looking comfortable, with a properly bandaged leg and a healthy visage which seemed grateful and welcoming towards his physician. The Minister of Finance, Dr Nigel Clarke, is represented as a physician, checking up on his patient dressed accordingly, seemingly confident and in control, pleased with the recovery of the patient, who reciprocates with a smile. The patient refers to the easing of pressure which suggests that it was high at one point and was now receding, contributing to a reduction in anxiety and renewed hope to get back on his feet. The physician with his arms akimbo suggests a feeling of pride, confidence and success that the diagnosis and treatment of the patient has been one that will ensure his recovery and will continue to improve overtime. This cartoon also helped or served to indirectly allay the fears of the

Fig. 7.8 Clovis Toon (2019) recovery of the dollar (*Jamaica Observer*, November 27, 2019, https://www.jamaicaobserver.com/tools/cartoons/20191127?profile=156)

Jamaican citizen who is anxious and fearful of being impacted negatively as the inevitability of the effects of devaluation on the prices of goods and services would materialize as a matter of course.

One of the concerns arising at the end of the 2013 EFF in 2016, concerned whether the Government under the JLP which had been elected to office would retain the Economic Programme Oversight Committee (EPOC) which emerged during the time of the PNP administration in 2013. See Fig. 7.9.

The concern reflected by the cartoon represents that of The Hon. Portia Simpson-Miller, Leader of the Opposition, PNP who asks the elected Prime Minister of Jamaica, The Hon. Andrew Holness of the JLP, whether he will essentially destroy or dissolve the two committees, represented as two crying babies in the basket—namely the Economic Programme Oversight Committee (EPOC) and the Electricity Sector Enterprise Team (ESET)—both created under the PNP administration by the then Minister of Finance, The Hon.Peter Phillips about one year prior.

Fig. 7.9 Clovis Toon (2016) don't destroy the progress (*Jamaica Observer*, April 19, 2016, https://encrypted-tbn0.gstatic.com/images?q=tbn:ANd9GcSPg6I4l-9EXzwuW9Gx-clCxK2gqI464eVg0g&usqp=CAU)

These 'babies' reflect EPOC and the ESET that The Hon. Portia Simpson-Miller, Leader of the Opposition, conversely suggests, should be nurtured and not abandoned by the new administration.

One of the unspoken fears not expressed publicly to any significant degree, was that EPOC would be abolished, having come to fruition under a PNP administration during the EFF 2013 after which they had lost the subsequent election and had been voted out of office. Further, that it has been the discourse and practice of the political parties observed over the years, that when a new administration is elected into office, it then dissolves or reconfigures some of the ongoing projects of its predecessor, irrespective of whether those projects or activities engendered real benefits. This occurrence can also be reflected in situations where the name of a project, started under one administration, is changed or renamed, with the election to office of the opposing administration in that, although the deliverables may remain the same, the credit goes to the incumbent.

EPOC had become a valuable tool of communication and transparency with respect to the status of the government's fulfilment of the commitments under the IMF programme over the years. EPOC would issue quarterly communications in both of the major newspapers making public, issues of concern and factors that could result in the government not being able to fulfil some of the targets or benchmarks specified in the IMF agreement, as implementation progressed.

The quarterly communiques issues by EPOC as one of their commitments towards transparency informs the business community and the ordinary citizen of how well the government was performing and any challenges arising to hinder the fulfilment of the requirements of the IMF programme, flagging issues before they grew to the point where they could actually derail the programme and the gains made. This Committee is still operational although there are signs, that at the end of the EFF Programme, its remit may be modified, or it may be dissolved in favour of the creation of a Fiscal Council instead.

Notably, in May 2019 a new six-member team of the Electricity Sector Enterprise Team (ESET) was named and designated to oversee the building of the 381—megawatt electricity generation plant. However, clarity is needed with respect to the functions and responsibilities, which was queried by the Executive Director of the National Integrity Action Committee (NIA) and its continuity in its original form is uncertain.

References

Arnesen, A., Clancy, J., Elliott, D., & Francis, K. (2019, December 5). *Venezuela, Petrocaribe, and the "Orgy of corruption"*. Caribbean Investigative Journalism Network. https://www.cijn.org/venezuela-petrocaribe-and-the-orgy-of-corruption/. Accessed September 7, 2020.

Brown, A. (1981). Economic Policy and the IMF in Jamaica. *Social and Economic Studies*, 1–51.

Duncan, N. (2017). *Jamaica's plan—Not the IMF's plan*. https://epocjamaica.com/blog/jamaicas-plan-not-the-imfs-plan/. Accessed November 12, 2020.

Glickhouse, R. (2013). *Explainer: What is Petrocaribe*? American Society/Council of the Americas AS/COA. https://www.as-coa.org/articles/explainer-what-petrocaribe. Accessed October 4, 2020.

Gupta, M. S., Schena, M., & Yousefi, M. R. (2018). *Expenditure conditionality in IMF-supported programs*. International Monetary Fund.

Higgins, G. (2015, October 3). *When will we stop blaming the IMF for our state of affairs?* Jamaica Observer. Retrieved 2020, from http://www.jamaicaobserver.com/columns/When-will-we-stop-blaming-the-IMF-for-our-state-of-affairs-_19231545.

International Monetary Fund. (2013). *Jamaica: Request for Extended Fund Facility*. Washington, D. C.: International Monetary Fund.

International Monetary Fund. (2013a). *Jamaica: Request for an extended arrangement under the extended fund facility*. Western Hemisphere Department, No. 13/126, Washington, DC.

International Monetary Fund. (2013b). *Jamaica: First review under the extended arrangement under the extended fund facility and request for modification of performance criteria*. Western Hemisphere Department, No. 13/304, Washington, DC.

International Monetary Fund. (2013c). *Jamaica: Second review under the extended arrangement under the extended fund facility and request for modification of performance criteria*. Western Hemisphere Department, No. 13/378, Washington, DC.

International Monetary Fund. (2014a). *Jamaica: Third review under the extended arrangement under the extended fund facility and request for modification of performance criteria—Staff report*. Western Hemisphere Department, No. 14/85, Washington, DC.

International Monetary Fund. (2014b). *Staff report for the 2014 Article IV Consultation and fourth review under the extended arrangement under the extended fund facility and request for modification of performance criteria*. Western Hemisphere Department, No. 14/169, Washington, DC.

International Monetary Fund. (2014c). *Jamaica: Fifth review under the extended fund facility and request for modification of performance criteria—Staff report*. Western Hemisphere Department, No. 14/295, Washington, DC.

International Monetary Fund. (2014d). *Jamaica: Sixth review under the extended fund facility and request for modification of performance criteria—Staff report*. Western Hemisphere Department, No. 14/359, Washington, DC.

International Monetary Fund. (2015a). *Jamaica: Seventh review under the extended fund facility and request for modification of performance criteria—Staff report, Press release; and Statement by the Executive Director for Jamaica*. Western Hemisphere Department, No. 15/95, Washington, DC. https://www.imf.org/external/pubs/cat/longres.aspx?sk=42834.0.

International Monetary Fund. (2015b). *Jamaica: Eighth review under the extended fund facility and request for waiver for the non-observance of performance criterion and modification of performance criteria—Press release and staff report*. Western Hemisphere Department, No. 15/150, Washington, DC.

International Monetary Fund. (2015c). *Jamaica: Ninth review under the arrangement under the extended fund facility and request for modification of performance criteria—Press release; Staff report; and Statement by the Executive Director for Jamaica*. Western Hemisphere Department, No. 15/270, Washington, DC.
International Monetary Fund. (2015d). *Jamaica: Tenth review under the arrangement under the extended fund facility and request for modification of performance criteria—Press release; Staff report; and Statement by the Executive Director for Jamaica*. Western Hemisphere Department, No. 15/343, Washington, DC.
International Monetary Fund. (2016a). *Jamaica: Article IV Consultation, eleventh and twelfth reviews under the extended fund facility and request for modification of performance criteria—Press release; Staff report; and Statement by the Executive Director for Jamaica*. Western Hemisphere Department, No. 16/181, Washington, DC.
International Monetary Fund. (2016b). *Jamaica: Thirteenth review under the arrangement under the extended fund facility—Press release and staff report*. Western Hemisphere Department, No. 16/297, Washington, DC.
Jamaica Observer. (2019, November 17). Concentrate on the inflation rate and not on the dollar slide—Holness. Sunday. https://www.jamaicaobserver.com/latestnews/Concentrate_on_the_inflation_rate_and_not_the_dollar_slide_-_Holness?profile=1373.
Nelson, C. (Ed.). (2019). *Social partnership and governance under crises*. IGI Global.
Perkins, W. (2002). *Wilmot "Mutty" Perkins—Transcript of live session*. https://go-jamaica.com/chat/ts_wilmotperkins.html. Accessed November, 2020.
Sullivan, M. P. (2010, July). *Jamaica: Background and US relations*. Library of Congress. Washington, DC: Congressional Research Service.
Wilks, A., & Lefrançois, F. (2002). Blinding with science or encouraging debate. How World Bank Analysis Determines PRSP Policies, Bretton Woods Project, London and World Vision International Monrovia, California.

CHAPTER 8

The International Monetary Fund and the Social

Introduction

The IMF was constructed ideationally, relationally and symbolically as a fully negotiated monetary order, embodying the confidence, 'real hope' and perception of being an enabler of transformation, which the world was in dire need of at the end of World War Two. The monetary and financial institution represented a conduit to further economic and financial resilience as well as engendering equitable global economic development. In the context of the global political economy, national interest remains the undercurrent and the means of constructing alternatives, so that, the platform for negotiating 'buy in' has no guarantees with respect to negotiating outcomes and the nature of engagements undertaken.

The global environment and economy have evidently become more complex, with the emergence of increased connectivity and the multiplicity of state and non-state global actors, with hegemonic, multi-level power relations. As globalization processes and technological innovation becomes expansive, this creates 'real time' connectivity and information flows between nations and global actors, across geopolitical and state boundaries, whilst simultaneously becoming invasive into domestic space. Likewise, the IMF, in responding to the global dimension of change has led, implicitly, as well as explicitly, to a morphing, widening and deepening of its construct.

C. Clarke and C. Nelson, *Jamaica's Evolving Relationship with the IMF*,
https://doi.org/10.1007/978-3-030-59204-2_8

This engenders greater reflection on its *raison d'etre*, and the contextual implications of its role as a participant in constructing macroglobal financial policy and decision-making, 'rolled out' and expressed within the micro-domestic, multifaceted domain of the diverse states with whom they are engaged in a partnership, in the economic, as well as navigating the geopolitical, sociopolitical spaces within which decisions are constructed and thereafter operationalized.

The IMF Actor Network

In cases, the IMF as an actor network, has had to negotiate and occasionally navigate the divides blurred, by the intermingling of subliminal actor networks of power, within the geopolitical, ideological and financial actor networks of interests operative, whilst brokering power relations pursued within the context of the governance, decision-making and execution of Fund interventions within states.

According to Strange (1999) the state required economic growth and the economic system was therefore required to reciprocate, by providing the state with credit finance to enable it to produce, trade and enjoy a degree of prosperity.

The state, in turn, is embedded within the capitalist market economy and is inseparable from it, within the framework of complex interdependence between economic growth and the credit creating system of finance. Other proponents such as Kindleberger (1978) concurs with the overall perspective that one of the weakest factors in the international economy is the international financial system and call for it to be regulated, in order to avoid the reoccurrence of crises.

Diverse criticisms have also arisen, from the perspective of the governance of the institution and its response as an outcome of external relations. Collectively, these have had multiple repercussions accompanied by the distilling of diverse perceptions with respect to hidden motives and spin off effects with respect to the consequences. These gaps, deficiencies and weaknesses have surfaced in the 'cut and thrust' of IMF operations, which has served to undeniably fray the image of the institution and character of the interface with diverse country regimes within the framework of operationalizing avenues of support from global, monetary and financial networks.

Overall, these criticisms have served to 'cast shade' and lend support to a perception, which signals the undermining of the expressed founding ideals and expectations constructed at the creation of the Institution, brought to the forefront, by the vagaries inherent in negotiating, leveraging and brokering arrangements within multiple, multi-level multilateral networks within global financial and monetary systems of power, which are always contested, conflictual and sometimes controversial.

In tandem with the ebb and flow of globalization processes, the IMF has had to respond to micro domestic as well as the macroglobal financial economic maladies and crises, through actioning and leveraging networks of power within geopolitical financial and monetary relations, which has engendered reflection. There has been a continual impetus to rethink, reassess recalibrate and reform in response to the changing global political economy, in terms of its role, raison d'etre, with respect to issues of modernization and maintaining relevance, within the space of flows of international, monetary and financial domains.

When one considers the IMF's global monetary and financial network of relations and the purposes of its construction, several 'game changing' events have surfaced within the actor networks of the global political economy, which have served undeniably, to play a role in fraying the confidence real hope and perception of the institution. Included in this, is the perception of its purposes as a conduit and accessible portal for financial support in the context of furthering global financial and monetary order and stability, to engender equitable global economic development.

Reflecting on the amendments of the IMF's Articles of Agreement, these arguably reveal outcomes of entertaining horizons of change to the point of effecting changes within the discourse and commensurately the practice of the Institution. It is noted that the First Amendment entailed the creation of the Special Drawing Rights (SDRs) as an international reserve asset, after the collapse of the Bretton Woods System. The Second Amendment served to legitimize the floating exchange rate system, also in the early 1970s, as well as encourage international financial flows and exchanges as a function of the international, concomitantly supporting the retention of the rights of members to regulate capital flows across their borders independently (Abdelal, 2006).

Supplemental provisioning for the IMF was also enabled by diversifying its sources of income by the establishment of an Investment Account (IA) which remained dormant until after the review of the financial structure of the IMF in 2004.

The Third Amendment of 1992 sought to shore up and maintain the liquidity of the IMF, in response to the problem of accumulating arrears and rising indebtedness of the members consisting of the poorer developing countries.

The latter 1999s revealed accelerated growth within emerging market countries and rising instability in the transitional developmental processes punctuated with fluidity of cross-border capital flows accompanied by increased interconnectedness as well as within the context of growing regional integration. Altogether, this precipitated an environment of turbulence within global economic financial flows evidenced by the incidence of crises and the heightened propensity for crisis conditions to blossom. Consequently, the Fourth Amendment sought to target the allocations of SDRs with a view to provide additional IMF liquidity for about 39 developing country members and the transitional countries in the throes of undertaking processes which enabled them to become more integrated within the global economy.

Amending the IMF's Articles of Agreement to provide for a central role in overseeing processes surrounding the orderly liberalization of capital accounts, remained dormant. However, one of the more controversial amendment proposals, which was heavily resisted, concerned allowing the IMF jurisdiction over the capital accounts of its members which would have become legally binding on members if an amendment to the IMF Articles was effected. This controversy was accentuated further by financial crises in Southeast Asia, Latin America and Eastern Europe as well as being compounded by issues of international politics (Abdelal, 2006). Further, one could argue also that it had implications for the role of the IMF which would engender a discoursal shift in some form and possibly crossing the divide of state sovereignty. However, the IMF was encouraged to retain an advisory capacity with respect to prudent regulation and assisting in the implementation of least distortionary capital controls as well as retain a posture of neutrality with respect to jurisdictional issues synonymous with exercises that build their expertise and the proffering of advice (Eichengreen, 2000).

The idea of orderly liberalization presented economic policy liberalization as both desirable and inevitable in terms of the economic performance benefits with respect to the normative dimensions, which had additionally procedural components in light of the type and scope of economic policies pursued to realize rewards from global financial integration (Moschella, 2012). Orderly liberalization was nevertheless posited as a desirable goal despite diverse outcomes with respect to the problems and consequences of uncontrolled short-term capital flows. Positions rest to a degree with respect to customizing capital account liberalization with due consideration being made to the individual country context on a phased basis, whereby there would be defined obligations and actions accordingly.

In 2006 there was notably a deterioration in the income position of the Fund which led to the activation of the Investment Account (IA) created prior in 2004, resourced in 2008, through the investment of income from gold sales and subsequent revision of the Rules and Regulations surrounding the management of the IA and investment authority. The Fifth Amendment that became effective in February 2011, further sealed the provisioning of supplementary resources and actioned the sustainable flow of income for the IMF in alignment with its activities for the long term. The amendment also enabled diversification in the use and types of investment instruments reflecting the expansion of investment authority.

However, the emergence and blossoming of systemic and potentially systemic, financial crises as outgrowths of interactive, economic, monetary and financial flows operative within the global capitalist market economy actor network, commensurate with the progress of globalization, has continually established contexts for change. The occurrence of crises has compelled, introspection, reflection and action on the part of the International Monetary Fund with the responsibility to respond to address anomalies in the global financial system. Thereby reducing the vulnerabilities and consequences associated with the unfettered nature, mobility and cycles juxtaposed in the management of capital flows and the framework of the norms of liberalization and self-regulation.

There are discursive aspects of social change and transformation as well as socially transformative effects emanating from discursive change. Consequently, there are discursive aspects within processes instigating changing social relations and transformation. The occurrence of crises as agents of transformation, presents opportunities for, or serve to catalyze processes towards horizons of change as manifestations, captured through the lens of changing and adopting norms, as well as changing discourse and discourse practice.

Surveillance

Core functions of the IMF entail the role of surveillance and regulator within the domains of the global, economic, monetary and financial order and network relations, capping and addressing the diverse flows and sources of destabilization that emerge, within the global political economy. Crises are the products of the relational interplay within and external to the global capitalist market economy actor network, which are juxtaposed with the IMF's response as a mitigator of such systemic occurrences and risks through surveillance.

The international monetary and financial system has been subject to a degree of turmoil, allegedly in the context of states pursuing orderly liberalization. The international monetary and financial system has been subject to a degree of turmoil, allegedly in the context of states pursuing 'orderly liberalization' resulting in the need for management and control, as in the context of resulting and emerging global financial crises.

Contemporary Crises

In the case of the Mexican financial crisis of 1994 to 1995 which was preceded by a currency devaluation and Mexico repurchasing its own Treasury securities to shore up its money supply in the context of an election. The resultant utilization of foreign exchange reserve acted to stymie increases in the interest rate and corollary effects. Subsequent devaluations and political violence, prefaced against changes in US monetary policy, precipitated the shift in investment perception, an appetite which triggered instead, capital flight and the depreciation of the Mexican peso. Corollaries contributed to destabilization such as the drop in value of foreign capital investments which enhanced the risk of contagion into emerging markets with implications for the overall global financial system (Musacchio, 2012).

A joint response by the United States and the IMF sought to stabilize the currency devaluations and deter contagion. The bailout was successful in terms of not fully utilizing the reserves made available and repaying obligations to the investors. It however, sparked controversy from the perspective of perception and the potential to engender moral hazard and setting a precedence for other countries to engage in imprudent macroeconomic and debt management practices within their economies. The optics of the bailout was defended and vindicated, being framed as a burden sharing, restructuring effort undertaken with the private sector in response to unique circumstances that required unconventional action, which would not be considered as a template for future interventions.

The Mexican financial crisis was followed by the more controversial, East Asian crisis which emerged in the summer of 1997, within Southeast Asian countries—Taiwan, South Korea, Thailand, Singapore and Hong Kong. This crisis emerged in the context of them vigorously undertaking neoliberal economic policies as well as pursuing rapid industrialization. The resultant, vigorous economic growth earned them the label the 'East Asian miracle' by the World Bank as well as the name 'the Asian Tigers' in the developing world. These countries enjoyed a vigorous rate development, fuelled by their economic openness and capital account liberalization which engendered trade, attracted foreign direct investments and financial flows which delivered successful macroeconomic growth.

The abrupt reversal of the 'miracle' to a 'debacle' was attributed to contagion, triggered by a series of currency devaluations which served to overturn the development trajectory of the region. There was a spilling over, in terms of its effect, to neighbouring states such as China and Japan threatening the stability of the wider global financial and monetary system overall.

Series of Accusations and Recriminations

Accusations flowed, as to the causes of the resultant financial contagion and economic collapse, culminating in the complete reversal of the economic growth formerly enjoyed by East Asian states. The economic collapse has attributed to the view that the East Asian states were engaged in crony capitalism (Hughes, 1999; Lee, 1999). Further, that the East Asian states were practising 'phased selective interventions' (Berhane, 2012, p. 3) into the market, which altogether further intimated the failure of the 'Asia Alternative' (Higgott, 1998).

Criticisms of the IMF rose to the surface with respect to issues surrounding the inadequacy of economic surveillance prior, such as in the case of South Korea and Indonesia, the speed and responsiveness of the international financial institutions, the nature of the 'structural reforms', and policy advice given in the aftermath, which was deemed as incorrect: Ito (2012) by several critics.

Contentions on the part of the IMF were that there were a number of critical misconceptions with respect to the Fund's role in the international monetary system and response to crisis, namely—the IMF's imperfect access to information in addition to the absence of assurances that by forewarning countries of crisis that they would so act upon the information given.

Recriminations included questions concerning the institutional legitimacy and role of the IMF which found itself constrained, being cognizant of the dangers of making any incursions beyond the divide of state sovereignty (Wolf) in addition to not being culpable for the outcomes where its overtures of warnings to states are ignored, for example to Thailand (Fischer, 1998) which ended up being the epicentre centre of the Southeast Asian crisis of contagion.

Perspectives raised, questioned whether the policy prescriptions were too tight, associated with degrees of intrusiveness and encroachment upon state sovereignty (Higgott, 1998) and procyclical (Ito, 2012) more so that the crisis was not attributed to issues of government expenditures and fiscal deficits.

On the part of the recipient Southeast Asian countries the crisis struck at the heart of the modalities of the development pathway of these economies which was intimated as being a failure of the Asian alternative. Lee (1999) waivered on the causes of the Asian crisis, being attributed to internal factors such as the crony capitalism, albeit that the 'Asian Way' entailed deviations from Western free market economic edicts or whether the factors were external ones. External factors would be indicative of a weakness or failure within the international financial system itself, more so, as standard interpretations of crisis experience could not provide a sufficient understanding of the event.

The Asian IMF stigma (Ito, 2012) that remained subsequent to the interventions made, resonated in the psyche of recipient Southeast Asian countries. Incursions according to (Higgott, 1998) beyond the state borders of autonomy and infringing upon political processes also engendered resentment and the legitimate reticence by Southeast Asian states to the wholesale buy-into the tenets of neoliberalism in the future and the unfettered movement of capital.

In the aftermath of the Asian financial crisis, criticisms were raised which questioned the efficiency of the existing governance of the system and the deliverables expected from the International Monetary Fund, resulting in calls for a new financial architecture and reforms. This inquiry precipitated proposals for new and novel remedies such as the creation of a world currency and for a global financial supervisor (Ffrench-Davis et al., 2000).

The Asian financial crisis signalled inefficiencies or weaknesses in the management of global financial systems. Overall, the diverse criticisms energized reflection on the modus operandi, appropriateness and efficacy of IMF discourse practices and the instruments used. The Asian financial crisis precipitated increased collaboration between the IMF and the World Bank which led to the creation of new financial designs with the recognition of the need for standard accounting practices and mechanisms to regulate the movement of international capital.

One of the instruments created as a response to the Asian crisis was the Contingency Credit Line (CCL) which was a precautionary lending programme for countries with sound policies but which were vulnerable to risks not of their own making in addition to contagion effects (Chweiroth, 2009). This Facility eventually expired partially to the stigma attached evidenced by no uptake from the intended recipients. The crisis, however, engendered introspection, with respect to querying the adherence to norms and discourse practices, regarding modalities of capital controls and the optimal policy and practice.

Immediately following the Asian crisis of 1997–1998, a series of capital account crises occurred in Russia, Brazil, Turkey and Argentina. The first IMF programme for each of them allowed the country to maintain the fixed exchange rate regime despite real exchange rate overvaluation. The crisis in Brazil 1998–1999, resulted in the decision to float the exchange rate as an alternative to capital controls and imminent default (Lopes, 2003) prompted a variety of interventions with respect to responding to the crisis and market fragility. Emerging calls and concerns with respect to the adequacy of IMF surveillance, brought to the forefront, coupled with additional concerns regarding the adequacy of governance within the institution (Gallagher & Tian, 2017)

The efficiency of IMF surveillance and interventions within the crises of Russia, Brazil and Mexico were decried as failures prompting criticisms surrounding the failure of the IMF's surveillance capabilities. Sachs (1997) criticized the handling and approach to the reforms in Russia being contingent upon the formation of a currency union of the 15 successor states which resulted in inflation and collapse of the GDP for some impacted economies due to the delay in effecting stabilization measures. In addition to this, there were a number of concerns and debates on certain rules regarding the role of capital controls.

Capital controls had been used in the early years of the IMF as a mechanism to harmonize exchange rate stability and economic policies, in addition to being used by developed countries such as the United States (1963) and Germany in 1961 to mitigate balance of payment crises. Chwieroth (2009) notes that the official orthodoxy of the Fund and supporting institutional framework since 1945, entrenched the right of governments to use capital controls within the required institutional framework. The impact of crisis engendered contending views, to the point where it was held by some, that capital account liberalization without requisite controls actually precipitated consecutive financial crises in the 1980s to 1990s. The Asian financial crisis did not result in an amendment to the IMF's Articles of Agreement (Eichengreen, 2000) but indirectly instigated a process of introspection with respect to capital control modalities operative within crisis scenarios.

The financial crises of the 1990s also precipitated considerations on the merit of free market controls as an optimal policy tool by countries, however a number of incidences deferred the wholesale adoption and change in the discourse practice (Chwieroth, 2009; Moschella, 2010). The initiative for change waned consequent upon a change in the staff complement away from Keynesian economists who supported capital controls as interventionist measures to those adopting new classical economic approaches and modalities positing that capital controls were counterproductive. Attempts in 1997 to amend the Articles of Agreement of the International Monetary Fund to reflect capital account convertibility (Gallagher & Ocampo, 2013) was resisted by the United States that threatened to withdraw IMF funding (Gallagher, 2011) reflective of divergent support among staff members. This was despite industrialized countries utilizing capital controls in the context of bilateral arrangements read by some, as demonstrating inconsistency with the stance taken in the context of IMF governance.

IMF surveillance was allegedly blindsided by the unexpected Sub Prime Crisis in the United States in 2007 due to an overconfidence in status, the systems and practices within designated financial institutions who were constituents of the centres of global financial capital, coupled with the scant likelihood or expectation of these entities triggering emergent crises, juxtaposed against the prevalence of the incidences of such events in developing and emerging economies.

The expansion of credit opportunities and the deregulation of the financial sector with concentrated, rampant speculation, seeking to capitalize upon investments in the housing sector, precipitated the crash and economic storm that ensued. There had evidently been compromises in terms of prudential and financial risks taken and the resultant crisis, which began in the United States as a developed economy and the bastion of neoliberalism itself. This irony encouraged opportunities to interrogate underlying beliefs underpinning the economic theory of neoliberalism and modalities thereof Crouch (2011) and Stiglitz (2013) which informed the discourse and practice of the Fund.

Nevertheless, for most banks in the United States and the United Kingdom, incentives to take excessive risks in investing in the sub-prime market in search of higher short-term profits were underpinned by strong competition in the domestic market and compounded by impatient capital. Structural and ideational factors conditioned informal institutions to favour market-based ideology over prudential regulation, which entrenched a faith perpetuated by agents in the ability of markets to correctly price risk and return, and thus self-regulate. These structural ideas both influenced and were reinforced by state-based agents over consecutive governments. As the global financial crisis demonstrated, the multiplicity of structural, institutional and agent-level processes that perpetuate risk aversion carry with them severe consequences.

Analysts surmise that underlying the global financial crisis were issues of growing inequality combined with deregulation, exacerbated by the expanded access and availability of credit to finance consumption (Stockhammer, 2015). These criteria that engendered the speculative mortgage crisis which grew out of proportion, precipitated a full-blown global financial crisis requiring remedial measures. Other questions arose with respect to whether the IMF had lost its relevance for the twenty-first century and whether it was equipped to meet the challenges based on lessons learned from the crisis and thereby effect meaningful change. Expansion of credit increased leverage with borrowers decline in standards and regimes of the lenders contributed to the vulnerabilities which precipitated into systemic risks (Claessens et al., 2014).

However, in the aftermath of the 2008 Sub Prime Crisis, the IMF again, became subject to intense criticism by the global community and programme recipients calling for remedial change. Critical debates concerned the IMF's response and alleged weaknesses with respect to its surveillance functions, speaking directly to its raison d'etre, the purposes of the Fund, and its functions within the context of rising instability and the growing complexity with regard to global financial and monetary networks.

The normative response to the Sub Prime Crisis or the global financial crisis of 2007–2009 led to the introduction of global financial safety nets and reforms which strengthened and complemented the traditional role of the IMF with respect to crisis prevention resolution and resilience to shocks. Several lending reforms were enacted, inclusive of tools for crisis prevention and resolution, buttressed by global financial safety nets to be able to respond to adverse shocks, which complemented the traditional function's role of the IMF.

However, the 2008 crisis proved to be a horizon of change beyond which the IMF was catalyzed and prompted to move beyond the established towards furthering additionality, in terms of discourse and practice to accommodate a new pattern. This movement allegedly originated within the IMF itself.

On reflection, the surfacing of crises, apart from introducing instability, has served to introduce degrees of uncertainty within the landscape of international financial flows in the global economy. Commensurate with this, the IMF's role of surveillance of the processes surrounding global capital flows has had to treat with degrees of uncertainty prompting introspections of efficacy, its modus operandi underlying the discourse and practice of the regimes instituted and understanding of these flows. The implications surrounding the validity of self-regulating markets were questioned heavily in spite of the recognition that markets had contributed to rapid economic growth on the part of several states (Rodriguez, 2017).

Blyth (2002) explores the relationship of the role of uncertainty, critical economic ideas and interests in making and forging institutional change possibilities and under what conditions, institutional change actually takes place. According to Gourevitch (1986), crisis can become the conduit or source of ideas which arise out of trying to diagnose and respond to the uncertainties and in constructing or devising a response. This collaborates with Grabel (2011) who argues that the crisis response on the part of the IMF portrayed uncertainty or 'incoherence'. At the outset the IMF's response did not reveal any consistent strategy or regime but left a vacuum, by the absence of a unified, consistent, universally applicable response to the crisis, considering the rhetoric and policy that emerged in comparison to the Asian crisis.

However, decrying the suggestion that the crisis signalled the demise of neoliberalism, Grabel (2011) asserted that it had however displaced certain ideological characteristics and the constraints of pure unbridled neoliberalism and instead opened the door to 'incoherence', in terms of proliferating chaotic responses, contradictory strategies and a plethora of ideas which eventually can become settled and productive, facilitated by the explorations outside of the box of the constraints of neoliberalism to etch out a solution or response.

In this case the determination of new institutional frameworks as a collective response to treat with crisis conditions enabled the entertainment of the methodology of capital controls as a response to treat with uncertainties intrinsic in interpreting and diagnosing the crisis condition, supporting an increased level of support for regulatory measures for capital controls as tools to broker and mitigate capital flows and avert crises.

Following the global financial crisis, research emerged, demonstrating that the IMF had begun accepting gradual capital account liberalization and the use of capital controls in the wake of the global financial crisis of 2008. Research which econometrically examined Article IV reports before and after the global financial crisis determined that the financial crisis impacted the behaviour of the IMF reflected by a degree of change in the manner in which advice was tendered to participating countries in Fund arrangements. There was demonstrably a change in patterns as well as attitudes with respect to supporting capital flow policies (Gallagher & Tian, 2017) inclusive of a heightened tolerance of the utility of price-based capital controls as a last resort for developing and emerging markets with the phased liberalization of the capital account (Takagi, 2005). Ostrey et al. (2010) noted that countries that had deployed capital controls going into crisies were among the least impacted, leading to an increased level of support for regulatory measures for capital controls as tools to broker and mitigate capital flows and avert crises.

However, one could argue that an Amendment of the Articles could have far-reaching effects with respect to entrenching capital controls as part of the agreement. There could be however, several issues in relation to the original mandate and raison d'etre of the IMF that arguably could shift or enlarge, signalling an inherent departure from neoliberalism and the founding ideas and the ideological basis which led to the framework of the institution at its inception.

One could also take the posture that the ideological divide between member states had diminished over time, coupled with relinquishing degrees of sovereignty within the construct of participating within the IMF as an institutional actor network, which has afforded levels of cooperation and pragmatism around regimes that further global coherence in the governance of capital flows that auger to the benefit of the network and state concerned.

The IMF has always been unequivocal in its support for capital account liberalization being cognizant of the risks especially in the absence of the required regulation and resilience capability within the financial sector of states. However, the need to centre diverse IMF state dialogues on the issues surrounding the risks inherent in the process, was highlighted in terms of either being deficient or disregarded at the points of interface with client states (Takagi, 2005).

Altogether, these opened the door for the IMF to engender the creation of a new inclusive, strategic response, tailored between participants and stakeholders instead. In addition to continuity in terms of a reassertion of the IMF authorities' maintenance and reiteration of procyclical policy adjustments and the maintenance of existing governance patterns.

The IMF demonstrated 'ideational change' in its discourse and discourse practice (Gallagher & Tian, 2017) evidenced by the manner in which the benefits and risks concerning global capital flows were framed in discussions and implementation thereafter. Discourse involves inculcation by actors-material aspects, in genres, styles, ways of using language, materialized in bodies, postures, gestures ways of moving (Fairclough, 2003). Advocacy continued to further the institutionalization of regulatory regimes in the management of cross-border flows and the need for minimum procedures or mechanisms to treat with fluctuations in the ebb and flow intrinsic in cross-border movements.

Network relations according to Fairclough (2003) cover all the dimensions—social practices, discourse and mechanism of inculcating processes, beyond textual elements to include social processes including discourses within discourse and discourse into context into actor networks. New relations and network dynamics are forged through the divergence in part and convergence in part with a degree of reflexivity in the network dynamic engendering inclusion around the solution.

The IMF in solidifying the changing discourse surrounding the treatment of risks and potential challenges in the processes concerning the liberalization of capital flows and related after-effects, facilitated the accommodation of change on two tracks. One initiative aimed to embed the changing discourse, without a legally binding commitment which would offset Article VI, Section 3 of the Articles of Agreement, was the promulgation of a document the 'New Institutional View' on capital flows in 2012.

This 'Institutional View' was couched from the standpoint of not encroaching sovereignty, being framed as a non-binding template to further decision-making concerning the management of capital flows in accordance with national policy choice. These Capital Flow Management Methods instituted should include residency-based measures that are not discriminatory, inclusive of measures to generally influence flows overall.

The IMF supports the use of Capital Flow Management Methods or Capital Account Regulations with regard to being applied to the deregulated portions of the capital account of states, once they accompany these actions with macroeconomic, countercyclical monetary and financial policies undergirded by macroprudential financial and foreign exchange reserve regulations (Gallagher & Ocampo, 2013).

The IMF furthered the retention and even consolidation of dimensions of its raison d'etre through the type of response which entailed capturing an accommodative posture, which served to enlarge the value and role of the institution as an interlocuter, with respect to discourse and practice arecapital controls. These efforts filtered, complemented and supported discoursal realignment of policy advice tendered to states with the revised discourse practice, through the Staff Guidance Notes around capital controls which furthered the embedding of a degree of certainty at the interface. The IMF concomitantly stayed anchored to its primary discourse, ideationally relationally and textually, consistent with and through the promulgation of guidelines. In this context, discourse suggests new ways of being, new identities and repositioning, to act, think, talk and see self in terms of the 'new discourse' (Fairclough, 2003).

Cerny (1994) reiterates that the dynamics of financial globalization are such, that it constrains the latitude of state policymakers to act, limiting policymaking capacity, which engenders the need for external interventions, management and control which speaks to the remit of the Fund, in the context of responding to emerging crises, more so due to the interdependence and connectivities within the global financial and monetary system and network of relations. There was a furthering of policy coherence accordingly, with changes that enabled the broadening of the IMF's governance capacity through an inclusive approach which networked autonomous institutions, other networks and actors (Jessop, 1990) which were integrated into the system through degrees of coordination and orchestration which in turn, enhances governability and furthers systemic integrity (Rhodes, 1997; Sørensen, 2006).

Jamaica and Change

One event captured in the Jamaican media, which was of symbolic significance, was the visit to Jamaica of Madame Christine Lagarde, the first woman to be made Managing Director of the International Monetary Fund (IMF) which speaks to a change away from the traditional. Her visit was captured and also reflected in the imagery of cartoons, which further resonated with the Jamaican society in several ways. One of which was the fact that, in her leadership capacity, as the head of the International Monetary Fund, that she had decided to visit Jamaica, being the first IMF Head to do so, which was also a change from the norm. More obvious was that, her visit served to further cement the relationship of the institution she represented with Jamaica's government and endorsement of the economic reform programme, signifying the solidarity and commitment between the IMF and the government and highlighting the benefits of programme implementation.

When Mme Lagarde presented her speech on behalf of the International Monetary Fund on the campus of the University of the West Indies in June 2014 there were a number of key themes as well as a strong logic in the communication which, apart from the political overtones, revealed salient efforts to understand and interpret the Jamaican and Caribbean societies. One critical theme expounded in different ways was that of change. She began by reflecting upon Jamaica's economic landscape commenting upon the efforts to restructure the economy and to achieve the macroeconomic targets in relation to the programme to tackle the debt, etc., and also the level of fiscal discipline exercised by the leadership of the country. She utilized various textual approaches in conveying a message and semiotics in her acknowledgement and affirmation that 'Jamaica had changed' and that Jamaica had 'lived with the change'.

Reiterating the change that Jamaica had gone through and the difficulties, Mme Lagarde, stated that efforts were made to spread the burden across the society, mentioning some of them—the debt exchanges, etc., and the various impacts in terms of what was endured, whilst trying to protect those who were the most vulnerable. Her speech demonstrated a degree of symbolism in terms of her communicative structures and conveyance of understanding and identifying with the pain of the Jamaica experience in undergoing change through the IMF programme.

Drawing upon her knowledge of the Caribbean and Jamaican icons such as Claude McKay, Bob Marley and Derek Walcott she mentioned some of their literary and musical works bringing to the fore modalities of connectivity showing a level of resonance with the Caribbean consciousness. Mme Lagarde spoke about the Caribbean and how it too had evolved in terms of economy, population and society. The theme of unity was highlighted and to ensure a certain level of inclusiveness, a degree of ownership and to foster participation around the resolution of issues, utilizing approaches that would enable the mutual sharing of the benefits thereafter for all participants.

The Caribbean and Jamaica would be able to benefit from continued partnership with various stakeholders to enable the change and to go through the reforms despite the immediate discomfort. An optimistic future was juxtaposed with addressing some of the features of the Jamaican economy that predisposed it to certain vulnerabilities, like climate change, etc., admonishing that Jamaica was still not quite out of the woods as yet and that the reform agenda should still be maintained, accelerated and strengthened. The speaker continued to speak about the issue of resilience and conveyed a sense of pride concerning Jamaica's progress juxtaposed against the issue of economic resilience and the need to strengthen this area.

Mme Lagarde made the point that development was essentially not an elusive dream and Jamaica had the potential to realize a degree of prosperity. The speech sought to inspire and give hope that Jamaica could become prosperous with hard work and the consistency of effort, and was in good hands (Fig. 8.1).

Mme Lagarde was able to connect with the audience in terms of Jamaica's change and the need to stick to the reform agenda along with the clear cognizance of the suffering that had been experienced by the society to further change and the challenges that lay ahead towards prosperity. But her presence, and character of her leadership also as the Head of the IMF, also signals that the IMF has also changed in some respects.

Future Horizons of Change

In the twenty-first century, the role of the IMF leadership becomes more critical, with a perceived liability to always be *en garde*, as the

Fig. 8.1 Clovis Toon (2014) Jamaica in Good Hands (*Jamaica Observer*, Saturday 28 June 2014)

first responder to global systemic symptoms to further resilience at the interface of possible crises, fluctuations in cross-border capital flows to engender stability and to instill normalcy at the interface of the multiple actors within the global political economy.

Accentuated by the momentum and inherent interconnectedness and interdependence of globalization processes, 'the nature of the beast' is such that vigilance is required to detect the myriad financial maladies that arise from within diverse, country circumstances—traversing the monetary, financial and macroeconomic—that possess systemic contagious potential.

Globalization is dialectical for states and other actors within the financial and monetary system with respect to responding and engaging with its transformative potential and the unfettered consequences for states with heterogeneity and diversity in terms of levels of economic development, capital and resource mobilization requirements and vulnerabilities. The inevitability of crises always presents the need for creativity and hopefully for horizons for change to unfold out of the uncertainty to embrace a new norm or higher modality of operations. Lagarde communicated a level of realism by stating that the journey was just beginning and would be a long one and admonished Jamaica as well as the Caribbean that gains would not be made overnight and consistency, change and patience would be required to engender lasting success. The same could apply to the IMF too.

References

Abdelal, R. (2006). The IMF and the capital account. *Reforming the IMF for the 21st Century, 19,* 185.

Berhane, E. (2012). The role of government in East Asian development: Lessons for Ethiopia.

Blyth, M. (2002). *Great transformations: Economic ideas and institutional change in the twentieth century.* Cambridge University Press.

Cerny, P. G. (1994). The dynamics of financial globalization: Technology, market structure, and policy response. *Policy Sciences, 27*(4), 319–342.

Chwieroth, J. M. (2009). Capital ideas: The IMF and the rise of financial liberalization. Princeton University Press.

Claessens, S., Kose, M. M. A., Laeven, M. L., & Valencia, F. (2014). *Financial crises: Causes, consequences, and policy responses.* International Monetary Fund.

Crouch, C. (2011). *The strange non-death of neoliberalism.* Cambridge: Polity Press.

Eichengreen, B. (2000). The International Monetary Fund in the wake of the Asian crisis. The Asian financial crisis and the architecture of global finance, 170–191.

Fairclough, N. (2003). *Analysing discourse: Textual analysis for social research.* London: Routledge. https://doi.org/10.4324/9780203697078.

Ffrench-Davis, R., Pietrobelli, C., Zamagni, S., & Ocampo, J. A. (2000). Financial globalization and the emerging economies. Economic Commission for Latin America and the Caribbean (ECLAC).

Fischer, S. (1998, March). The IMF and the Asian crisis. In Forum Funds Lecture at UCLA (Vol. 20).

Gallagher, K. (2011). *Regaining control? Capital controls and the global financial crisis* (PERI Working Paper, 250). Political Economy Research Institute, University of Massachusetts at Amherst.

Gallagher, K. P., & Ocampo, J. A. (2013). IMF's new view on capital controls. *Economic and Political Weekly*, 10–13.

Gallagher, K. P., & Tian, Y. (2017). Regulating capital flows in emerging markets: The IMF and the global financial crisis. *Review of Development Finance, 7*(2), 95–106.

Gourevitch, P. (1986). *Politics in hard times: Comparative responses to international economic crises*. Cornell University Press.

Grabel, I. (2011). Not your grandfather's IMF: Global crisis, 'productive incoherence' and developmental policy space. *Cambridge Journal of Economics, 35*(5), 805–830.

Higgott, R. (1998). The Asian economic crisis: A study in the politics of resentment. *New Political Economy, 3*(3), 333–356.

Hughes, H. (1999). Crony capitalism and the East Asian currency and financial' crises'. *Policy: A Journal of Public Policy and Ideas, 15*(3), 3.

Ito, T. (2012). Can Asia overcome the IMF stigma? *American Economic Review, 102*(3), 198–202.

Jessop, B. (1990). *State theory: Putting the capitalist state in its place*. Penn State Press.

Kindleberger, C. (1978). *Manias, panics and crashes: A history of financial crisis*. New York: Basic Books.

Lee, E. (1999). The debate on the causes of the Asian crisis: Crony capitalism versus international system failure. *Internationale politik und gesellschaft*, 162–167.

Lopes, F. L. (2003). Notes on the Brazilian Crisis of 1997–99. *Brazilian Journal of Political Economy, 23*(3), 91.

Moschella, M. (2010). *Governing risk: The IMF and global financial crises*. Springer.

Moschella, M. (2012). Seeing like the IMF on capital account liberalisation. *New Political Economy, 17*(1), 59–76.

Musacchio, A. (2012, May). *Mexico's financial crisis of 1994–1995* (Harvard Business School Working Paper, No. 12–101). http://nrs.harvard.edu/urn-3:HUL.InstRepos:9056792.

Rhodes, R. A. W. (1997). *Understanding governance: Policy networks, governance, reflexivity and accountability*. Buckingham, UK: Open University Press.

Rodriguez, C. (2017). *The case of the International Monetary Fund and the 2008 Global Financial Crisis*. https://www.e-ir.info/2017/11/29/the-case-of-the-international-monetary-fund-and-the-2008-global-financial-crisis/.

Sachs, J. (1997, December 11). IMF is a power unto itself. *The Financial Times*. https://www.uv.es/~fores/AcosoTextual/sachsbio.html.

Sørensen, E. (2006). Metagovernance: The changing role of politicians in processes of democratic governance. *American Review of Public Administration, 36*(1), 98–114. https://doi.org/10.1177/0275074005282584.

Stiglitz, J. E. (2013). *The price of inequality*. St Ives: Penguin Books.

Stockhammer, E. (2015). Rising inequality as a cause of the present crisis. *Cambridge Journal of Economic.*, *39*(3), 935–958.

Strange, S. (1999). The westfailure system. *Review of International Studies*, *25*(3), 345–354. Retrieved October 20, 2020, http://www.jstor.org/stable/20097604.

Takagi, S. (2005). *The IMF's approach to capital account liberalization*. International Monetary Fund.

CHAPTER 9

History Made? The Precautionary Stand-By Agreement (PSBA)

Introduction

Pleased with the performance of the Jamaican economy throughout the course of the 2013 Extended Fund Facility (EFF) with the Fund, the Prime Minister of Jamaica and the Director of the IMF's Western Hemisphere Department announced that the Fund would be continuing to support Jamaica's economic programme through a thirty-six month Stand-By Agreement (International Monetary Fund, 2016a). This agreement with the Fund was historic for Jamaica as it was not anticipated that any drawdown would be made on the funds the agreement would make available based on the robust levels of reserves that were at the Bank of Jamaica. The SBA was therefore to be a precautionary one—some form of insurance against the types of unforeseen but potentially devastating crises that could overtake small island developing nations such as Jamaica once underway—and, given the agreement of Fund staff with the premise of the precautionary nature, represented an open affirmation of the confidence with the IMF of Jamaica's progress and proposed programme. The Precautionary Stand-By Agreement (PSBA) inked between Jamaica and the IMF provided access to 312% of Jamaica's quota equivalent to US$1.7billion. The programme consisted of twenty-two structural benchmarks to be implemented throughout the thirty-six months of the agreement. Of note is the fact that this was the only one of the three since the year 2010 that did not specify any prior actions for the government to

C. Clarke and C. Nelson, *Jamaica's Evolving Relationship with the IMF*,
https://doi.org/10.1007/978-3-030-59204-2_9

complete before the agreement would be signed a further confirming the substantial advances Jamaica had made in its management of the economy and the quality of results in the six years prior.

Transitions in Conditionalities

The 2013 EFF had supported several important institutional reform efforts in the area of fiscal policy. As noted in Chapter 4, special attention was paid under the EFF on the fiscal policy areas of: (a) tax policy reform to streamline, rationalize and specify clear and precise eligibility criteria for persons and entities wishing to benefit from tax incentives as well as the formalization of the tax treatment for the special economic zone that was being created for interested investors; and, (b) re-engineering of key aspects of tax administration to facilitate the transition to electronic filing for many tax types and fees as well as for large taxpayers that tended to create bottlenecks inside tax collectorate locations. On the real expenditure side, the entire landscape as it related to whole-of-government budgeting was transformed. From the level of the macroeconomic fiscal space, a formal fiscal rule was specified in the context of the established Fiscal Responsibility Framework inclusive of the fiscal responsibility law that put the responsibility of ensuring that the fiscal trajectory implied by the budget was credible, consistent with the economic programme and sustainable. Within this context, the 2013 EFF also addressed long-standing issues of weak public financial management that led to multiple dysfunctionalities in the conduct of government business which then caused distortions in the operation of fiscal policy and hamper growth.

Capital expenditure budgeting is another major area that was reformed and now uses a mechanism to score all proposed public sector investment in order to facilitate scrutiny and ensure prioritization of projects based on objective criteria and verifiable information sources. There was also a spotlight on the operations of public bodies that were largely divorced from the central government budgeting process. Many of these entities had become obsolete or duplicative in their functions and/or mandates and some had ceased to operate but were still being recorded on the books. The thrust in relation to these entities during the 2013 EFF was to clean up the records, enforce the production of outstanding Annual Reports to the Houses of Parliament inclusive of for the entities that were to be closed. Importantly the EFF continued the drive advanced under the 2010 SBA—the divestment of those public bodies that are habitual loss-makers that create unbudgeted contingent liabilities that needed to be terminated to support fiscal discipline and promote fiscal stability.

In an effort to control the running costs of the government, efforts were also focussed on understanding and developing plans to control public sector employment and the public sector wage bill. This issue was flagged as being of critical relevance to economic performance as the widely held view is that wage-to-GDP ratios that exceed 9% are typically associated with countries that have low rates of economic growth. Whilst wage freezes as were previously used to provide governments with time to contend with this issue, wage freezes without reforms in the underlying economic programme management will only result in sharp increases once employees are out of the freeze and demand adjustments to compensate for the high rates of inflation and other changes in their living standards that might have occurred during the period of the wage freeze. In order to get a handle on the potential dynamics that were driving this area of expenditure, the government set about undertaking a census of all posts across the public sector including the public bodies. This enabled the later construction of a comprehensive database of public sector employees, their emoluments, qualifications, skills and other attributes that can be used in strategic human resource management and planning that is useful to the public sector as it restructures itself.

Rules regarding hiring and firing of public sector worker, the contracting of debt through government guarantees and other implicit agreements that have a similar impact were designed and implemented. Finally, the government devised an action plan for the implementation of the planned transformation of the public sector. This was submitted to Parliament inclusive of a detailed timeline and indication of the areas that would generate the largest efficiency gains and was focussed on the plans to implement shared corporate services built on a platform of rich data and information in order to reduce the duplication of services such as human resource management and development, accounting and communication thereby increasing efficiencies and effectiveness of these functions for the government service.

A pilot was also to be developed and implemented in a two-parts that would support the building of a comprehensive database of all emoluments paid to employees in the Ministry of Finance, Health, Security and Education. The previously developed e-census database was to be updated and expanded to cover all employees in all ministries, departments and agencies. The employment policy of the government was to be developed using information arising from a review of public sector employment and remuneration that would be done as part of the 2013 EFF. Finally, there was a major reform of the government pension system which transitioned to a contributory defined benefit scheme in an effort to improve the funding of the system and was implemented on a phased basis during the transition period. In this regard, draft legislation was developed to facilitate this transformation of the pension system.

Another important dimension of the reform of the public financial management system was the implementation of a Central Treasury Management System (CTMS). This arose in response to the discovery that whilst central government attempted to address its time inconsistency problem—where tax revenues are not collected in the same time period and in the same dollar value as its current liabilities such as the payment of the salaries of teachers and nurses fall due—the government was borrowing at increasingly higher rates on the domestic market rather than utilising the surplus of cash available in the various bank accounts held by many public sector entities. With proper accounting of the stocks and flows, the preliminary analysis revealed that were this approach to be utilised, the government would have available to it surplus cash with which to meet the needs of both central government and each entity. Government's appetite to debt was unnecessarily crowding out the private sector and it's potential investment activity and driving up the cost of interest.

The CTMS was established to provide cash flow support to the central government whilst ultimately preserving institutional ownership over the funds as a means of smoothing out the timing issues between the collection of tax revenues and the maintenance of government expenses that come due almost daily. A major benefit of the CTMS is the reduction in the need for issuing government debt instruments to cover basic operational expenses as well as debt servicing costs. This project was initiated in the 2010 SBA and implementation continued throughout the 2013 EFF and provided an important pillar in the foundation to correct Jamaica's weak public financial management and fiscal deterioration identified in 2011 and 2004 World Bank Country Economic Memorandum as binding constraints to growth, respectively. Through the provisions of the 2013 EFF, the cash management function was transferred from the Fiscal Policy Management Unit of the Ministry of Finance to the Cash Management Unit in the Accountant General's Department (AGD). The transfer of these responsibilities was followed by the restructuring of the AGD to a new organizational structure and a training needs assessment was completed in order to identify the priorities needed by the staff that would be translated into a medium-term training program.

Further strides were made during the 2013 EFF in terms of the reform and strengthening of the financial sector. In order to modernize the financial sector, the government authorized the Bank of Jamaica to become the regulator for the entire system with the Financial Services Commission providing specialized regulation for the non-deposit-taking institutions and pensions. During the 2013 EFF, the Banking Services Act was passed and implemented to facilitate this effective supervision. Additional legislation and regulation were also passed in relation to the prohibition of unlawful financial operations and, instead, provisions were made to address the issues that prevent the introduction of Collective Investment Schemes through the list of appropriate legal and regulatory frameworks to facilitate their introduction into the landscape. The final component of the financial sector reform was the development of a framework for the resolution of entities in the sector in the event of systemic failure. The framework specified the responsibilities of each entity and stakeholder have clearly outlined as well as the legal structure for the resolution process.

Understanding the Precautionary Stand-By Agreement (PSBA)

The Stand-By Agreement (SBA) offered by the IMF was developed in 1952 as part of the tools that the Fund would extend to countries that needed financing support to address the balance of payments problems that tend to occur during an economic crisis. The SBA is to be a rapid response mechanism that countries can access to support their ability to emerge from a crisis and re-enter their economic growth cycle. Despite the fact that all member countries are eligible to access and utilize the SBA modality, the IMF reports that low-income countries typically opt to access concessional financing that is tailored to their individual needs and that the SBA is typically used by middle and high-income countries (International Monetary Fund, 2016b). Given that the SBA is intended to provide short-term support to countries with balance of payments problems, it is typically implemented over a period of twelve to twenty-four months but it can be extended up to a maximum of thirty-six months. The agreement terms are usually driven by the needs for financing, repayment capacity of the member and the extent to which previous agreements between the member and the Fund were discharged. The terms extended to member countries were improved in early 2016 as a result of the review of quotas that occurred during that year. The Fund can lend more than the newly approved limits in exceptional circumstances such as existed during the 2008 global economic and financial crisis based on the Exceptional Access Policy. The current SBA lending framework also facilitates increased front-loading of the funds approved for countries in the event that country conditions, depth of the financial need and the strength of the policies to be implemented throughout the programme justify such front-loading. As needed, countries can also access funds through the SBA on a rapid access basis through the IMF's Emergency Financing Mechanism.

The new framework of the SBA approved in 2016 revises the focus of the prior action and structural benchmarks of the programme. SBA programmes would typically focus on the objectives of the economic programme crafted by member countries and would minimize the number of conditions required for the review period. The overarching goal of SBAs is to support countries in their efforts at reforming the policies and practices that contributed to the deterioration or threat of deterioration due to external conditions. The revised framework significantly reduced the criteria used by the Fund to adjudge the performance of borrower members as the only performance criteria for SBAs would now be the quantitative programme targets that would be tied to disbursements from the Fund. Despite this, the Executive Board could decide to waive the targets as deemed necessary. Targets in this category typically include those relating to the level of the international reserves, fiscal deficits, the level of public sector borrowing and other critical variables that are programme contingent and can provide an indicator of the source of any variance from programme objectives due to operational or other changes. Importantly the new framework for the SBA has eliminated the need for countries to also satisfy structural performance criteria in exchange for the identification of structural benchmarks in critical policy areas that would indicate that policy and other organizational and operational reforms are proceeding according to plan and therefore that the economic programme is being supported by corrective measures to prevent regression once the agreement is concluded.

Revisions were also made in relation to the periodicity of programme reviews and this was made to be subject to the strength of the country's policies and the required financing based on the pace of programme implementation and any developments that may have arisen in the member's economy. Repayment of disbursed SBA funds is anticipated to be completed within five years of completion as repayment typically occurs 3¼ years after each disbursement is received. Lending rates are a composite of a market-determined interest rate based on the Special Drawing Rights with a minimum floFor of five basis points and a margin of 100 basis points along with a surcharge that increases as the time for which credit is outstanding increases.

A country with outstanding credit of more than 187.5% of quota after three years would attract a surcharge of 300 basis points—the intention being to discourage the granting of overly large programmes and the use of IMF programmes over extended periods. The Fund also charges commitment feeds on the amounts that can be drawn down during each twelve month period of the agreement at a rate of fifteen basis points for amounts up to 115% of a members' quota, 30 basis points on amounts between 115 and 575% of quota and 60 basis points on amounts in excess of 575% of quota. Fees can be refunded if a country utilizes the full amount committed by the Fund for its SBA, however, if portions of the committed amounts are not used then the commitment fees paid would not be refunded depending on the proportion that was unused. Additionally each amount drawn is subject to a fee of 50 basis points.

The final reform of the SBA was the development of a high-access precautionary arrangement (HAPA) that would provide insurance for members who may face a large financing requirement with a low probability. Typically, countries who participate in these Precautionary Stand-By Agreements (PSBA) do not intend to draw down the amounts that are approved however they are able to if the need arises. In obtaining an approval for a thirty-six month PSBA on 11 November 2016, Jamaica joined a handful of countries who had previously engaged in this type of agreement with the IMF. A recent review of the various programmes offered by the IMF indicated that given the precautionary nature of PSBAs, they tend to have fewer conditionalities that ordinary SBAs and they often rely more heavily on the quantitative aspects of the programme rather than prescribing the normal-sized slate of structural benchmarks (European Central Bank, 2019). Perhaps as a result of the combination of these three features, countries tend to have better compliance rates than under regular non-precautionary SBAs. The European Central Bank also indicates that countries that engage in PSBAs tend to have more stable rates of economic growth, lower than average levels of public debt and the size of the adjustment that countries have to make under the PSBA is typically small.

Table 9.1 indicates that seven countries had accessed the PSBA prior to Jamaica's agreement in 2016. Ukraine and the Republic of Croatia had received the PSBA in the pre-crisis period between 2004 and 2005 whilst Serbia and St. Kitts and Nevis had engaged the Fund in this regard between 2011 and 2013.

Only Georgia, Romania and Honduras obtained a PSBA in 2012, 2013 and 2014, respectively. During 2016, both Jamaica and Kenya accessed the PSBA. In each year up to 2019 only Greece, Argentina and The Republic of Armenia accessed the PSBA in 2017, 2018 and 2019, respectively. Over the period considered there was no discernible trend in the dollar value of the agreements although generally speaking, countries receiving the PSBA engaged the IMF for a period of two years. Eight of the twelve counties were able to maintain the precautionary nature of the agreement whilst four countries—St. Kitts, Georgia, Honduras and Argentina did utilize the funds allocated by the IMF. Of the four, Honduras's PSBA was also accompanied by a Standby Credit Facility (SCF).

Colombia entered into a two-year PSBA with the Fund on 15 January 2003 for 100% of its quota (International Monetary Fund, 2004a). At the third review of the programme,[1] Fund staff reported that the country's macroeconomic programme had demonstrated an out-turn that exceeded the forecasted targets. Growth in real GDP was recorded at 3.7% in 2003 and 3.8% during the first quarter of 2004 and the rates of inflation declined to 5.4 by May 2004. The staff also indicated that these results could be attributable to the very design of the programme at the outset to enable the economy to recover from the 1998 recession and to improve resilience to the impact of external shocks. The fiscal data indicates that the fiscal policy trajectory is consistent with the programme targets nevertheless there were concerns regarding the strengthening of the local peso that was feared could contribute to a slowdown in the growth of exports. There were also concerns regarding the interest rate

[1] Prior documents for the programme were not available on the Fund website at the date of writing.

Table 9.1 Countries qualifying for the IMF Precautionary Stand-By Agreement (PSBA) 2003–2020

					Context the countries were operating during the first year of agreement						
Countries with PSBA	*Agreement Period*	*Mon ths*	*Amount*	*Used*	*External debt-to-GDP (%)*	*Fiscal balance-GDP (%)*	*GDP growth (%)*	*Inflation (%)*	*Poverty (%)*	*Total debt-to-GDP (%)*	*Standby Credit Facility (SCF)*
Colombia	2003	24	1548m (SDR)	No	52	2.5	3.9	7.13	50.9	75.1	No
Paraguay	2003	15	50m (SDR)	No	44.9	−0.3	4.3	14.24	40.5	50	No
Republic of Croatia	2004 (successor to a failed 2003 PSBA)	20	US$137m	No	36	−5	4.2	2.06	11	41.7	No
Peru	2004	26	255m (SDR)	No	42	−2	5	3.66	51.6	46.74	No
Ukraine	2004	12	US$607m	No	32.514	−2.0	12.1	9.05	29.50	65	No
Paraguay	2006	27	$65m (SDR)	No	13.2	1.67	4.8	9.59	39.5	27.7	No
Peru	2007	25	172.37m (SDR)	No	28	3	8.5	1.78	41.1	31.87	No
Honduras	2008	12	38.85m (SDR)	No	16	1.5	4.2	11.4	49.9	22.32	No
Costa Rica	2009	15	US$740m	No	25.16	5.6	4.3	4.88	15	30	No
El Salvador	2009	15	US$800m	No	40	5.7	-2.1	0.54	42.8	58.14	No
Honduras	2010	18	129.5m (SDR)	No	17.2	2	3.7	4.7	43	23.55	Combined SCF

(continued)

Table 9.1 (continued)

					Context the countries were operating during the first year of agreement						
Countries with PSBA	*Agreement Period*	*Mon ths*	*Amount*	*Used*	*External debt-to-GDP (%)*	*Fiscal balance-GDP (%)*	*GDP growth (%)*	*Inflation (%)*	*Poverty (%)*	*Total debt-to-GDP (%)*	*Standby Credit Facility (SCF)*
Serbia	2011	18	€1b	No	75.6	4.9	2	12	6.8	96.36	No
St. Kitts & Nevis (2011 data)	2011	36	US$84.5m	Yes	105.32	5	1.8	5.84	21.8	135.02	No
Georgia (2014 data)	2012	24	US$387m	Yes	17.7	3.5	6.4	−0.94	19.2	31.26	No
Romania (2013 data)	2013	24	€1.98b	No	17.8	−2.1	3.5	4	31.2	43.3	No
Honduras (2016 data)	2014	36	US$188.6m	Yes	27.8	−0.4	3.6	2.73	66	48.7	Combined two year SCF 2014–2016
Jamaica	2016	36	US$1.64b	No	113.64	−0.19	1.4	2.35	17.1	122.7	No
Kenya	2016	24	US$709.3m	No	27.6	8.8	5.9	6.32	36.1	54.5	SCF combined 2016–2018
Greece	2017	12	€1.6b	No	181.8	0.7	1.5	1.2	4.40	224.1	No
Argentina	2018	36	US$50b	Yes	51.3	−5.5	−2.48	34	9.6	86.06	No
Republic of Armenia	2019	36	US$248.2m	No	50.07	0.5	7.6	1.44	22.2	83.3	No

Source Collated by Authors from: International Monetary Fund. (2019a). *Republic of Armenia: 2019 Article IV Consultation and Request for a Stand-by Arrangement*. Washington, DC: International Monetary Fund; International Monetary Fund. (2002, January 18). *Peru: Letter of Intent and Technical Memorandum of Understanding*. Retrieved from International Monetary Fund: https://www.imf.org/external/np/loi/2002/per/01/index.htm; International Monetary Fund. (2004a). *Colombia: Third Review under the Stand-by Arrangement and Request for a Waiver of Nonobservance of Performance Criterion*. Washington, DC: International Monetary Fund; International Monetary Fund. (2004b). *Paraguay: Request for Stand-By Arrangement—Staff Report*. Washington, DC: International Monetary Fund; International Monetary Fund. (2004c). *Peru: First Review under the Stand-By Arrangement and Requests for Modification of Performance Criterion and Waiver for Nonobservance of Performance Criterion*. Washington, DC: International Monetary Fund; International Monetary Fund. (2004d). *Republic of Croatia: 2004 Article IV Consultation and Request for Stand-By Arrangement*. Washington, DC: International Monetary Fund; International Monetary Fund. (2007). *Peru: 2006 Article IV Consultation and Request for Stand-by Arrangement—Staff Report*. Washington, DC: International Monetary Fund; International Monetary Fund. (2008). *Honduras: Request for Stand-By Arrangement—Staff Report*. Washington, DC: International Monetary Fund; International Monetary Fund. (2009). *El Salvador: Request for Stand-by Arrangement—Staff Report*. Washington, DC: International Monetary Fund; International Monetary Fund. (2010). *Honduras: Request for a Stand-By Arrangement and an Arrangement under the Standby Credit Facility*. Washington, DC: International Monetary Fund; International Monetary Fund. (2012, March 28). *Press Release: IMF Reaches Staff-Level Agreement with Georgia on Request for Stand-By Arrangement and Standby Credit Facility*. Retrieved from International Monetary Fund: https://www.imf.org/en/News/Articles/2015/09/14/01/49/pr12108; International Monetary Fund. (2013b). *Romania Request for a Stand-by Agreement*. Washington, DC: International Monetary Fund; International Monetary Fund. (2013c, May 20). *Serbia- 2013 Article IV Consultation Concluding Statement of the Mission*. Retrieved from International Monetary Fund: https://www.imf.org/en/News/Articles/2015/09/28/04/52/mcs052013b; International Monetary Fund. (2014a). *Honduras: Request for a Stand-by Arrangement and an Arrangement under the Stand-by Credit Facility*. Washington, DC: International Monetary Fund; International Monetary Fund. (2014b, March 7). *Press Release: IMF Executive Board Approves US$127.6 Million Extended Arrangement for Armenia*. Retrieved from International Monetary Fund Web site: https://www.imf.org/en/News/Articles/2015/09/14/01/49/pr1488; International Monetary Fund. (2015, February 2). *Press Release: IMF Executive Board Approves US$497.1 Million Stand-by Arrangement and US$191.2 Million Stand-by Credit Facility for Kenya*. Retrieved from International Monetary Fund: https://www.imf.org/en/News/Articles/2015/09/14/01/49/pr1529; International Monetary Fund. (2019b, May 6). *IMF and Honduras Reach Staff-Level Agreement on a Stand-by/Credit Facility Arrangement*. Retrieved from International Monetary Fund: https://www.imf.org/en/News/Articles/2019/05/06/pr19143-honduras-imf-reaches-staff-level-agreement-stand-by-credit-facility-arrangement; Ministry of Finance of Ukraine. (2020, September 15). *Ministry of Finance of Ukraine*. Retrieved from International Monetary Fund: https://mof.gov.ua/en/mvf

as well as capital flows leading to considerations about introducing capital controls. Despite these concerns, the likely out-turn for the 2004 fiscal year was viewed at the time of the third review to exceed the expectations under the programme particularly for growth in real GDP which was expected to be 4% in comparison to the 3.3 in the original programme document. Despite the expectation that potential risks could materialize due to the pending constitutional amendment campaign and follow-on presidential elections during 2006, Fund staff were confident that the authorities would have been capable of controlling fiscal policy on a sustainable path, implement budget, pensions and fiscal decentralization reforms in a sustainable manner and they were in support of the authorities request for a waiver of their non-observance of performance criteria, the completion of the third review of the SBA and allowance of multiple currency practices.

Paraguay experienced 0% economic growth during the six-year period between 1997 and 2002 that has been attributed to a number of issues including a political administration that was not duly elected and therefore had difficulty in achieving consensus to implementing any needed of the well-needed changes in the policies and frameworks of the government (International Monetary Fund, 2004b). Other governance-related issues such as dealing with corruption, transparency, property rights and taxation tended to be difficult to implement and enforce. There were also a series of banking crises dating back to 1995 that left significant levels of non-performing loans in the system that was complicated by the dollarization of the economy. There are threats to the fiscal accounts due to the fact that public enterprises control the majority of the public utilities, which were operating suboptimally and at a loss, were providers of transportation, electricity and water inter alia making it impossible for them to be closed or brought under reasonable control. The private sector was also battling with the issue of declining and low levels of productivity due to issues relating to the formation of human capital and sectoral inefficiencies associated with the structure of various tax expenditures. Finally, poverty and unemployment were high without an adequate social protection system to support life whilst persons attempt to create a livelihood. According to the International Monetary Fund (2004b), the economy eventually entered the deepest recession of its history until that point as a result of a combination of a regional crisis, poor performance in the agriculture sector and inadequate economic policies to support domestic activity. As a result there was a decline in real GDP of 2.5%, inflation rates of 14%, depreciation of the local currency by 34% and the collapse of its then third-largest bank resulting in capital outflows.

The PSBA was granted in 2003 as a result of the improvements in various aspects of Paraguay's economic and governance climate in the wake of the implementation of a newly elected president whose legitimacy enabled the implementation of critical reforms that tackled corruption successfully, initiated the reform of the critical public sector institutions, as well as a series of laws that reformed the structure of the economy and fiscal policy inclusive of customs. Turnarounds in agricultural output and restoration of the economic activity across the region facilitated a return to growth, appreciation of the currency and improved reserves at the central banks and buoyancy in bank deposits. Fund staff was therefore supportive of the reform agenda that had the potential to set the Paraguayan economy on the right footing in the medium term and the staff supported two extensions on the agreement that was to end in March 2005.

Peru entered into a twenty-six month PSBA for 21% of its annual quota or SDR287.279m on 9 June 2004 (International Monetary Fund, 2004c). The 2004 PSBA followed a previous 24 month PSBA negotiated on 18 January 2002 for SDR255m or 20% of its annual quota (International Monetary Fund, 2002). This prior PSBA was expected to generate adequate resources to support debt servicing of external debt on time. Prior to this, Peru had weathered significant uncertainty and disruptions due to El Nino weather, changes in trade terms due to the negative impact of the Asian crisis on demand for Peruvian products by Asian countries; and other external shocks to critical areas of its economy. Complicating the impact of these shocks was the domestic turmoil associated with the removal of the country's president and the installation of an interim government. The economic environment was somewhat stagnant during this period with real GDP growing by 1% between 1998 and 2000 and inflation was below 4%. The financial sector was weakened during the period as non-performing loans doubled, the profitability of the institutions declined and the availability of credit to the private sector declined.

There was also an associated deterioration in the fiscal accounts and the balance previously recorded in the public sector accounts became a deficit of 3.2% of GDP in 2000, 1.2 percentage points higher than permitted under the fiscal responsibility legislation. There was also pressure on the reserves at the central bank however they were still sufficiently comfortable to cover short-term needs if necessary. The programme implemented by the interim government during the year 2000 was also supported by an SBA with the IMF to help support the efforts at restoring macroeconomic stability ahead of the installation of a new government. The 2000 SBA was implemented successfully as all targets were met and the initiatives to support structural reforms were implemented. Despite this, the economic out-turn was not as strong as anticipated and the new government attempted to jump-start economic activity through a tax-relief driven and labour market enhancing stimulus package. Despite this, there were only moderate changes in the economic activity during the first half of the year however in the second half the sluggishness in the key indicators returned. As a result, the Fund provided support to the country through an SBA in the last quarter of 2000 with a goal of establishing the enabling environment to facilitate high growth rates in the medium term. The structural reforms to be implemented included measures to address inefficiencies in the productive process, measures to increase investment from the private sector, and controlling the need for borrowing by the public sector. Importantly, the government planned to reform the tax system to provide it with the neutrality and equity through reforms of both policy and administration (International Monetary Fund, 2002).

The Republic of Croatia is the only country in the sample to have received two consecutive PSBAs in 2003 and 2004 despite the 2003 agreement having not been successfully completed (International Monetary Fund, 2004d). Whilst there was relatively strong economic growth and low inflation between the mid-1990s however the continued gap between savings and investment and the large current account deficits and build-up of foreign debt led to a crisis arising from a demand boom fuelled by credit. The 2003 PSBA's derailing was attributed to the changes in fiscal policy arising from the campaign leading up to the late November elections during 2003 which resulted in a waning of government buy-in to the programme. The successor 2004 PSBA was developed to provide SDR97m over twenty months intended to support the country reform process as it navigated accession into the European Union (EU). The 2004 PSBA continued the programmes of the 2003 agreement alongside new fiscal policy measures that were designed to implement the necessary measures to support the Republic's entry into the EU. Measures included thrusts to ensure the transparency of the budget, a curtailing of the lending by the Croatian Development Bank, the introduction of a single treasury account, improvements in the area of debt management, the development of a medium-term fiscal framework in addition to the usual SBA terms relating to the government deficit and indicative ceilings on borrowing. The programme would be supported by 26.6% of the country's quota with the IMF over seven tranches and is perhaps an indication of the low likelihood that the authorities would draw down on the allocated amount regardless of which Fund staff indicated their perception that even if Croatia was to access the resources that it would be able to repay any amounts used.

With respect to Ukraine, the authorities had decided to continue to engage them on a precautionary basis because of its very positive economic performance due to a series of successful relationships between 1994 and 2002. The plan was to use the PSBA as a bridge to resume active borrowing from the Fund later on in the decade whilst also providing insurance to the turn of 30% of the Ukraine's quota in the event that there was pressure on the country's balance of payments. However, the authorities did not adhere to the terms of the agreement and the agreement was therefore suspended until it expired at the end of March 2005. The authorities decided to proceed for the next three years on a technical assistance programme with the Fund (Ministry of Finance of Ukraine, 2020). Despite this, sharp declines in export prices and weak global demand, sent Ukraine back to the IMF and they were able to secure an SBA in November of 2008 for 802% of its quota and the global financial crisis only worsened the economic crisis forcing a renegotiation of the agreement in 2010.

In the immediate wake of the global financial and economic crisis, the Serbian authorities inked a deal with the IMF for a PSBA that would support the economy in its perceived nascent recovery from the crisis. The authorities were able to secure SDR935m under an 18 month precautionary programme with the Fund. The authorities did not think there would be any need to draw on the funds based on the anticipated positive improvements in the performance of the economy. Whilst there was some recovery it was short-lived and the Serbian economy would be plunged into a recession by 2012 due to a combination of negative shocks as well as alterations to the fiscal trajectory as a result of election pressures. State-owned banks received capital injections from the public purse and expansionary fiscal decentralization caused an escalation in the fiscal deficit. In its statement arising from the concluding mission with the authorities, the Fund concluded that the outlook for Serbia was one that was dependent on the revitalization of its agriculture sector that would contribute to the achievement of the targeted inflation band (International Monetary Fund, 2013c). Mission staff indicated that the direction of policy over the medium term will determine the extent to which growth would recover. In particular, there was the need for definitive and fundamental changes in the conduct of fiscal policy and the management of the public finances in order to reset the current imbalances, restore confidence and enhance the country's growth potential. Fiscal policy, monetary policy and structural reform had to work together to ensure the correction of the underlying problems in the economy. Nevertheless, the external conditions could disturb the growth trajectory even if policies were properly implemented and private sector fallout could still be possible.

Peru explored the parameters for a second PSBA during an October 2006 mission with Fund staff that was intended to provide support for its economic programme for the fiscal year 2007/2008 (International Monetary Fund, 2007). The PSBA would provide support for the programme over a 25 month period and would provide 27% on the country's quota with the Fund. The planned programme for the fiscal year was based on four main pillars. The authorities intended to consolidate their previous efforts at establishing macroeconomic stability by: maintaining the fiscal targets below the ceiling of 1% as established in the Fiscal Responsibility and Transparency Law; reducing distortionary taxes and exemptions; improving the quality of public expenditure; and, attempting to infuse more flexibility in the framework used to target inflation. The second priority was the intention to firmly address high rates of poverty by restructuring the existing social assistance programmes and improving their effectiveness. The pursuit of dollarization would be reduced with particular emphasis on the mortgage loan market in order to improve the banking system's ability to be resilient. The fourth and final pillar was the intention of the government to reform regulatory requirements towards a simplified regime, support the flexibility of the labour market and to ensure that economy was opened even further to international trade. Fund staff supported the programme as Peru had implemented sound policies that had been paying dividends and the positive global environment proved favourable for the Peruvian economy as it experienced the longest period of economic growth to that date. Nevertheless, Fund staff was cognizant of the impending challenges that would need to be navigated by the authorities and were therefore supportive of the granting of the PSBA especially given the fact that the political administration was newly elected but still committed to achieving the targets identified.

In 2009, the government of Costa Rica requested a 15 month PSBA that would provide a total of SDR492.3m or 300% of quota to support its implementation of an adjustment programme that would support its ability to cope with the emergent harsh external environment whilst it attempted to safeguard its potentially negative impacts on the rates of economic growth and household level incomes. In response to the deterioration of the external environment, the country's monetary authorities had restricted the money supply and facilitated the ability of the exchange rate to adjust. The goal of fiscal policy will be to continue to mitigate the impact of the adjustment process that was underway on the robustness of domestic activity with emphasis on the most vulnerable groups. The support provided by the IMF under the PSBA would be used to instill stability in the domestic financial market to reassure investor confidence in the programme outlined by the authorities and release additional monetary flows from other multilateral that will provide a stock of foreign exchange liquidity—as a substitute for the potential reduction in foreign direct investment flows as well as reductions in tourist visits and associated expenditures as well as reductions exports—that would help to cushion the potential impact on the balance of payments and support the move to make the exchange rate more flexible. The Fund staff opined that the Costa Rican economy was likely to return to its medium-term growth path of approximately 4.5% growth rates after the year 2010 whilst the current account deficit would decline to 5.5% of GDP. In order to support this strategy, financial support under the PSBA would be front-loaded to the authorities with two-thirds being available upon approval of the agreement and more than 200% of the country's quota being available within twelve months of the agreement. Nevertheless the authorities would be alert to the risks associated with deeper shocks to the balance of payments, tax revenues and GDP growth rates that were far lower than had been projected and delays by the legislative assembly in approving access to the supplementary financial flows from the other international financial institutions.

Similar to Costa Rica, the El Salvadorian economy was being negatively impacted by the global economic and financial crisis in 2009 which was compounded by issues relating to their pending elections as well as the impact of the downturn in the economy of the United States. In an effort to shore up the liquidity of their banking systems, the government negotiated a PSBA for SDR513.9m or 300% of quota through a high-access arrangement that would also support confidence in the domestic financial sector by both investors and depositors (International Monetary Fund, 2009). Fund support would thereby enable the authorities to reduce uncertainty in the strength, validity and sufficiency of the economic and other efforts to reform the society on the heels of election that appointed a new administration. The main pillars of the programme were to ensure the implementation of sufficient measures to provide contingencies to the financial system issues through keen monitoring of system indicators relating to short-term borrowing and the liquidity positions of the banks. Controls would also be placed on the operations of the nonfinancial public sector to reign in the deficits to below 2.8% of GDP and the authorities would implement additional expenditure on social issues and infrastructure development by creating fiscal space through the elimination of subsidies on non-residential electricity consumption and if they were able to secure additional support from the international financial institutions. Finally there would be reforms to improve the regulation and supervision of the financial sector and improve the resilience of the banking sector to shocks. The programme would be able to provide support to help calm the financial markets as it would provide front-loaded and exceptional access to 200% of the country's quota upon approval of the agreement and the remainder allocated equally over the remainder of the period. It is notable that El Salvador had four SBAs between May 1993 and February 2000 all of which had been treated as precautionary and supported a range of programmes intended to restore economic growth through a series of reforms aimed at macroeconomic stability. The agreements were reportedly for small amounts (less than 40% of quota) and would enable the authorities to maintain macroeconomic discipline and implement structural reforms. The programme was approved on 16 January 2009 for a fourteen and a half month period and would provide SDR513.9m to El Salvador.

The Republic of Georgia engaged in a twenty-four month combined SBA and Standby Credit Facility (SCF) with the Fund on 28 March 2012 for a combined SDR250m in total and both components were intended to be treated as precautionary (International Monetary Fund, 2012). They were granted access to this combination financing option because they had successfully completed a thirty-three month SBA that had focussed on the establishment of economic stabilization, restarting economic growth and promoting the necessary fiscal adjustment. This agreement expired in June 2011. The performance was stronger under the 2011 SBA and during 2011 there was real GDP growth of 7%, single digit inflation, and, government debt to-GDP was 34% and the net international reserves were at a record US$2.8b. Nevertheless, changes in the world economy created significant uncertainties in the market exacerbated the vulnerabilities in the economy and was anticipated to lead to a reduction in growth rates to 6% and continued low inflation. In order to reduce the scale of these vulnerabilities the 2012 PSBA/SCF was intended to shore up the buffers for the fiscal account, support Georgia's adjustment to the changes in the external environment, restore confidence within the markets and act as a basis for the government to benefit from complementary resource mobilization from official sources. The authorities remained committed to the maintenance of a flexible exchange rate and rooting of monetary policy in the pursuit of price stability. There was also a commitment to implement sector-specific policies that would help to reduce the problems regarding high unemployment and the current account deficit when combined with the overall economic programme to maintain macroeconomic stability. In the concluding mission, it was noted that despite the faithfulness of the government in implementing the programme, external events led to a lower than programmed growth rate which inevitably constrained growth and required measures to ensure the budget deficit was maintained. This was accomplished by curtailing administrative expenditures that were complemented by specific increases of specific tax types.

Having successfully completed a twenty-seven month SBA, the Government of Romania requested a twenty-four month SBA for 170% of its quota that it intended to have access to on a precautionary basis (International Monetary Fund, 2013b). The authorities simultaneously obtained the support of two billion euros from the European Union and one billion was being provided through a policy loan from the World Bank. This substantial array of funds was being provided because of Romania's high degree of vulnerability to external shocks despite the fact that it had accumulated fiscal buffers and corrected imbalances in the macroeconomy. These shocks were associated with the issues in the Euro area particularly as it relates to capital flows that impact emerging markets more severely than others. The substantial financial support for the Romanian economic programme was meant to provide a policy anchor and support for the continued implementation of its reform agenda for the

2013–2015 period. The PSBA was also to empower Romania to so establish its economic foundations so that they will not need support from the Fund. As with other SBAs, the programme pillars are: reforms of the fiscal institutions and systems; expansion of buffers based on monetary and fiscal reform; public sector process reforms to enhance the country's ability to grow.

Honduras secured staff-level agreement to three successive PSBAs with the IMF between 7 April 2008 and 3 December 2014 (European Central Bank, 2019). The first two of the three PSBAs valued at only 30 and 100% of quota, respectively, went off-track and the second and third PSBAs that followed were enhanced by an SCF. The first PSBA was intended to provide a bridge until the planned access to the Fund's Poverty Reduction and Growth Facility (PRGF). The last of the three PSBAs spanned a three-year period in contrast to the previous two-year agreements and was designed as a successor to the second failed PSBA. The 2008 programme was aimed at supporting fiscal strengthening in order to support monetary focus on the inflation targeting and containing credit growth to reduce the emergence of a credit bubble (International Monetary Fund, 2008). The PSBA would have provided substantial financing and the gap could have been covered by the concessional flows that would be available through the PRGF. The 2010 programme added the authority's intent to place added emphasis on the operating accounts of public sector entities in order to further enhance the strength of the fiscal reforms previously implemented. The programme—which was blended with a SCF—was meant to enhance investor confidence and mobilize additional resources to support financial flows within the programme in order to reduce instability and provide sufficient foreign exchange flows (International Monetary Fund, 2010). As a result of a softening of the fiscal accounts between 2011 and 2013 due to slippages in government spending and significant deficits at the state-owned electricity company. Macroeconomic policies were also expansionary and the balance of payments had also deteriorated. As a result, the 2014 blended PSBA/SCF was scheduled to provide support over three years and would provide SDR129.5m (International Monetary Fund, 2014a). A significant portion of the programme effort was to be focussed on correcting the fiscal affairs of the country with other emphasis on shoring up support for the social protection system, the monetary and exchange rate, the financial sector, and, other reforms that had significant positive fiscal implications.

These three programmes were then followed by the most recent agreement approved by staff on 6 May 2019 (International Monetary Fund, 2019b). The PSBA would be blended with the Standby Credit Facility and provide a total of SDR224.8m or 90% of quota to support the economic programme outlined by the authorities to ensure macroeconomic stability through reforms of their public electricity company and to enhance investment and financing of the social safety net in a context of fiscal sustainability. Improvements in the area of governance and ensuring that the business environment was one which fostered economic growth that was not only sustainable but also inclusive were important planks of the planned economic agenda. Reforms were implemented to enable the creation of more fiscal space whilst maintaining the prescriptions of the fiscal responsibility legislation. In order to ensure that these reforms impact the poor and vulnerable positively, the focus on controlling inflation at low levels was to be the focus of monetary policy along with ensuring that adequate international reserves are maintained and the entire financial sector would be strengthened through the implementation of a wide range of market development activities aimed at improving the efficacy of inflation control and thereby strengthen the ability of the monetary authorities to effectively and credibly transition to the increasingly popular inflation targeting modality of operations. In addition, regulatory systems would be strengthened and reoriented to encompass the recommended macroprudential framework to prevent systematic contagion and therefore improve the resilience of the financial sector.

Kenya's PSBA received staff-level approval on 2 February 2015 and was combined with a Standby Credit Facility for SDR352.82m and SDR135.6m, respectively, representing 180% of Kenya's quota in the Fund (International Monetary Fund, 2015). It was designed to be a one year provision and to provide a visible policy anchor that would support the authority's continued effort at reforms to the macroeconomic structure, the implementations of various reforms relating to institutions, reducing the potential impact of exogenous shocks on the society through various mitigation efforts. The programme developed by the authorities was anticipated to support their efforts at maintaining their record of strong economic growth and the results of their efforts at reducing poverty. Although the IMF had authorized that an amount of SDR379.96 is made available to the authorities immediately, the authorities expressed their intention to treat the entire amount on a precautionary basis and that they would only initiate a drawdown in the event that external shocks generate a significant gap in the balance of payments. The fiscal reforms were concentrated in areas that would strengthen public financial management as they included the intention to implement a central treasury management system to smooth out cash flow challenges, specifying policy parameters for local counties that wish to engage in borrowing, and ensuring that all contingent liability are subject to intense surveillance in order to suppress the emergence of any fiscal risks during the period. In terms of monetary policy the focus would remain on maintaining control of inflation by paying close attention to the potential for pressure to arise from credit expansion that could be spurred in a low inflation environment and also one in which investments in infrastructure was planned. Regulators would also be using the time to improve the scope and scale of their regulatory regime by expanding prudential oversight with particular emphasis being placed on the area of rules relating to bank capital, enhancements of the system for conducting stress-tests for the financial sector and significantly improving the ability of the domestic regulators to interface with their international counterparts in order further strengthen the quality of the regulatory system as well as affirm the soundness of domestic banks.

Grecian authorities were able to secure a three-year PSBA with the IMF providing 1.6b euros—approximately 55% of quota—for the one-year period July 1, 2017 to 31 August 2018. The approval was initially granted in principle as it was subject to the receipt of credible assurances that the rest of Europe would support debt sustainability in Greece as well as the maintenance of progress to programme targets. Measures included an expansion of the base of the income tax system and implementing critical reforms to the pension systems as these were determined to be critical to the needed transformation of the fiscal accounts and necessary to enable sustainable growth in GDP. This was indicated alongside the need to protect the vulnerable groups in the society within the context of maintaining fiscal discipline whilst also ensuring that the burden of the reforms were shared fairly. The financial sector was also scheduled for reform in order to ensure that it could restore credit availability and therefore facilitate and support economic growth. The changes would address the legal framework within which non-performing loans were addressed as well as the broad regulatory framework for capital, supervision, asset quality and bank capitalization. The Fund programme, nevertheless, was understood to be insufficient to provide sustainability and would require the provision of support from the rest of Europe and therefore the Fund's support was contingent on the settling of this type of agreement.

Argentina's PSBA lasted between 2018 and 2020 for US$50bn and was the only country in this review to have utilized its allocation. The Argentinian authorities indicated that they would have accessed the first tranche and leave the remainder of the financing as precautionary. The authorities had approached the Fund because of their declining rates of economic growth, double digit inflation and the more than 50% decline in the value of their domestic currency to the US dollar in the first eight months of 2018. This sharp decline in the value of their currency was due to the negative effect of a drought on agricultural production simultaneous with high global energy prices and tight global financial conditions that would negatively interact with the large external financing and fiscal gaps faced by the authorities. The end-result was market pressure on the domestic currency, fears relating to the possible treatment of outstanding central bank paper, and, increases in the risk premium associated with Argentina. The objective of their three-year SBA was to support the strengthening of the economy in an effort to restore confidence in the markets and to enable the authorities to reduce the country's debt levels. The agreement provided Argentina with a veritable arsenal to restore confidence and settle the markets to the tune of over UD$50bn which is reputedly the largest loan in this history of the Fund. This translated 1110% of Argentina's quota and SDR35.379b. The immediate amount that Argentina was allowed to purchase was US$15bn of which one-half was to be used to support the budget at the outset. The other dimensions of the economic programme included the transition to a macroeconomic programme that provides clear indicators of a sustainable decline in the debt, reduced inflation through the setting of more realistic inflation targets, and re-establishing the central bank's independence. The programme also addresses the issue of social protection as it enabled the government to continue its social sector spending with a provision to increase the allocation if there was a deterioration in the social indicators. Argentina had to restore the internal consistency of its inflation targeting regime by providing credible targets, strengthening the independence of the central bank and terminating central bank financing of government expenditure.

The Republic of Armenia secured board approval for its 2019 PSBA on May 17 of that year for an amount of SDR180m or approximately 139.75% of quota (International Monetary Fund, 2019a). The Republic had maintained the economic and financial stability that had been supported in the previous 2014–2017 EFF programme valued at 89% of quota that was focussed on engendering a revitalization in the economy and thereby contribute to poverty reduction, inflation stabilization and increased fiscal and external resilience (International Monetary Fund, 2014b). The PSBA was designed to provide support to the authorities as they attempted to further improve their economic foundations including policy reform as well as changes that would help them to enhance their enabling environment for business as well as their governance. Fund staff supported the agreement because the authorities had been successful in maintaining the necessary conditions of macroeconomic and financial sector stability whilst simultaneously promoting economic growth through a range of structural reforms. The PSBA was approved for three years and would support reforms in the area of tax administration and the modernization of the country's property tax; strengthen the effectiveness of monetary policy in order to enable them to retain support of their medium-term inflation target; enhance the safeguards available for the financial system whilst developing capital markets and access to finance thereby enabling the emergence of a more inclusive economy.

Jamaica's 2016 PSBA

During a mission to Kingston between 21 and 30 September 2016, Jamaican authorities and the staff of the IMF arrived at an agreement where the Fund would continue to support the country's economic programme in the form of a PSBA for 312% of quota or approximately SDR1.2b or US$1.7b over a 36 month period (International Monetary Fund, 2016c). The economic programme was intended to provide insurance in the event that external shocks arose that jeopardized the balance of payments beyond what was available from domestic resources. Whilst the previous two agreements—the 2010 SBA and 2013 EFF—contained prior actions that had to be implemented before the programme was fully approved and disbursements made, the 2016 PSBA was not preceded by any prior actions. Comments during the board discussion of the Jamaica programme noted the commendable efforts and now track record established by Jamaica in terms of the demonstration of programme ownership and commitment to implementation under the 2013 EFF (International Monetary Fund, 2016c). The board was informed that Jamaica had successfully entrenched macroeconomic stability—long sought-after milestone—as inflation was low and under control, there were adequate reserves and reductions in the current account deficit. Importantly, there was evidence that the companion levels of fiscal discipline and proper debt management were being adhered to and overall public sector debt was sustainably on a downward path. Despite these accomplishments the board considered the continued low growth environment in the context of relatively high rates of poverty as well as unemployment with attendant issues of high crime and violence.

The IMF Resident Representative, Constant Lonkeng Ngouana wrote an Op-ed on the successes of the EFF as being emblematic of the macroeconomic stability that has settled fears about uncertainty in the domestic and international markets about the credibility of the reform agenda outlined by the Government of Jamaica (Ngouana, 2016). He pointed to the ability of the authorities to have doubled the amount of international reserves over the thirty-six month period of the EFF as a major indicator of the success of the EFF and interprets this as removing the need for continued borrowing from the IMF to support its balance of payments. Ngouana (2016) notes that this achievement has enabled the government to graduate to a programme arrangement in which the financing available from the IMF is merely precautionary and therefore will only act as protection in the event that some unforeseen or particularly volatility-generating shock were to emerge and disrupt the trajectory of the economic programme. Despite the fact that the country had not planned to utilize the funds made available under the successor 2016 PSBA, the Res Rep noted that the insurance was useful for SIDS such as Jamaica that was vulnerable to a wide range of disasters and shocks, and that Jamaica would have to maintain sound policies in three key areas—fiscal, monetary and exchange rate policy—that are consistent with the overall reform agenda proposed by the government. The other indicator of this elevated status is the fact that the newly approved PSBA would only be reviewed semi-annually in contrast to the quarterly reviews under the regular SBA or EFF modalities. Finally, the cumulative funds that would be available under the PSBA were double what was allocated under the EFF.

The 2016 PSBA was focussed on supporting the government in its attempt to make substantive progress on reform of the monetary policy and financial sector frameworks as well as in the area of public sector transformation. The monetary policy framework had to be reformed through the tabling of a new Bank of Jamaica Act to acknowledge the fundamental and explicit change in policy to inflation targeting, changes in the mandate of the bank to include financial supervision, the transformation of the bank into a super-regulator of the entire financial sector and changes in the governance framework at the board level. These changes represent a significant transformation of the policy landscape and pave the way for the independence of the central bank subject to proper capitalization of the balance sheet and settling of sundry outstanding balances with the Ministry of Finance. Complementarily, there would also be the operationalization of the Financial System Stability Committee to provide additional levels of oversight for the financial system. There were also to be advances in the area of financial inclusion through the establishment of a commission that would implement the activities in this area that had been approved by the Cabinet.

The public sector reform agenda was centred around restoring control in the expenditure and debt profiles of all of the government with particular emphasis on public bodies. In particular, the permitted stock of arrears for public bodies would be limited to a maximum of J$6.4b focussing on the major debt or deficit creating public bodies. Performance of these public bodies in this area would be monitored and reported to the Fund on a monthly basis. Several entities were scheduled to be closed due to the fact that the entities no longer played a role in the current strategic focus of the government as well as the fact that several had been out of operation for periods of time. Legislative changes were to be effected to channel earmarked funds from revenue-generating public bodies such as the Tourism Enhancement Fund and the CHASE Fund to the central government's Consolidated Fund. The government also intended to make changes to the operational status of some public bodies by changing those that could be reintegrated into central government where this proved consistent with good-practice in public financial management. Mergers were also to be effected for the HEART/NTA, Jamaica Foundation for Lifelong Learning and the National Youth Service. In a bid to reduce operationalize costs, duplication of functions across multiple organizations in the public sector and to improve overall operational efficiencies, the government intended to implement shared corporate services based. This would be preceded by an identification of the currently staffed positions that would be impacted by the implementation of shared corporate services in the area of human resource management, public relations and communications and internal audit and to support the affected workers with opportunities for training.

Beyond this, the government also intended to build a comprehensive database of the various occupations in government along with information relating to pay and other dimensions of emoluments across the entire public sector but with a strategic focus on the Ministries of Health, Education and the Police Groups that constitute approximately 60% of total employment in government as well as the staff across the Ministry of Finance and the Public Service. This database would then enable strategic human resource deployment, post upgrading, upskilling and other decisions that would be difficult in its absence. Complementing this was the intended creation of clear, unambiguous rules to guide the Post Operations Committee that would be required to opine on all types of employment status and decisions in the public sector including the appointment of persons to act in a post. The Committee was intended to control the rate of employment whilst simultaneously ensuring that the public sector is properly resourced. Any persons opting for early retirement would be prohibited from being rehired in the public sector for at least five years after such retirement unless they repay any incentive payments provided. Simultaneously, rules and standards were to be developed to limit the continued hiring of persons being employed post-retirement in all capacities inclusive of contractual workers. The system of performance-based pay was to be reviewed with a view to developing a medium-term policy and an associated implementation plan to better and more meaningfully align the pay with the performance. Overall, the government intended to implement specific rules for hiring, promotion and exit from the public sector. As far as compensation in the public sector is concerned, there was an intention to develop a framework within which the government and public sector workers would negotiate wage adjustments.

When combined, the Jamaican authorities hoped that these reforms would enable them to consolidate significant gains that would then facilitate increased expenditure on infrastructure, social protection and increased provision of security. The Economic Growth Council would also play an important role in the anticipated programme that would provide a fillip to growth and increased employment through private sector jobs. Most notably, the Fund expressed its anticipation of a productive engagement and support for the government's reform programme.

Conclusion

Jamaica's journey to the PSBA represents a story of triumph over a significant reform agenda to correct decade long gaps in policy and administration as well as to modernize operational aspects of the public sector in order to simplify the ease of doing business for individuals and the private sector as well as to increase the efficiency and effectiveness of policy decisions. The road began with national disquiet about the certain impending doom of the then newly elected administration utter the words 'International Monetary Fund' (see Clarke & Nelson, 2020). Over time, public commentators opined on the transformation of the Fund to being more sensitive to the needs of authorities to support vulnerable groups during periods of economic reform, ensuring that the burdens created by reforms were equitably shared and allowing authorities to make their own decisions regarding timing and other dimensions of the structural reforms intended to correct long-standing constraints to economic development and growth (see Chapter 4 in this volume). Although the country successfully re-engaged with the IMF in the form of a 27 month SBA in 2010 by completing all prior actions and three reviews, fiscal slippages arose due to the inordinate pressure on the authorities to honour commitments made by the previous administration as well as on the campaign trail to three main employee groups in the public sector that comprise over 60% of public sector employees. These unprogrammed and unapproved payments by the government contravened the underlying tenets of the agreement and led to a suspension of the review and disbursement schedule (see Clarke & Nelson, 2020). Complicating events in the political arena gave rise to distractions that also delayed programme implementation and undermined the credibility and authority of the implementation of the reform agenda.

This reform agenda was revived after a protracted period—more than twelve months—of negotiations and a change in the political administration. The succeeding EFF of 2013 did not follow the level of front-loading of resources afforded under the previous agreement the reform agenda was front-loaded in an attempt to escalate the positive benefits arising from its implementation (International Monetary Fund, 2013a). The authorities had to demonstrate that there was a higher degree of commitment to the full implementation of the complete programme agreed upon with the Fund. Whilst there was a successful implementation of the 2013 EFF programme from the start, the true test of the validity of the reform agenda and commitment of the Jamaican government were embodied in its continued implementation after a change of government in 2016. This demonstrates the high degree of ownership of the programme by country authorities and cemented the partnership between the Government of Jamaica and the IMF. After more than two decades of aloof indifference from Jamaica that had chosen to engage with the international capital markets that had since been closed to developing countries due to the global economic and financial crisis, the IMF could join with the government in true celebration of the strides that had been made in fostering a true partnership with Jamaica and successfully administering the economic reform programme. Supporting the administration in accessing and completing its first ever PSBA in 2016 was a landmark moment for Fund staff and the Executive Board of the IMF. The biggest signal of this is the historic visit of the IMF Managing Director—Madame Christine Lagarde—to Jamaica where she made visits that included the academic community along with the usual technical, political, private sector and trade union stakeholders. The visit was highly publicized and was accompanied by the publication of a volume on improving.

At the closing mission for the PSBA, the Fund and authorities issued a joint statement noting that the successful completion of the agreement reflected the commitment of the authorities to establishing and maintaining economic independence through the establishment of 'a home-grown' programme of economic reform that has generated significant gains in the form of lower rates of unemployment, reductions in taxes, high levels of business confidence and low inflation, with economic conditions combining to create US$3.5b of reserves (*The Jamaica Observer*, 2019a). Despite these gains, the mission indicated the need for the authorities to address the long-standing issue of crime and other dimensions of human and social capital such as the quality of education and health care and to improve the resilience of the agricultural sector. In order to enable the vulnerable populations to maintain their livelihoods during this process, the authorities indicated their intention to continue to maintain and possibly expand the social safety net offerings. Other priorities signalled by the government included continued efforts at public sector transformation with a focus on improving service delivery and effective compensation for public sector employees. The creation of strong fiscal institutions—such as the fiscal council—and the reinforcement of the strength of the financial sector through finalizing the regulatory and statutory authorities of the BOJ and FSC—will be important components of the success of the economic independence that has been won (*The Jamaica Observer*, 2019b). Prime Minister Holness admonished his colleague Ministers and leaders in government to ensure that fiscal discipline and fiscal responsibility are both now characteristics of the culture of government that would enable the continued implementation of the ambitious reform agenda planned for the upcoming fiscal years (*The Jamaica Gleaner*, 2019). Would Jamaica break from the commitment made by the Minister of Finance (Campbell, 2018) that Jamaica would not seek another borrowing relationship with the IMF once the PSBA had been successfully completed? Has the economy and society developed sufficient resilience and buffers to contend with any potential external shocks due to its nascent economic independence? This resolve would be tested within half-a-year of the closure of the PSBA and Chapter 11 provides insight into the economic programme in 2020.

References

Campbell, E. (2018, April 11). Jamaica should avoid going back to the IMF—Clarke. *The Jamaica Gleaner*.

Clarke, C., & Nelson, C. (2020). *Contextualising Jamaica's relationship with the IMF*. Cham: Palgrave Macmillan.

European Central Bank. (2019). *Conditionality and design of IMF-supported programmes* (Occasional Paper Series No. 235). Frankfurt: European Central Bank.

International Monetary Fund. (2002, January 18). *Peru: Letter of Intent and Technical Memorandum of Understanding*. Retrieved from International Monetary Fund: https://www.imf.org/external/np/loi/2002/per/01/index.htm.

International Monetary Fund. (2004a). *Colombia: Third Review under the Stand-by Arrangement and Request for a Waiver of Nonobservance of Performance Criterion*. Washington, DC: International Monetary Fund.

International Monetary Fund. (2004b). *Paraguay: Request for Stand-By Arrangement—Staff Report*. Washington, DC: International Monetary Fund.

International Monetary Fund. (2004c). *Peru: First Review under the Stand-By Arrangement and Requests for Modification of Performance Criterion and Waiver for Nonobservance of Performance Criterion*. Washington, DC: International Monetary Fund.

International Monetary Fund. (2004d). *Republic of Croatia: 2004 Article IV Consultation and Request for Stand-By Arrangement*. Washington, DC: International Monetary Fund.

International Monetary Fund. (2007). *Peru: 2006 Article IV Consultation and Request for Stand-by Arrangement—Staff Report*. Washington, DC: International Monetary Fund.

International Monetary Fund. (2008). *Honduras: Request for Stand-By Arrangement—Staff Report*. Washington, DC: International Monetary Fund.

International Monetary Fund. (2009). *El Salvador: Request for Stand-by Arrangement—Staff Report*. Washington, DC: International Monetary Fund.

International Monetary Fund. (2010). *Honduras: Request for a Stand-By Arrangement and an Arrangement under the Standby Credit Facility*. Washington, DC: International Monetary Fund.

International Monetary Fund. (2012, March 28). *Press release: IMF reaches staff-level agreement with Georgia on request for Stand-By Arrangement and Standby Credit Facility*. Retrieved from International Monetary Fund: https://www.imf.org/en/News/Articles/2015/09/14/01/49/pr12108.

International Monetary Fund. (2013a). *Jamaica: Request for an Extended Arrangement under the Extended Fund Facility*. Washington, DC: International Monetary Fund.

International Monetary Fund. (2013b). *Romania: Request for a Stand-by Agreement*. Washington, DC: International Monetary Fund.

International Monetary Fund. (2013c, May 20). *Serbia- 2013 Article IV Consultation Concluding Statement of the Mission*. Retrieved from International Monetary Fund: https://www.imf.org/en/News/Articles/2015/09/28/04/52/mcs052013b.

International Monetary Fund. (2014a). *Honduras: Request for a Stand-by Arrangement and an Arrangement under the Stand-by Credit Facility*. Washington, DC: International Monetary Fund.

International Monetary Fund. (2014b, March 7). *Press Release: IMF executive board approves US$127.6 million extended arrangement for Armenia*. Retrieved from International Monetary Fund Web site: https://www.imf.org/en/News/Articles/2015/09/14/01/49/pr1488.

International Monetary Fund. (2015, February 2). *Press Release: IMF executive board approves US$497.1 Million Stand-by Arrangement and US$191.2 Million Stand-by Credit Facility for Kenya*. Retrieved from International Monetary Fund: https://www.imf.org/en/News/Articles/2015/09/14/01/49/pr1529.

International Monetary Fund. (2016a, October 13). *IMF reaches staff-level agreement with Jamaica on three-year Precautionary Stand-By Arrangement*. Washington, DC.

International Monetary Fund. (2016b). *IMF Stand-By Arrangement. International Monetary Fund Factsheet*. Washington, DC: International Monetary Fund.

International Monetary Fund. (2016c, November). *Jamaica: Request for Stand by Arrangement and Cancellation of the Current Extended Arrangment under the Extended Fund Facility*. Retrieved from International Monetary Fund Web site: https://www.imf.org/external/pubs/ft/scr/2016/cr16350.pdf.

International Monetary Fund. (2019a). *Republic of Armenia: 2019 Article IV Consultation and Request for a Stand-by Arrangement*. Washington, DC: International Monetary Fund.

International Monetary Fund. (2019b, May 6). *IMF and Honduras reach staff-level agreement on a Stand-by/Credit Facility Arrangement*. Retrieved from International Monetary Fund: https://www.imf.org/en/News/Articles/2019/05/06/pr19143-honduras-imf-reaches-staff-level-agreement-stand-by-credit-facility-arrangement.

Ministry of Finance of Ukraine. (2020, September 15). *Ministry of Finance of Ukraine*. Retrieved from International Monetary Fund: https://mof.gov.ua/en/mvf.

Ngouana, L. C. (2016, November 12). What does the new precautionary stand-by arrangement mean for the Jamaican people? *The Jamaica Observer*.

The Jamaica Gleaner. (2019, September 19). Jamaica praised as IMF concludes final review—Holness pleads for consensus to tackle crime, corruption crises *The Jamaica Gleaner*.

The Jamaica Observer. (2019a, September 22). An unqualified success for Jamaica. *The Jamaica Observer*.

The Jamaica Observer. (2019b, November 7). IMF lauds Jamaica govt's commitment to sustaining policy discipline. *The Jamaica Observer*.

CHAPTER 10

Built to Last: Sustainability, Growth and Development—The Road to Vision 2030

Introduction

Beginning with the five-year Independence plan of the 1960s to the National Industrial Plan of the 1990s, Jamaica has developed and pursued several short-term plans intended to spur the development of its economy and society. During the decade of the 2000s it was recognized that this type of planning cycle was not providing the maximum benefit as it was too short; centred around the electoral cycle, and, was also not continued where there was a change of ministers or administration. The plans were also not integrated across sectors and therefore were not able to bridge the silo approach to development that does not take advantage of the synergies required for sustainable levels or catalytic types of development.

The wheels of the plan development process were set in motion at the celebratory conference to mark the fiftieth anniversary of the Planning Institute of Jamaica (PIOJ) in November 2005 when the then Minister of Finance challenged the PIOJ to produce national development plans that were more consistent with and relevant to the national realities and that were achievable. By 2006, the Minister added to this mandate by asking the PIOJ to build a model that was consistent with the structure of the Jamaican economy and utilize this model to support the development of a long-term national development plan. In developing the plan, the PIOJ was to use the existing policy statements in the form of sector plans, programmes of work, development-related commitments such as

C. Clarke and C. Nelson, *Jamaica's Evolving Relationship with the IMF*,
https://doi.org/10.1007/978-3-030-59204-2_10

the Millennium Development Goals as the springboard to the development of the plan and the strategies would then be validated and/or selected using the model. Staff from the PIOJ and Ministry of Education were selected to be trained in the development and further customization of the identified Threshold 21-Jamaica model that was identified as the most comprehensive planning and analysis tool that could support the development of a long-term national development plan for Jamaica.

At the strategic level, a Plan Advisory Group was established to give strategic direction to the plan development process and its membership included the private sector and civil society groups. In taking up the call, the PIOJ established a core team to drive the plan development process in the Director General's Secretariat and all technical and executive staff of the PIOJ were appointed as drivers of the Task Forces that were later established to develop sector plans. Using the support of a wide range of sectoral experts—both internal and external to the PIOJ—across 31 sectors, the process began with visioning exercises through workshops and scoping exercises across the island to elicit and identify the approach that Jamaica would utilize to establish and implement the country's sustainable development framework. This process resulted in an agreement on the desired ultimate goal of the final plan, a shared national vision to make *Jamaica, the place of choice to live, work, raise families and do business.*

Recognizing the extensive nature of the development agenda, the lessons learnt from previous development plans that suffered from lack of buy-in and the absence of a strategic framework buttressed by a plan for monitoring and evaluating progress, the plan development process (PDP) was based on the development of sector plans for the thirty-two identified sectors. The drafting of these sector plans was done using the combined efforts of specially convened Task Forces with members from the ministries, departments and agencies of government, the private sector, civil society, the International Development Partners with the chairperson coming from either the public or private sector. Simultaneously, the team trained in the development of the T21 Jamaica model continued the model development process to ensure it would support the development of the plan as best as possible and also to train persons from the public sector in the use and utility of the model. In addition, various forms of communications and consultations were implemented by the Plan Development Unit (PDU) in an attempt to expand the participatory nature of the PDP and expand the validation of the plans being specified for each sector. This process was initiated with the launch of the

PDP in October 2007. The consultative process continued throughout the two-year PDP with a range of stakeholders and the general public to provide updates as well as to maintain their engagement and interest. Presentations were made to key stakeholders from the Prime Minister and Cabinet, the Opposition Party and its Shadow Cabinet, leaders, technical and policy representatives of all Ministries, Trade Unions, Civil Society, clusters of upper high school students, the media, the private sector and the international development partners. The feedback from these wide consultations was then utilized in the internal peer reviews of each sector plan and infused into the documents after the deliberations within the Task Force and the PIOJ.

The next task was the infusion and integration of the 32 sector plans into one integrated national development plan for Jamaica. In order to ensure the robustness of the process, the PDU clustered sector plans and invited a small set of critical thinkers to critique and review the plans. These review teams were multi-disciplinary and considered the cross-cutting themes as well as whether there were issues that were inadequately addressed in the plans or that needed to be considered in multiple plans. Most importantly, the external review process focussed on identifying the main themes that were emerging from the strategic framework that would indicate the achievement of the vision statement. In addition, the external review supported the efforts of the PDU to identify any inconsistencies, duplications or matters requiring clarification in either of the sector plans or across sector plans. The results of these cluster reviews were further validated through additional literature reviews and consultations and infused into the sector plans. Following this, another round of consultations was initiated with all levels of government to ensure that the results were infused in the policy development process and programme implementation activities.

This iterative process was completed and resulted in the preparation of the integrated national development plan which was laid in the Houses of Parliament by Prime Minister Bruce Golding during his Budget Presentation along with the first corresponding three-year medium-term socio-economic policy framework. The final plan document specifies that Jamaica's people were put at the centre of the PDP and this was embedded in the entire strategic framework. Four national goals were specified: (1) Jamaicans are empowered to achieve their fullest potential; (2) The Jamaican society is secure, cohesive and just; (3) Jamaica's

Table 10.1 Alignment between Vision 2030 Jamaica national goals and national outcomes

National Vision Jamaica, the place of choice to live, work, raise families and do business	
National Goals	*National Outcomes*
Goal 1: Jamaicans are empowered to achieve their fullest potential	NO1: A Healthy and Stable Population NO2: World-class Education and Training NO3: Effective Social Protection NO4: Authentic and Transformational Culture
Goal 2: The Jamaican society is secure, cohesive and just	NO5: Security and Safety NO6: Effective Governance
Goal 3: Jamaica's economy is prosperous	NO7: A Stable Macroeconomy NO8: An Enabling Business Environment NO9: Strong Economic Infrastructure N10: Energy Security and Efficiency N11: A Technology-Enabled Society N12: Internationally Competitive Industry Structures
Goal 4: Jamaica has a healthy natural environment	N13: Sustainable Management and Use of Environmental and Natural Resources N14: Hazard Risk Reduction and Adaptation to Climate Change N15: Sustainable Urban and Rural Development

Source Planning Institute of Jamaica (2009)

economy is prosperous; and (4) Jamaica has a healthy natural environment (Table 10.1).

Vision 2030 Jamaica and the International Monetary Fund Agreements 2010–2019

The development of Vision 2030 Jamaica occurred during the worst financial and economic crises globally. The strategic and long-term nature of this plan is perhaps most commendable during such a context as it will ensure that the country does not only address stemming the impact of the short-term crisis but that it also simultaneously implements a strategic framework that corrects structural imbalances whilst entrenching the principles of sustainability through a reorientation of the development paradigm. During this period, the government was pursuing a policy of re-engaging the multilateral development partners as the conditions in the international capital markets were once again un-favourable to highly indebted small island developing countries like Jamaica who had been caught in debt traps due to a range of issues including domestic financial sector crises. The onset of the global financial crisis in 2008 also instigated the country's return to the International Monetary Fund. The authorities utilized the support to initiate reforms in the area of fiscal policy which focussed on instilling fiscal discipline and reforming the financial sector in the wake of the failure of a series of unregulated financial institutions. The return to the IMF also served to catalyze the desired support from the multilateral institutions. As Clarke and Nelson (2020) indicate this was a courageous move on the part of the new administration, as Jamaica's borrowing relationship with the Fund was characterized by significant levels of tension that had led previous administrations to deliberately avoid entering into borrowing relationships with the Fund or to even be taking advice on economic policy from the institution.

Jamaica's return to the International Monetary Fund unlocked significant sums of policy linked financial support from the European Union, Inter-American Development Bank and the World Bank who were incentivized by the IMF's so called 'seal of approval' given to Jamaica's economic programme and reform agenda. The government was faced with the implementation of a debt exchange, the imposition of a tax package, and the need to be far advanced in auctioning divestment plans for the major loss-making public bodies that would tend to be major contributors to the build-up of contingent liabilities in the public sector in the form of prior actions that had to be completed for the programme to be approved officially. In recognition of the significant effort required by the government to implement these signal transactions and to initiate its agenda for economic reform, the programme provided a large portion of the total funds available from the IMF as well as the multilateral partners upfront.

In the context of the popular perception and the experience of countries who have engaged in borrowing relationships with the Fund as being negative, an important concern was the extent to which Jamaica would be able to successfully implement both an IMF-supported programme and its well-developed and fully articulated NDP, Vision 2030 Jamaica.

The underlying issue being, how would the conditionalities and economic reforms prevent or complement the strategies needed to be implemented to achieve progress towards Vision 2030.

2010 Standby Agreement (SBA)

Given the urgency of the international and domestic economic environment and the low levels of macroeconomic stability that characterized the Jamaican economy, it is not surprising that the 2010 SBA focussed heavily on the implementation of a small range of activities that contribute to Jamaica's ability to achieve Goal 3—Jamaica's Economy is Prosperous. The 2010 SBA specified a total of forty-nine conditionalities of which three were prior actions and the remainder were structural benchmarks.

The three prior actions that were implemented under the 2010 SBA were all intended to establish the fiscal discipline required to support the structural reforms that were critical to the economic reform programme being supported by the IMF. Two of the prior actions required the successful implementation of a comprehensive debt exchange and progress in relation to the divestment or agreement regarding the divestment of Air Jamaica—a major source of contingent liabilities for the government. Table 10.2 illustrates that these two reforms aligned with National Outcome 7—*Stable Macroeconomy*—and the National Strategy focussed on *Ensuring Fiscal and Debt Sustainability*. The third prior action was also aligned with restoring a *Stable Macroeconomy* but was instead focussed on national strategy 7-2 *Develop an Efficient and Equitable Tax System* the implementation of a tax package based on relatively secure bases in order to increase revenue flows available to the fiscal authorities. Once these three prior actions were implemented, the SBA was signed and Jamaica received the agreed inflows the task remained to implement the structural benchmarks over the upcoming eight quarters. There were forty-six such structural benchmarks of which forty-one were related to Goal 3. The remaining five structural benchmarks were aligned with Goal 2 *Jamaican society is secure, cohesive and just* and they were intended to support *Effective Governance* (National Outcome 6) and the aligned National Strategy 6-5 *Strengthen Public Institutions to Deliver Efficient and Effective Public Goods and Services.*

Unfortunately, the authorities were not able to complete the implementation of the 2010 SBA due to slippages on the fiscal side related to the payment of additional salaries to three public sector groups that

Table 10.2 Alignment between the conditionalities in the 2010 Standby Agreement and Vision 2030 Jamaica National Development Plan

National Outcome	*National Strategy*	*Prior actions (number)*	*Structural benchmarks (number)*
Goal 2: Jamaican society is secure, cohesive and just			
6 Effective Governance	6-5 Strengthen Public Institutions to Deliver Efficient and Effective Public Goods and Services	0	5
Goal 3: Jamaica's economy is prosperous			
7 Stable Macroeconomy	7-1 Ensure Fiscal and Debt Sustainability	2	16
	7-2 Develop an Efficient and Equitable Tax System	1	2
	7-3 Maintain Financial System Stability	0	21
8 Enabling Business Environment	8-2 Increase Access to Capital	0	2

Source Compiled by authors from Planning Institute of Jamaica (2009) and International Monetary Fund (2010)

represented 60% of public sector employment. These payments had not been included in the economic programme and therefore were viewed as being in contravention of the spirit and letter of the SBA. Only three of the eight scheduled tests were undertaken and as a result the official records related to the SBA indicate only partial completion of the agreed benchmarks. Of the five agreed activities relating to Goal 2, only one item was met relating to the preparation of the Prime Minister's Committee Report on Public Sector Reform; two others relating to the completion of a census of employment in the public sector and the design of a public sector employment and compensation reform were classified as being in progress in the final review document; and, the remaining two were delayed (See Table 10.2). In terms of the structural benchmarks that would have contributed to the advancement of three National Strategies, there were also mixed results. Only ten of the forty benchmarks were achieved of which eight related to benchmarks that would *Ensure Fiscal and Debt Sustainability* and one each related to *Develop an Efficient and Equitable Tax System* and *Financial System Stability*, respectively. Eleven national strategies remained in progress, six of which related to *Financial System Stability*, four to *Ensure Fiscal and Debt Sustainability*, and, one to *Increased Access to Capital*. Nineteen of the programmed benchmarks were delayed or not yet due; fourteen of these related to the national strategy titled *Financial System Stability*, three to *Ensure Fiscal and Debt Sustainability*, and one to *Develop an Efficient and Equitable Tax System*.

Overall, it would appear that the authorities successfully implemented the largest number of benchmarks under the national strategy that reflected its most urgent economic need to establish fiscal and debt sustainability in order to establish a stable macroeconomy. The need to have a stable macroeconomy is well established in the literature and has been utilized in well known indices of economic performance such as the Global Competitiveness Index (GCI) calculated annually by the World Economic Forum. The GCI clearly establishes the primacy of macroeconomic stability as a necessary prerequisite for the competitiveness and therefore growth of an economy however, it clearly acknowledges that macroeconomic stability is not sufficient to guarantee this competitiveness. Other complementary characteristics will also be required for the economy and society in order to get the improvements in competitiveness desired by countries globally. Nevertheless, the critical state of the economy required dedicated focus on establishing macroeconomic stability. Despite the fact that the 2010 SBA was not implemented in full, the wheels were set in motion with the eight benchmarks that were met. As indicated in Chapter 2 of this volume, Jamaica would eventually have to return to the Fund as the need to properly entrench fiscal discipline, transform the public sector and support the implementation of necessary changes in the financial sector required continued support from the multilateral institutions that would not be granted in the absence of an agreement with the IMF.

2013 Extended Fund Facility (EFF)

Chapter 3 of this volume outlines the Second Return to the Fund and indicates the structure of the programme and the intention of the Fund to ensure that more reforms were frontloaded in the agreement in contrast to the 2010 SBA. Whilst the Jamaica Debt Exchange was a success by all measures upon its implementation, the progress achieved was not to be sustained as the supporting measures had not been completed due to the suspension of the agreement between the third and fourth quarterly review. As indicated above, only one half of the benchmarks that would address and support the establishment of fiscal and debt sustainability was implemented.

As indicated in Table 10.3, the number of prior actions to be completed before the official start of the programme doubled from three to six. These prior actions were now evenly split between the

Table 10.3 Alignment between the conditionalities in the 2013 Extended Fund Facility and Vision 2030 Jamaica National Development Plan

National Outcome	*National Strategy*	*Prior actions (number)*	*Structural benchmarks (number)*
Goal 1: Jamaicans are empowered to achieve their fullest potential			
3 Effective Social Protection	3-4 Promote Greater Participation in and Viability of Social Insurance and Pension Schemes	0	1
Goal 2: Jamaican society is secure, cohesive and just			
6 Effective Governance	6-5 Strengthen Public Institutions to Deliver Efficient and Effective Public Goods and Services	0	8
Goal 3: Jamaica's economy is prosperous			
7 Stable Macroeconomy	7-1 Ensure Fiscal and Debt Sustainability	3	17
	7-2 Develop an Efficient and Equitable Tax System	3	17
	7-3 Maintain Financial System Stability	0	13
8 Enabling Business Environment	8-1 Ensure a Facilitating Policy, Regulatory and Institutional Framework for Business Development	0	4
	8-2 Increase Access to Capital	0	1
10 Energy Security and Efficiency	10-2 Promote Energy Efficiency and Conservation	0	1

Source Compiled by authors from Planning Institute of Jamaica (2009) and International Monetary Fund (2013)

first two national strategies aligned to National Outcome 7—*A Stable Economy* under Goal 3. Under National Strategy 7-1: *Ensure Fiscal and Debt Sustainability* the authorities successfully implemented another debt exchange dubbed the National Debt Exchange that effected critical changes in the repayment structure of certain debt instruments. The focus during this exchange was the use of accretion and other mechanisms to alter the repayment schedule of these instruments and thereby secure the sustainable decline on the amortization of existing debt and the accumulation of new debt issue used previously to make these payments. In addition, Jamaica also successfully implemented a national Public Debt Law and, expectedly, the final prior action aligned with this national strategy required the government to secure a multi-year agreement with at least 70% of its employees that would limit any wage increases to 2.5% in the first year and no more than a combined 5% in the following years. The other three prior actions were taxation related and were aligned to National Strategy 7-2 *Develop an Efficient and Equitable Tax System.* All three were geared towards curtailing tax expenditures through: (1) a cessation in the granting of discretionary waivers by the Minister of Finance; (2) capping the value of total monthly discretionary waivers granted to non-charities at J$80m in contrast to J$250m for charities; and, (3) the adoption of a decision not to approve or renew any waivers or tax incentives except those prescribed by legislation and to initiate the process of developing an Omnibus Incentive Law that would harmonize and streamline the provisions in a manner that minimized the distortions to economic activity, respectively.

The sixty-two structural benchmarks under the 2013 EFF were aligned to three of the four Vision 2030 Jamaica Goals albeit to varying degrees. Under one benchmark, the authorities agreed to and tabled legislation to amend the public sector pension scheme in order to improve the extent to which it was funded/financed. This is aligned to National Strategy 3-4 Promote greater participation in and viability of social insurance and pension schemes under the *Effective Social Protection* national outcome for Goal 1: Jamaicans are empowered to achieve their fullest potential. In relation to Goal 2: Jamaican society is secure, cohesive and just, focus was placed on implementing benchmarks that are to National Strategy 6-5 *Strengthen Public Institutions to Deliver Efficient and Effective Public Goods and Services* through eight benchmarks. These benchmarks centred around developing a database to support the human resource function across the public sector, making strides to rationalizing common activities across the public sector the implementation of shared services and an improved understanding of the total compensation of public sector employment in order to improve the competitiveness of public sector salary packages. In addition, an action plan for the merger, abolition, divestment, outsourcing and realignment of entities in the public sector was developed to guide future efforts at public sector transformation. Submissions regarding these benchmarks were to be presented to Cabinet for further review, approval and implementation.

In terms of National Strategy 7-1 *Ensure Fiscal and Debt Sustainability* aligned to Goal 3, the emphasis in the 2013 EFF was on correcting cash management in central government; the budget process and its inadequate alignment with the macrolevel budget ceiling; development and adherence to five-year capital expenditure plans; further entrenchment of fiscal discipline and finalization of the divestment plans for the public sector. Efforts to address cash management were necessary when a review of the bank accounts across government revealed that there was enough cash available to meet intertemporal needs however as they were held in proprietary accounts that were not accessible to the Treasury leading to additional debt issues to make payments that are due. In order to reduce the inefficiencies generated by this coordination failure, the government initiated a comprehensive reform of the treasury function. One outcome of this reform is the appropriate transfer of the function to the Accountant General's office and the implementation of a Central Treasury Management System (CTMS) that supports the accounting for the funds of each entity and forecasting the cash needs across the entire public sector to facilitate planning or allowable support from the central bank.

The reforms to the budget function were comprehensive with the establishment of a budget calendar that was designed to ensure the development of complete and comprehensive estimates of expenditure for central government. These estimates were produced using multi-year expenditure plans to ensure that the various Ministries, Departments and Agencies (MDAs) were aligning their individual budgets to their strategic and operational plans and that the financial implications of these plans over the medium term were adequately accounted for. The budget authorities would then utilize a range of tools to prioritize the various submissions based on the socio-economic context, the available fiscal space, the implications for the medium- to long-term debt trajectory, and stated government priorities. Emphasis was also placed on the policy and programmatic aspects of the capital budget of the government which has implications in the medium to long term for the recurrent aspect of the government—requiring provisions for maintenance, upgrades, monitoring and regulation. A process based on quantitative analysis was implemented to introduce objectivity and comparability into the development and implementation of the public sector investment programme. This strengthened the support available to MDAs in the development of capital projects aligned to their mandates and increase the extent to which the MDAs could be more certain that their projects would be eligible and viewed worthy of inclusion in the budget. Finally, based on the established budget calendar, the budget process is to be sufficiently advanced to facilitate discussion and further prioritization and revision at the January retreat of the Cabinet. These discussions are expected to facilitate final deliberations regarding the proposed focus areas for the upcoming fiscal year and support tabling in advance of the official opening of the Houses of Parliament in April. When combined with the recently implemented parameters of fiscal responsibility assigned to the Minister of Finance, these changes support a stronger system of alignment of budget with government priorities and the long-term national development plan and reduces the possibility that ad hoc, unapproved and inadequately analysed expenditure can occur and compromise budget administration and performance as discussed in Chapter 5 of this volume.

Despite the discontinuation of the 2010 SBA after the third quarterly review, the authorities were still able to advance the work required to support the entrenchment of fiscal discipline and continue the efforts at fiscal consolidation. One of these efforts was in the specification of the Financial Administration and Audit (Fiscal Responsibility Framework) Regulations, 2012, that guided MDAs and the Ministry of Finance operationally. It prescribed specific processes that must be followed prior to an MDA receiving either a grant or a loan from any source and criteria for these processes can be prescribed by the Financial Secretary. Breaches of this are subject to a written reprimand by the Financial secretary for a first offence providing that there is no financial loss to the government as a result of the contravention. The Financial Secretary must also submit a written report on the matter outlining the circumstances of the breach and the number of such offences committed by the particular MDA to the Public Service Commission who can take further action (Government of Jamaica, 2012). The Regulations also allow the Minister to suspend, withdraw or impose conditions on any previously approved expenditure warrant and must provide Cabinet with a report indicating the basis for either decision including insufficient funds and any potential negative impact that the decision could have on agreements with domestic or international partners. The reason for and impact of these changes need to be presented to the Financial Secretary and must indicate the implications for the fiscal expenditure and revenue profile over the year at the national and the MDA level. Where the change will result in an increase in MDA expenditure, the responsible officer must indicate an offsetting reduction in expenditure elsewhere in the budget of their entity. Having completed this, the Financial Secretary will share the information with the Minister of Finance and provide a recommendation for consideration. The MDA must implement the change in compliance with section 16(3) of the Act, failing which the Financial Secretary is empowered to roll back or cease the implementation of the change until the entity complies in full and a report is to be prepared and sent to the Public Service Commission for appropriate action. The Regulations also prescribe the need to ensure that the debt-reduction trajectory is adhered to and that when the target is achieved, the Fiscal Policy Paper will demonstrate that there will be fiscal balance on average over the medium term (Government of Jamaica, 2012).

Each Permanent Secretary is required to submit a three-year business plan that presents a three-year financial summary which ought to be consistent with the expenditure ceilings in the Budget Call Circular and consolidates the plans of the departments, agencies and any on-budget public bodies aligned to the portfolio ministry. The Financial Secretary is permitted to make a minimum provision in the budget for entities that do not adhere to this requirement. The Financial Secretary must be presented with a request from the Permanent Secretary responsible for an entity requesting additional expenditure that includes the rationale, the expenditure profile for the next two years, and, any corrective action that can minimize the planned excess expenditures. The Financial Secretary then submits the request and recommendation to the Minister of Finance who then presents it to Cabinet (Government of Jamaica, 2012). If supported by the Minister and Financial Secretary, the Cabinet Submission must include a financing plan demonstrating how the expenditure will be accommodated. If approved by Cabinet, the Financial Secretary will send the report to the Public Administration and Appropriations Committee where either the Financial Secretary or the Ministry may be required to appear. If the accounting officer does not adhere to the regulation or exceeds the budgeted allocation without prior approval the Financial Secretary must submit a report regarding the same to the Public Services Commission. Where a Financial Secretary is remiss and does not respond to the request from an accounting officer, the officer may take the matter to the Cabinet Secretary who will instruct the Financial Secretary to act within a specified time which if not abided by will be referred to the Public Services Commission.

The Regulations also indicate that the fiscal policy measures to be outlined in the Fiscal Responsibility Statement signed by the Minister of Finance must meet nine (9) criteria. Firstly, the measures must reduce and maintain prudent Government debt levels. The financial implications of policy decisions on future generations must be given due consideration and must support the building of sufficient levels of national saving. Fiscal policy measures being proposed must support stability and predictability in the levels of taxation and spending and should support the moderation of cycles in economic activity. The FRS must also minimize the granting of tax expenditures, support expenditure policies that contribute to the achievement of economic growth, poverty reduction and improved welfare in Jamaica. The final two requirements are the proper maintenance of the physical assets of the government and alignment between the proposed expenditure plan and the targeted fiscal outcomes (Government of Jamaica, 2012).

Beyond this, the Minister of Finance must also present sufficient detail on how the measures satisfy the overarching fiscal and macroeconomic framework, outline the overall fiscal trajectory; ensure that the current programme being proposed is fiscally consistent over the three-year fiscal plan; and, describe the extent to which the fiscal plans are prudent and consistent with sustainability over the long term. The Minister must also present information on the benchmarks that will be used to assess the performance of the proposed fiscal policy. Indications must be made of the measures that will be taken to address any cyclical fluctuations or emergencies of any type that require a fiscal response and any compensating measures to reverse the impact of the intervention(s) made. The risks likely to impact the programme, other key assumptions, consistency of the estimates with sound fiscal management principles and any noteworthy disclosures and changes in classification or standards used to prepare or present the fiscal accounts. The macroeconomic context and forecasts must be presented in the statement in order to demonstrate the consistency across government policy and present the implications of these and any changes in government policy can have on the macroeconomic variables. In addition, the Ministry is required to submit a Fiscal Management Strategy and an independent analysis of the Fiscal Policy Paper is to be conducted by the Auditor General. Confidential information can be withheld but must be indicated to the Auditor General and the Ministry may publish interim reports focussing on different time points based on the point in the year that the report is being prepared.

Therefore the overarching and most far-reaching reform aligned to National Strategy 7-1 is the establishment of the fiscal rule in law. Under the five structural benchmarks related to the implementation of the fiscal rule, the government developed the conceptual framework and set a target for the implementation of the fiscal rule for 2014/2015. The purpose of the fiscal rule is to ensure that the budget balance being planned by the government—through the tabling of its estimates of expenditure and revenue plans—is sustainable over the medium to long term as a major emblem of macroeconomic stability and signal that the national debt will not increase sharply. Having been identified in 2009 as an important element needed to establish the credibility of the country's fiscal trajectory, an initial form of the fiscal rule was promulgated as part of the 2010 SBA as an important step in the process of fiscal consolidation by streamlining expenditure to match revenue forecasts in order to support the achievement of the fiscal targets (Jamaica Information Service, 2010).

The 2010 fiscal rules specified both a budget balance rule and a debt rule. The changes effected under the 2013 EFF included a new rule that established a floor on the overall balance of the public sector in order to ensure debt-to-GDP would decline to 60% by the fiscal year 2025/2026 (Lledo et al., 2017). In addition, a constraint was placed under the 2013 EFF on the loan values to a cumulative ceiling of 3% of GDP; if this limit were exceeded the 2014 update to the fiscal rule prescribes the need for annual adjustments to correct the deviation. The 2014 rule set a target for fiscal balance by the end of the fiscal year 2018 and a debt rule target of 60% of GDP or below by the fiscal year 2025/2026. This trajectory represented a more incremental approach to the achievements of the balanced budget and debt rules than the very sharp adjustments set under the 2010 SBA targets. The 2010 SBA had programmed for a balanced budget and a debt-to-GDP ratio of 100% by the end of the 2015/2016 fiscal year. Beyond these two rules, targets were also introduced in the framework for the wage-to-GDP ratio to 9% however, the achievement of this target was contingent on the reform, modernization and transformation of the public sector which would require significant preparatory work prior to any realignment of functions that would generate savings. In addition, the target was in respect of a ratio indicating also that growth in GDP could contribute to the reduction of the ratio. This target was not achieved in the expected timeframe, nevertheless, the fact that the government was implementing nine structural benchmarks relating to the achievement of reformation efforts of the public sector under the 2013 EFF. Through these benchmarks, the authorities indicated their commitment to the overarching principle of the 9% target and their intention to meet the target through a well-thought out and comprehensive reform of public sector employment policy and administration. It is important to note that both the 2010 and 2014 fiscal rules were drafted with the provision of escape clauses that allow the Minister to bring to Parliament any necessary deviations due to national security, national emergency or other exceptional grounds for affirmative resolution (Lledo et al., 2017).

The remaining benchmarks aligned to National Strategy 7-1 related to the continued efforts to divest Clarendon Alumina Partners (CAP)—a major source of contingent liabilities in previous fiscal years and the requirement for the government to ensure that CAP did not receive any new financing from any source relating to the government, or government guarantee, or receive permission to use public assets as collateral for third-party financing. In light of the changes to public financial management, a policy regarding the operation of public bodies was to be developed and submitted for approval to Cabinet. New property tax rates were also to be calculated and submitted to Cabinet.

Under the 2013 EFF, emphasis was also placed on the reform of several administrative dimensions of the tax system and these efforts were aligned to National Strategy 7-2 *Develop an Efficient and Equitable Tax System*. The authorities undertook the development of new productivity indicators for measuring the effectiveness and efficiency of the tax system. Key reforms included the removal of large taxpayers with more complicated tax liabilities from the general collectorate and to deal with their issues at a dedicated Large Taxpayer Office (LTO). In addition, the fiscal authorities also implemented mandatory online tax filing and payment for all income taxes and the consumption tax collected by retailers and wholesalers. Aligned with the e-filing was the accomplishment of a benchmark relating to the amendment of the Revenue Administration Act to facilitate the necessary access to the third-party information this would generate and to enable the use of the information to facilitate compliance management. Simultaneously structural benchmarks included efforts to expand the staffing of the LTO and strengthening the capacity of Tax Administration to conduct all types of audits. Whilst there was a delay in the meeting of the structural benchmark relating to the promulgation of the Omnibus Tax Incentive Act (OMTIA)—one of the five benchmarks regarding tax incentives/expenditures—it represented the culmination of the efforts to control the issuance of discretionary waivers and other special incentives by the Minister of Finance. The OMTIA provides the overarching legal framework regarding the entities that are eligible for incentives and the manner, type and value of the incentives that can be accessed and how they are to be utilized. The other structural benchmarks aligned to National Strategy 7-2 related to the amendment of the GCT act and the tabling of legislation regarding the special economic zones framework currently being established.

In terms of the financial sector, twelve of the implemented structural benchmarks are aligned to National Strategy 7-3 *Maintain Financial System Stability*. The major area in which the reforms occurred related to the tabling and enactment of the Omnibus Banking Law/Banking Service Act to facilitate the effective supervision of the financial sector by establishing the Bank of Jamaica as the organization with overall responsibility for financial stability. Prior to occurrence of the global financial crisis, supervision of the financial sector was split along the lines of deposit and non-deposit taking financial institutions. However, the lessons of the financial crisis indicate that both macro- and micro-prudential regulation that has sight of the entire financial system is critical in order to be able to stress test the system and to identify and prevent potential system-wide contagion. To bolster the financial stability mandate, the monetary authorities developed a consultation paper on the resolution framework for the entire financial sector. The draft resolution framework outlined the entire process of the resolution regime and indicate the legal structure that should prevail in the particular situation as well as the roles and responsibility of the entity implementing the resolution. The reforms also treated with curtailing the existence and operation of 'unlawful financial operations' and to implement a legal and regulatory framework that would allow the establishment and operations of Collective Investment Schemes. Retail repo clients have also benefitted from a reform that transitioned them to a trust-based framework.

The remaining six structural benchmarks supported two additional National Strategies supporting the attainment of Goal 3. Four of the benchmarks are aligned to National Strategy 8-1 *Ensure a Facilitating Policy, Regulatory and Institutional Framework for Business Development*. One of these benchmarks related to the implementation of a tracking system for development applications for construction permits in all parish councils. Work was also done to improve the operations of customs through the overhauling of the customs act that would support the implementation of the ASYCUSA World system at the Port of Kingston. In addition, capacity building efforts were implemented in order to improve the Post-Clearance Audit processing by customs. In order to *Increase Access to Capital* National Strategy 8-2, efforts were made through a benchmark in which the government would establish and operate a central collateral registry through which holders of non-traditional asset types would be able to securitize them as collateral and use them to support their desired form of economic activity.

Whilst the overwhelming focus in the 2013 EFF was on the successful implementation of structural reforms associated with the macroeconomic stability, efficiency of the tax system, and the entrenchment of financial stability, there were clear—though numerically small—attempts to address long-standing structural challenges. The overall outcome of the implemented benchmarks contributed to the fostering of a more stable economic platform from which all economic actors would be able to make their savings and investment decisions more securely. The efforts at reforming and achievements in the area of customs for example are noteworthy and have extensive impact on manufacturers and the wholesale and retail trade whose interface with customs and the tax system at the border is a normal part of their operations. The development approval process is another progressive advance as the process has in the past been characterized as being fraught with challenges and perhaps corrupt practices. In addition, the accountability of the various entities required to participate in the approval process was improved through implementation of the tracking system. Whilst these reforms are not sufficient or do not guarantee higher levels of economic growth, they were necessary to provide the basic framework within which complementary reforms and activities could spur transformation of the economic growth trajectory.

2016 Precautionary Standby Agreement (P-SBA) (Subhead)

Jamaica made significant progress in its economic reform agenda as it completed all fifteen reviews over the four-year period inclusive of an Article IV review. The nature of the reforms as indicated in the previous subsection, though largely focussed on three key national strategies relating to the economy, were substantive and far reaching in terms of changing the structure of the economy and some of the ways that the private sector interacts with the government in a variety of ways. Based on the success of the programme from both an implementation perspective as well as in terms of the trends in the high-level macroeconomic indicators such as inflation and debt-to-GDP growth, the Jamaican authorities indicated their commitment to leverage the achievements and to continue with the next tier of reforms. Given the nascent nature of the economic stability that had been instituted, the Jamaican authorities discussed the potential for continued support from the IMF that would be appropriate to the needs of the country (International Monetary Fund, 2016a). At the conclusion of the 2013 EFF, the IMF indicated that whilst the reforms were critical to restoring economic stability, emphasis would need to be placed on implementing structural reforms that would be growth-enhancing (International Monetary Fund, 2016a). Further, the programme was acknowledged as a turning point for the economy as the reforms addressed the high debt overhang that has impacted the economy since the early 2000s along with long growth rates. The IMF reported that more than 95% of the established and agreed structural benchmarks were met as the programme benefitted from a strong partnership that supported monitoring of implementation and communicating results to citizens (International Monetary Fund, 2016a). The achievements occurred in the context of a new political administration leading the government that had affirmed their support to continue the IMF programme (Table 10.4).

In order to take advantage of the momentum generated by the successful reforms, the GOJ was able to secure the support of the international partners to facilitate the structural areas that were considered as important constraints to development and also to support the operations of the private sector. The IMF also supported this second wave of reforms through a Precautionary Standby Agreement (PSBA) (See Chapter 9 for more on the PSBA). As noted in Chapter 9, the PSBA

Table 10.4 Alignment between the conditionalities in the 2016 Precautionary Standby Agreement (P-SBA) and Vision 2030 Jamaica National Development Plan

National Outcome	*National Strategy*	*Prior actions (number)*	*Structural benchmarks (number)*
Goal 2: Jamaican society is secure, cohesive and just			
6 Effective Governance	6-5 Strengthen Public Institutions to Deliver Efficient and Effective Public Goods and Services	0	9
Goal 3: Jamaica's economy is prosperous			
7 Stable Macroeconomy	7-1 Ensure Fiscal and Debt Sustainability	0	5
	7-2 Develop an Efficient and Equitable Tax System	0	1
	7-3 Maintain Financial System Stability	0	7

Source Compiled by authors from Planning Institute of Jamaica (2009) and International Monetary Fund (2016b)

did not require Jamaica to implement any prior actions and this type of agreement is usually extended to countries that have accomplished substantive reforms but who would prefer to enter into their next phase of reform with support from the IMF in the event that there is some unforeseen economic challenge—hence the precautionary prefix. The funds allocated under the US$1.7bn 2016 PSBA would provide a buffer against any unforeseen shocks to the economy that are not caused by actions taken by the authorities (International Monetary Fund, 2016c). In Jamaica, the PSBA was used to implement structural benchmarks aligned with four national strategies from Vision 2030. National Strategy 6-5 *Strengthen Public Institutions to Deliver Efficient and Effective Public Goods and Services* was aligned to nine of the twenty-two structural benchmarks targeted under the 2016 PSBA. The nine structural benchmarks focussed on strengthening the ability of the Permanent Secretaries in each Ministry and the Financial Secretary with the requisite database and informational foundation necessary for decision-making regarding the management, skilling and redeployment of human resources within and across the public sector. Focus was placed on the development of a database that would provide comprehensive information on all employees within the public sector. The information detailed would include the types of compensation received by each employee as part of the information that would help the Ministry of Finance to be able to accurately measure and track changes in the wage bill as part of its efforts to reduce the wage-to-GDP bill to 9% of GDP for sustainability.

Complementary to this is the strengthening of the operation of the Post Operations Committee to oversee all types of employment in the public sector including positions for which the employee is acting. The committee was expected to act to support the reduction in the growth of employment in the public sector whilst ensuring that the entities within the public sector were properly resourced and could meet their mandate. Rules were to be implemented that would prohibit the rehiring of participants in the early retirement programme from being rehired until after five years. Rules were to be developed and submitted to the Governor General that would limit the extent to which persons could receive continued employment in the public sector after they have passed the retirement age. Under the 2016 EFF, efforts were also made to increase the extent to which the performance management appraisal system was aligned to the performance-based merit increases, through the development and submission of a medium-term policy and implementation plan to Cabinet. Cabinet also received a proposal that outlined clear rules for hiring, promotion and exit in the public sector. Another dimension of the reforms aligned to National Strategy 6-5 related to the implementation of shared corporate services in the area of human resources, public relations and communications and, internal audit functions. The structural benchmarks in this regard focussed on identifying the positions across the public sector that will be affected and the development of a costed transition plan and schedule for such a transition. The final structural benchmark aligned to National Strategy 6-5 was the closure of five public bodies and the integration of the Children's Registry into the Child Development Agency.

As indicated in Table 10.3, five structural benchmarks were implemented in relation to National Strategy 7-1 *Ensure Fiscal and Debt Sustainability* under the Stable Macroeconomy National Outcome of Vision 2030's Goal 3: Jamaica's economy is prosperous. These benchmarks further entrenched fiscal consolidation by ensuring that all earmarked revenues from public bodies such as the Tourism Enhancement Find and the Chase Fund were paid into the Consolidated Fund of the government. Eligible public bodies would be reintegrated into central government in order to ensure consistent application of the relevant public financial management principles based on a time-bound plan. Mergers prescribed in the Public Sector Transformation Master Plan were implemented between HEART/NTA, Jamaica Foundation for Lifelong Learning Plan and the National Youth Service. All public bodies that tended to generate large domestic arrears found their ability to accrue such arrears capped at a combined J$6.4billion for the duration of the 2016 PSBA.

More reforms aligned with National Strategy 7-3 *Maintain Financial System Stability* were implemented to strengthen and advance the financial sector reforms and build on the results from the reforms initiated in the 2010 SBA and 2013 EFF. Further to the expanded mandate of the BOJ to include financial stability, the two benchmarks were implemented geared towards improving the governance structure of the bank and enabling it to operate under the rubric of an independence central bank. These reforms were consistent with the recommendations of technical assistance provided by the IMF and would result in the proper capitalization of the bank based on the established literature regarding central bank capital levels and paved the way for the BOJ to pay dividends to the fiscal authority. Institutional strengthening and other forms of support were provided to establish the foundations for inflation targeting. In terms of governance, appointments to the BOJ Board and terms regarding the provision of financing to the government by the BOJ were outlined in the revised framework and included in the revised BOJ Act submitted to the Parliament for approval. Complementary to the revised BOJ mandate for financial stability, a Financial System Stability Committee was operationalized by the appointment of the two required external members. The resolution framework for the financial system that was drafted under the 2013 EFF, was issued for comment from and consultation with the public. Having gone through the consultative process, the finalized proposal for the framework was submitted to Cabinet for consideration and approval. Based on the modernization of the financial sector that was achieved under the 2013 EFF, and the recognition that a large portion of Jamaica's citizens were not regular users of basic services provided in the formal financial sector, a council was established to spearhead the financial inclusion agenda approved by Cabinet.

Conclusion

Since the drafting of the National Development Plan, there have been concerted efforts to ensure that all policy documents are consistent with Vision 2030 Jamaica. After the adoption of the United Nation's Sustainable Development Goals (SDGs) by country leaders globally in September 2015, efforts were made to assess the extent to which Vision 2030 Jamaica was sufficiently addressing the range of development objectives that had been identified in the SDGs. The analysis indicated that overall the Plan was more than 90% aligned to the SDGs (Planning Institute of Jamaica, 2018). The fact that the three IMF-supported economic reform programmes implemented by Jamaica have multiple points of alignment with Vision 2030 Jamaica, and that the strategic framework underpinning Vision 2030 Jamaica extends beyond the relatively and expectedly narrow focus of an IMF Agreement. Nevertheless, the authorities' plans extended beyond these benchmarks in recognition of the fact that the reforms encapsulated in the benchmarks were necessary but insufficient to generate the needed levels of economic growth. As a result, the request for the 2013 EFF included highlights of the components of the intended growth strategy that would include labour market reforms such as allowances for flexible work, a stronger social protection framework to support out-of-work workers, and opportunities for training and certification (International Monetary Fund, 2013).

The 2016 PSBA also supported the establishment of a leaner and more efficient public sector through the reform of the public sector pension. Whilst not a structural benchmark, the government submitted a draft bill to Parliament in July 2016 that envisaged the plan transitioning a contributory one with reduced benefits as benefits would now be calculated using the previous five years of salary rather than the most recent years (International Monetary Fund, 2017a). In terms of the financial sector, the government also indicated their plan to address the risk issues highlighted in the Caribbean Financial Action Task Force report that indicated major gaps in Jamaica's Anti-money laundering and counter-financing of terrorism framework by expanding the scope of the central banks monitoring in the money service sector and improve on the extent to which the ownership structure of legal entities clearly reflects persons and entities with beneficial ownership. The government also indicated that it would prioritize financial inclusion in order to kick-start private sector led through a series of actions. The Economic Growth Council was also established in order to support efforts at generating high rates of economic growth. The government also made strides to improve its adherence to globally accepted data standards.

Along with the success of the 2013 EFF and the substantive vote of confidence represented in the sizable SDR allocations to Jamaica under the 2016 SBA, the two visits made to Jamaica by Madame Lagarde, the IMF's Managing Director—in November 2017—signalled to participants in all markets—local and foreign—that Jamaica had done substantial work on its economy that were bearing fruit and providing scope for social and other broad societal interventions (International Monetary Fund, 2017b). Lagarde is the only IMF head to have visited the Caribbean and Jamaica since the establishment of the Bretton Woods institution in 1945. The significance of her visit is further enshrined in the extensive nature of her engagement whilst in Jamaica that included meeting with Prime Ministers from across the Caribbean along with Ministers of Finance, Governors of the regions' central banks and private sector and representatives of international organizations who attended the sixth High Level Caribbean Forum. In addition to the conference, the Managing Director met with technocrats, visited with academia at the University of the West Indies and the launch of the IMF publication *Unleashing Growth and Strengthening Resilience.* Consultations on the issue of the challenges being faced regarding correspondent banking were facilitated through a roundtable with major stakeholders. Whilst the ownership of the two successive agreements was lauded, the authorities were reminded of the need to expand the potential to support the social dimension of the society to ensure that opportunities are created for all.

Early in November 2019, the IMF Board announced the completion of the final review of the 2016 PSBA and the success of the programme was attributed to the high degree of policy discipline. The IMF noted that Jamaica's successful economic reform was due to the commitment reflected by its implementation of two successful IMF-supported programmes over an almost seven-year period. The continued success of the reform agenda was linked to the completion of the central bank independence project and the establishment of a fiscal council. At the end of the almost seven years of far-reaching reforms, Jamaica was able to reduce its debt significantly in a manner that portends well for the future. The IMF affirmed that Jamaica's debt-to-GDP ratio should meet the target of 60% by the start of FY2026/2027. The expected fallout from the programme was not reflected in high unemployment rates, high inflation, instability in the financial sector or depleted reserves.

The IMF attributes the success of the two consecutive agreements to the combined commitment of Jamaicans from all segments of the society and the strong support of the international development partners (International Monetary Fund, 2019). The IMF credits the historic programme outcomes to sustained policymaking efforts given the previous failure to achieve the targets sets in multiple IMF agreements since the 1970s (Scott, 2018) and indicates that this puts Jamaica in good stead as an example for other small island developing states (International Monetary Fund, 2019). Despite these achievements, the need for the authorities and private sectors to do everything possible to generate rapid and where possible sustainable economic growth cannot be overstated. The strong economic reforms must not only be complemented with adequate social safety nets that can help the various categories of vulnerable persons in the population but it must also be leveraged to generate growth in which an increasing proportion of the population can participate in. If this is not done, there is increased possibility that societal cohesion will be jeopardized as will the hard-won economic gains. Having committed to leaving no one behind as per Agenda 2030 and making *Jamaica, the place of choice to live, work, raise families and do business*, the authorities will need to revisit the structure of the economy and attempt to improve the levels of human capital of the average citizen in order to be able to claim success on these goals. Will Jamaica return to the IMF? Has economic resilience in order to prevent a return to the debt overhang and other measures of macroeconomic stability that were addressed through the 2013 EFF and 2016 PSBA? What rewards would Jamaica reap from more than half-a-decade of implementing deep reforms?

References

Clarke, C., & Nelson, C. (2020). *Contextualizing Jamaica's relationship with the IMF*. Cham: Palgrave Macmillan.

Government of Jamaica. (2012). *The Financial Administration and Audit (Fiscal Responsibility Framework) Regulations*. Kingston: Government of Jamaica.

International Monetary Fund. (2010). *Jamaica: Letter of Intent, Memorandum of Economic and Financial Policies, and Technical Memorandum of Understanding*. Washington, DC: International Monetary Fund.

International Monetary Fund. (2013). *Jamaica: Request for an Extended Arrangement under the Extended Fund Facility*. Washington, DC: International Monetary Fund.

International Monetary Fund. (2016a). *IMF Mission concludes visit to Jamaica—Discusses modalities of possible future engagement. Press Release o 16/350.* Washington, DC: International Monetary Fund.

International Monetary Fund. (2016b). *IMF reaches staff-level agreement with Jamaica on three-year Precautionary Stand-By Arrangement*. Washington, DC: International Monetary Fund.

International Monetary Fund. (2016c, June 21). *IMF survey: Strong recovery in Jamaica but bold reforms still needed*. Retrieved from International Monetary Fund Web site: https://www.imf.org/en/News/Articles/2015/09/28/04/53/socar062116a

International Monetary Fund. (2017a). *Jamaica: First Review under the Stand-by Arrangement, Request for waiver of a Performance Criterion and Request for Modification of Performance Criteria*. Washington, DC: International Monetary Fund.

International Monetary Fund. (2017b). *Statement by IMF Managing Director Christine Lagarde at the conclusion of her visit to Jamaica*. Washington, DC: International Monetary Fund.

International Monetary Fund. (2019, May). *IMF lending case study: Jamaica*. Retrieved from International Monetary Fund Web site: https://www.imf.org/en/Countries/JAM/jamaica-lending-case-study

Jamaica Information Service. (2010, January 20). *Shaw promises Fiscal Responsibility Framework this year.* Retrieved from Jamaica Information Service: https://jis.gov.jm/shaw-promises-fiscal-responsibility-framework-this-year/

Lledo, V., Yoon, S., Fang, X., Mbaye, S., & Kim, Y. (2017). *Fiscal rules at a glance*. Washington, DC: International Monetary Fund.

Planning Institute of Jamaica. (2009). *Vision 2030 Jamaica National Development Plan*. Kingston: Planning Institute of Jamaica.

Planning Institute of Jamaica. (2018). *Jamaica: Voluntary National Review Report on the Implementation of the 2030 Agenda for Sustainable Development*. Kingston: Planning Institute of Jamaica.

Scott, S. (2018, May 13). 2018 marks 41 years of IMF 'rescue' of Jamaica. *Jamaica Observer*.

CHAPTER 11

There and Back Again: The Journey Continues

Introduction

Jamaica entered the year 2020 in high spirits. The country had been lauded throughout the financial media globally as having achieved the impossible. With the memory of a tumultuous period in the 1970s and 1980s, due to tensions between the IMF and Jamaica the latter attempting to navigate the combined effect of attempting to finance an expanded social policy agenda and an economic crisis spurred by the international oil price crisis and a maturing bauxite industry, the political rhetoric was in direct opposition to the then unwavering posture of the IMF (see Clarke & Nelson, 2020). As the need for the infusion of real economic resourced impacted the average citizen, the political administration of the 1970s struggled to maintain its legitimacy. Despite the widespread losses suffered by the political administration at the polls at the end of the 1970s, the new government experienced its own difficulties as it struggled to maintain a fixed exchange rate in the context of weak productive and export capacity through which to earn foreign exchange in the early-1980s.

For a small island developing state that experienced many economic shocks and other hazards that jeopardized the accomplishment of various development plans since independence, the accomplishments of the decade 2010–2019 appear impossible. Jamaica's ability to implement its

C. Clarke and C. Nelson, *Jamaica's Evolving Relationship with the IMF*, https://doi.org/10.1007/978-3-030-59204-2_11

development plans has been constrained by the absence of macroeconomic stability, the impact of pressures related to the electoral cycle, the need to rebuild infrastructure in the wake of natural disasters of various magnitude and the social conditions such as high rates of violent crime (Overseas Security Advisory Council, 2019; Harriott & Jones, 2016; Leslie, 2010), high rates of outmigration and 'brain drain' of highly skilled Jamaicans (McPherse, 2017; Jamaica Observer, 2018; Negron, 2012) and, an informal sector estimated to be 60% of GDP (Torero et al., 2006).

Despite the challenges facing the government regarding the need to kick-start high rates of economic growth, a feat that has not been accomplished in Jamaica since the 1960s, the government entered 2020 with a high degree of optimism having said 'ta-taa' to the IMF (Hamilton, 2012) on a far stronger economic footing than it did at the last successfully completed IMF Agreement in the 1990s. The Jamaican government and its technical team demonstrated high levels of technical competence, commitment to the programme implementation, and, the resolve to advance even deeper and more fundamental structural reforms that would spur economic activity and ultimately growth. In addition to the stronger economic footing and improvement in the technical capacity of various dimensions of the public sector through the administration of the various reforms, the IMF staff and Board have also developed a deeper appreciation of the Jamaican landscape that enabled it to have been so responsive to the needs of the society. Chapter 10 indicates that simultaneous with successfully completing two consecutive IMF Agreements, Jamaica made strides in achieving components of Vision 2030 Jamaica with the largest proportion being in the area of Goal 3 Jamaica's Economy is Prosperous. Fewer, though highly impactful, reforms were implemented during the 2013 and 2016 agreements that are aligned with Goal 1 Jamaicans are empowered to achieve the fullest potential and Goal 2 Jamaica' society is secure, cohesive and just.

On the policy front, based on the reforms initiated and completed since 2010, the Jamaican society was thought to be in good stead as it entered the year 2020. As detailed in Chapter 4 Jamaica has implemented significant reforms that have enabled the strengthening of the economy since 2010. According to the Government of Jamaica (2020a), these reforms have led to the entrenchment of macroeconomic stability and as a result three major areas of economic vulnerability have been improved: the external viability of the economy, the credibility of the budget process and therefore the budget and the sustainability of the fiscal programme. This resulted in the reduction in and improved control over the debt-to-GDP ratio and has complemented the impact of the reforms to the monetary framework to transition to an independent central bank with the appropriate governance structure and the financial sector strengthening efforts.

The impact of the policy agenda began to be reflected in the trends observed in the economic and social indicators. The indicators of central government performance reflected significant ease in the ability of the fiscal authorities to meet the targets under the economic programme. Macroeconomic indicators included low inflation rates consistent with the targeted range, tax revenues were relatively robust despite the provision of an estimate J$14bn reduction in taxes and fees related to real estate transactions (Government of Jamaica, 2020a). Debt-to-GDP had declined to 91.5% during the fiscal year and in terms of growth, there had been several quarters of growth in real GDP. On the social side, the labour market recorded the lowest unemployment rates of 7.2% during October 2019 (Statistical Institute of Jamaica, 2020a) in comparison to 8.7 and 10.5% in October 2018 and October 2017, respectively.

Overall, the fiscal rules implemented during the 2013 EFF (see Chapter 2 of this volume) supported the ability of the fiscal authorities to accomplish these results. The rule, though clear in its limits on the ways in which government expenditure should be developed and amended, reflects the awareness of the fact that Jamaica is a small island developing state, that trades openly with the rest of the world in terms of goods and services, and is subject to multiple natural hazards, the impact of which cannot be precisely estimated. As a result, it provides the Minister of Finance with options that can be engaged in the event that these shocks materialize in a way that jeopardizes the economic and social viability of the society through its effect on livelihoods given the fact that the informal sector is estimated to be 60% of the economy (Torero et al., 2006). The Minister of Finance, is therefore empowered with the appropriate Cabinet and Parliamentary approvals to act proactively and smartly in order to reduce or where possible avoid the potential impact of shocks through the provisions of either the Public Financial Management of Jamaica Disaster Risk Policy or through reallocations from central government to address the impact of other shocks. Importantly, the fiscal rules and the accompanying regulations require the identification and implementation of compensating measures to any unavoidable increases in expenditure as a result of shocks.

As Jamaica moved into the next decade in 2020, the horizon looked promising. Growth was set to increase given the extensive reforms undertaken in the previous decade. As growth returned and was sustained, other indicators such as debt-to-GDP and unemployment *inter alia* would improve and even more fiscal space would be provided to support the government's efforts to achieve Vision 2030 Jamaica, leave no one behind whilst making *Jamaica, the place of choice to live, work, raise families and do business.* Despite the successes of the partnership and borrowing relationship with the IMF under the 2013 EFF (see Chapter 2 of this volume) and 2016 PSBA (Chapter 9 of this volume), there were still fears about the ability of the technocrats and the political leadership of the country to manage the economic affairs outside of the security associated with a borrowing relationship with the Fund. Would Jamaica return to the Fund in the near future? Would the fiscal responsibility framework and the fiscal rules be sufficient to control government expenditure whilst unleashing economic development and growth? What of Vision 2030 Jamaica and the commitment to leaving no one behind, what was the likelihood that Jamaica could still make progress to either of these without the presence of the IMF?

The Year of Possibilities?

The Minister of Finance provided a consistent message of fiscal discipline and consolidation that would prevent the need for Jamaica to return to the IMF at the end of the 2016 PSBA (Government of Jamaica, 2019). There was a prevailing disbelief that the Jamaican authorities thought and continued to think themselves capable of managing the Jamaican economy without the IMF. Despite this disbelief the Minister continued to stay on message and assure the citizens of Jamaica that there was no need and no intention for Jamaica to return to a borrowing relationship with the Fund. 'This time is different' appears to be the basis of the Minister's statements because Jamaica had successfully implemented and completed two consecutive agreements with the IMF, one of which was precautionary and entered into only as insurance against possible deterioration in the financial markets that would require more reserves than the Bank of Jamaica could afford to expend. This would be hard to manage whilst implementing the intended reform agenda that deepened the landscape changes in the administration of the public sector and public bodies, furthered fiscal reforms in terms of public financial management and intensified the moves to strengthen the resilience of the financial sector and the ability of the Bank of Jamaica to deliver on its expanded core mandates (International Monetary Fund, 2016). Emphasis continued to be placed on reiterating the government's expressed and demonstrated commitment to conducting policy and implementing projects in fiscally prudent ways—a distinctly different tone from the pronouncements that tended to be made in previous governments. The government indicated that the establishment of economic independence through the proper conduct of fiscal policy was its unwavering commitment to the Jamaican population as this would provide the basis on which it would be able to increase the availability of economic opportunities to all and support the further expansion of the countries safety net to the vulnerable portions of its population (Government of Jamaica, 2019).

As Jamaica entered into the new decade, the Cabinet retreated on 16 January 2020 to consider the high-level strategic direction that the critical institutions within the government would be pursuing in light of the projected trend in the key macroeconomic and social indicators (Jamaica Information Service, 2020a). The three-day retreat provided an important part in the analytical process related to the budget for the 2020/21 fiscal year as each Minister would be required to justify and support the relevance of their programmes and projects in relation to the context within which the country was operating and the stated strategic priorities of the government. It also provides an opportunity for Cabinet Ministers to deliberate on any emerging trends presented by their colleagues or the leadership of several public sector organizations. This event would enable the Prime Minister to provide the nation with a summary indication of the plans for the calendar and fiscal year and signal the key components that would feature in the Governor General's Throne Speech and those that followed the official opening of the Houses of Parliament for the new fiscal year.

On the final day of the January 2020 Cabinet Retreat—a black swan event was emerging in China that would soon threaten to overturn all plans for rapid growth that were considered by Cabinet. The WHO data portal (2020) reports that as at 18 January 2020, China reported 49 cumulative cases and two deaths from the COVID-19 disease. According to the WHO data, within almost three days the number of cases had almost tripled to 125 and the cases continued to increase almost exponentially with another doubling of cases by 22 January 2020 in China. As the number of reported cases in China increased, and positive cases began to be recorded across the European continent, SIDS such as Jamaica heightened their alert. After having issued Infection Prevention and Control Guidelines for the COVID-19 virus on 24 January 2020 (Ministry of Health and Wellness, 2020), the Jamaican Ministry of Health issued its first advisory in the form of a travel advisory on 28 January 2020 and issued its first action to prevent the entrance of the virus into the island by placing a travel restriction on persons whose records indicated their presence in China within 14 days prior to their arrival in Jamaica (Government of Jamaica, 2020b). By Friday 31 January 2020 all travel between Jamaica and China was banned in the wake of the World Health Organisation's declaration that the outbreak of COVID-19 originating from China had been classified as global emergency. The move by Jamaica followed that of many countries globally and occurred despite the initial assessment by the Caribbean Public Health Agency (CARPHA) that the risk to the region from COVID-19 was low (Loop News, 2020). Blanket travel restrictions, evacuation of diplomatic and consular staff and citizens, and termination of flights originating or terminating in China represented some of the measures that started being implemented globally by end-January 2020.

The imminence of the first detected case in Jamaica on 10 March 2020 was foreshadowed by continuous speculation about the potential impact of the existing and likely policy responses to the contagious nature of the virus. The patterns globally was the termination of travel to regions with certain patterns in the number of cases and Jamaica's own attempt to delay the recording of its local patient zero would cause it to reduce the admission of persons coming from countries where the number of cases of the virus was increasing. The number and frequency of press briefings regarding the detection of the first case of COVID-19 intensified towards the end of February and into early March. By this time, the virus had infected close to one million persons globally and had been making its way around the world due to highly integrated nature of the Chinese economy and society into the business, academic and government sectors in almost every country. Transportation patterns also appeared to play an important role in the spread of COVID-19. The list of countries expanded to include South Korea, Iran and Italy to name a few and dual citizens or those with marriage exemptions coming from these countries would be subjected to a mandatory 14-day quarantine period (Government of Jamaica, 2020b). As the country came to the end of the first quarter of 2020, the Planning Institute of Jamaica (PIOJ) and the Bank of Jamaica provided initial insights into the potential scale of the devastation that could be wrought on the Jamaican economy as the virus impacted the health of Jamaican citizens directly. In terms of Jamaica's economic performance, the IMF revised its growth forecast of 1% positive growth to a contraction of 5.6% (Jackson, 2020). According to Jackson (2020) the Minister of Finance had indicated his projection that the Jamaican economy would experience a large economic shock due to COVID-19 in his comment on the IMF forecast. The IMF sought to ensure its relevance in the context of this crisis through its Rapid Financing Instrument[1] or Rapid Credit Facility depending on the income classification of the member. All member countries were eligible to access either mechanism; however, the latter facility was more likely to be accessed by those countries that have access to the Poverty Reduction and Growth Trust due to its concessionary nature. The quota available under the RFI was temporarily doubled to 100% of quota per year between 6 April and 5 October 2020 (International Monetary Fund, 2020a). In contrast to the normal borrowing facilities, the RFI is not accompanied with the normal reviews or programming, instead the assistance takes the form of direct purchases and the country must ensure that its efforts solve the balance of payments problems. Nevertheless, the Fund may require the implementation of prior actions and countries can benefit from technical assistance to support the implementation of policies in various areas.

In addition to establishing a COVID-19 Recovery Task Force chaired by the Minister of Finance, the Government of Jamaica provided multi-pronged support to various vulnerable groups in the population. The support termed the COVID-19 Allocation of Resources for Employees (CARE) Programme which included: compassionate grants to those who were unemployed or informally employed prior to the onset of the pandemic and temporary cash support for employees laid off after 10 March 2020 through the Supporting Employees with Transfer of Cash (SET Cash) (McIntosh, 2020; International Monetary Fund Country Focus, 2020). Those who are self-employed also benefitted from grants to support their small businesses. The SET Cash payments were made for April and May to 19,000 additional applicants whose employment status was verified by Tax Administration as their information would have been excluded from the initial information submitted by their employer

[1] The Rapid Financing Instrument (RFI) replaces two instruments: the Emergency Natural Disaster Assistance (ENDA) and the Emergency Post-Conflict Assistance (EPCA) (International Monetary Fund, 2020a).

in March. The eligibility of 337,000 persons were confirmed for the Compassionate Grant whilst only 12,000 of the original 30,000 applicants for the SET cash were also approved for payment. The CARE Programme also provided J$1.1 billion to the Ministry of Labour and Social Security as additional resources to the Programme of Advancement Through Health and Education (PATH) programme. The funds would be used to provide a third payment to beneficiaries between April and June without them needing to apply. Grants and appropriations in aid were also extended to: businesses operating in the tourism sector; and, tertiary students with student loans (The Ministry of Finance and the Public Service, 2020).

Calls for the authorities to return to the IMF emerged as the potential for a snowball effect across the economy became apparent (Ricketts, 2020). Jamaica accessed the IMF support to the tune of US$520m on 15 May 2020 through the RFI in response to the clear multi-dimensional impact that the crisis was shaping up to effect on the Jamaican economy and society. The IMF expressed their satisfaction with the government's economic policy responses to the impact of the crisis and was of the view that the authorities had made good provisions for crisis events through the economic reforms begun since 2010 (International Monetary Fund, 2020b, May). The government indicated that the proceeds from the RFI would be included as part of the reserves at the central bank since there was no current need for budgetary support.

On 20 May 2020 the Bank of Jamaica reported an estimated decline in Jamaica's economy by between 4 and 7% for the fiscal year, predicated on a containment of the spread of COVID-19 by the end of the June quarter. The expected recovery of economic activity would then facilitate growth between 2.5 and 5.5% in FY2021/22 (Bank of Jamaica, 2020). On 27 May 2020 the PIOJ reported that based on the preliminary data they received the Jamaican economy contracted by 1.7% during the first three months of 2020 which they attributed to the policy changes that were implemented in relation to the closure of the borders, the implementation of curfews that restricted after and before work economic activity, along with slowdown in Mining and Quarrying and the end-stage of the construction of significant road infrastructure projects. Looking ahead the PIOJ projected that growth would continue to be negative and their estimate of the contraction was between 12 and 14% for the April to June quarter of 2020 (Planning Institute of Jamaica, 2020b). As expected this decline would be driven by contraction in tourism and allied activities due to the border closures as well as the limited movement for social activities and early closure of all businesses to enable workers to return home before the curfew cut off. Their estimate of the decline in real GDP for the fiscal year was pegged at between 4 and 6%.

In order to ensure that adequate fiscal space would be available for any possible further emergency responses, the Minister of Finance utilized the escape clauses permitted in the Fiscal Responsibility Framework and the Financial Audit and Administration Act and suspended the fiscal rules through the end of FY2020/21 (Clarke, 2020). Suspensions can be countenanced in the event of occurrences that are beyond the control of the government such as natural, health and other disasters, public emergencies and the emergence of a severe economic downturn and must be agreed to by the Auditor General who certifies that the impact of the occurrence will exceed 1.5% of GDP. The forecasts of the IMF, BOJ and PIOJ indicated contractions in GDP of between 10 and 12% and therefore the anticipated savings from excess tax revenue above planned expenditure would not materialize. The final step is the approval by affirmative resolution by the House of Parliament. The rules needed to be suspended to facilitate the expenditure on the CARE Programme, almost all dimensions of the health sector, and other critical expenditures. The suspension of Jamaica's fiscal rules gave the authorities an additional two fiscal years on the original 2025/26 fiscal year deadline to achieve a debt-to-GDP ratio of 60% or lower. As part of Jamaica's application for the RFI, the IMF reviewed and consented to Jamaica's intention to suspend the fiscal rules. In presenting the suspension of the fiscal rules, the Minister contrasted the approach taken by Jamaica versus that of Peru that bypassed their rules and enacted new legislation to facilitate their economic response. Jamaica amended the Fiscal Responsibility Legislation to include suspension in response to potential economic contraction rather than manifested economic contraction, and, in light of the fact that Jamaica had been declared a disaster area due to the then imminent spread of COVID-19 consistent with the general trend among countries that do have these rules in place.

Whilst this outlook was extremely devastating for the entire population, the population would come to wish for these original forecasts to prevail. By 26 August 2020, the BOJ would revise its forecast for the economy downward to a decline in real GDP of between 7 and 10% for the fiscal year due to the resilience of the spread of the disease despite the enormous effort to curtail it. The BOJ indicated that partial recovery could emerge during the next fiscal year; however, this recovery would not allow the economy to return to its pre-COVID-19 levels until the year 2022 (Bank of Jamaica, 2020a, August 26). The report of the PIOJ on 9 September 2020 concurred with the estimates released a few weeks earlier by the BOJ. The PIOJ reported an estimated decline in real GDP of 10.2%. The July to September quarter was forecasted to decline between 8 and 10% due to the continued travel and other policy measures. The revised forecast for the fiscal year was pegged at between 8 and 10%. Recovery was pegged to resumption of activity in the Mining and Quarrying sector; however, there was no expectation of a return to pre-COVID-19 GDP levels until the year 2022 as telegraphed by the BOJ (Planning Institute of Jamaica, 2020c, September 9). The official data released by the Statistical Institute of Jamaica (STATIN) certified the decline during the April to June quarter of 2020 at 18.4% (Statistical Institute of Jamaica, 2020b). In addition, their data reflected a 12.6% unemployment rate during July 2020 which represented an almost doubling from 7.8% associated with July 2019 (Statistical Institute of Jamaica, 2020a). The BOJ in November revised its forecast for the economic decline to 10 to 12% for the current fiscal year but maintained the projection for possible growth of 3% in 2021/22 or higher depending on the size of the recovery in the tourism sector (Bank of Jamaica, 2020b, November 19).

Conclusion

The PIOJ has indicated that it will be undertaking a review of the impact of COVID-19 on the country's ability to make progress in relation to achieving Vision 2030 Jamaica. In March 2020, the PIOJ reported that Jamaica had made progress in accomplishing Vision 2030 Jamaica, the majority of which are associated with the stable macroeconomy that is aligned with Goal 3—Jamaica's economy is prosperous (Jamaica Information Service, 2020b). In terms of the medium-term targets set for 2018, the PIOJ indicated that the tourism sector had achieved all its targets whilst the agriculture sector was also reported to have made progress. The low unemployment rate was interpreted as an indicator of the improved business environment, nevertheless, concern was expressed regarding the inability to observe these improvements in the form of economic growth. In spite of this the PIOJ reported that gains were also made with respect to Goal 1—Jamaicans are empowered to achieve their fullest potential with gains made in the area of child poverty and national food poverty. Despite these gains, the targets relating to reduced prevalence of non-communicable diseases and attendance across all levels of the education sector were not achieved. Progress was made towards the achievement of Goal 2—The Jamaican society is secure, cohesive and just—crime remained an important issue across the society. The environmental domain encapsulated under Goal 4—Jamaica has a healthy natural environment, was the only goal for which the indicators reflected a decline due to a decline in all the components of the 2018 Environmental Performance Index (EPI). Overall progress has been made in 66.7% of the 75 national outcome indicators contained within the various three-year medium-term frameworks aligned with Vision 2030 Jamaica (Jamaica Information Service, 2020b).

By September 2020, given all that transpired in the Jamaican society in the intervening months due to the emergence and impact of the COVID-19 disease, the PIOJ indicated that there are likely to be slippages in the achievement of the development indicators and targets associated with Vision 2030 Jamaica (Planning Institute of Jamaica, 2020c). It is yet unknown the precise impact that: (a) COVID-19; and, (b) the policy measures implemented both to curb the spread of the virus and to support the most vulnerable, will have on the ability of the government to achieve the targets set for 2020 and 2021 under the most recent medium-term socio-economic framework developed to support the implementation of Vision 2030 Jamaica. Surprisingly and quite counterintuitively, remittances have been extremely buoyant throughout the crisis, the PIOJ reports an increase in real remittance inflows of 38.5% for July 2020 when compared to July 2019 (Planning Institute of Jamaica, 2020d). This is likely due to a combination of issues including *inter alia*, possibly, increased use of bank transfers rather than in-person and therefore information capture due to the travel restrictions as well as the fact that many in the Jamaican diaspora perform roles such as nurses, doctors and teachers, that were in high demand during this crisis as opposed to the 2008 global economic and financial crisis.

Will Jamaica's development trajectory be fundamentally altered as a result of the impact of COVID-19? And, if so, in what way? Will Jamaica need to re-enter a borrowing relationship with the IMF contrary to its intention and proclamation not to do so? Can the authorities demonstrate sustained and truly institutionalize economic independence in Jamaica? Will the hurricane season wreak unfathomed impacts based on the volume and impact of rain from various hydro events, whether or not the country experiences a direct hit? How will the government restore the quality of infrastructure in a way that supports both the physical recovery as well as the recovery of livelihoods across the island? The extent to which the trajectory positively or negatively alters is heavily dependent on the quality of and foresight with which decisions are made on a daily basis. Will the policy and technical elites be able to support the recently re-elected government in steering policy and projects in ways that are synergistic and reduce the negative impacts whilst contributing to the achievement as many outcomes as possible? Policy will need to be both proactive and reactive—it must anticipate critical societal needs given the trends observed both locally and globally and implement projects and programmes that solve any emergent needs whilst addressing long-standing development challenges. In doing this, the authorities must engage its international development partners in identifying solutions and alternative sources and modalities of financing them in order to continue to move the development needle. Further government must take the bold decision to fully digitalize itself and therefore provide a filip to the private sector to do the same—without this, incremental applications of technology will only increase the frustration of the populace and worsen the divides that have become more apparent since the emergence of COVID-19.

References

Bank of Jamaica. (2020a, August 26). *Monetary policy press statement: QMPR press conference*. Kingston: Bank of Jamaica.

Bank of Jamaica. (2020b, November 19). *Monetary policy press statement*. Kingston: Bank of Jamaica. http://boj.org.jm/uploads/news/qmpr_press_conference_may_2020_speech_-_governor_richard_byles.pdf.

Clarke, C., & Nelson, C. (2020). *Contextualising Jamaica's relationship with the IMF*. Chaum: Palgrave Macmillan.

Clarke, N. (2020, June 7). *COVID-19 and suspension of Jamaica's fiscal rules*. http://jamaica-gleaner.com/article/commentary/20200607/nigel-clarke-covid-19-and-suspension-jamaicas-fiscal-rules#:~:text=JAMAICA'S%20FISCAL%20RESPONSIBILITY%20FRAMEWORK,per%20cent%20by%202027%2D28.

Government of Jamaica. (2019, April 11). *Minister looks to positively different post-IMF Era for Jamaica*. https://mof.gov.jm/mof-media/media-centre/press/2542-minister-looks-to-positively-different-post-imf-era-for-jamaica.html.

Government of Jamaica. (2020a). *Fiscal Policy Paper FY 2020/21*. Kingston: Ministry of Finance and the Public Service.

Government of Jamaica. (2020b, March 3). *Jamaica's travel advisory for COVID-19*. https://www.moh.gov.jm/jamaicas-travel-advisory-for-covid-19/.

Hamilton, C. (2012, August 5). 'We hesitated too long'—PJ Patterson. *Sunday Observer*. http://www.jamaicaobserver.com/news/-We-hesitated-too-long—PJ-Patterson_12098810.

Harriott, A. D., & Jones, M. (2016). *Crime and violence in Jamaica*. Washington, DC: Inter-American Development Bank.

International Monetary Fund. (2016, November 11). *IMF Executive Board approves US$1.64 billion Stand By Arrangement for Jamaica*. https://www.imf.org/en/News/Articles/2016/11/11/pr16503-IMF-Executive-Board-Approves-US164-billion-Stand-By-Arrangement-for-Jamaica.

International Monetary Fund. (2020a, April 9). *The IMF's Rapid Financing Instrument (RFI)*. https://www.imf.org/en/About/Factsheets/Sheets/2016/08/02/19/55/Rapid-Financing-Instrument.

International Monetary Fund. (2020b, May). *Jamaica: Request for Purchase under the Rapid Financing Instrument—Press Release; Staff Report; and Statement by the Executive Director for Jamaica*. Washington, DC: International Monetary Fund.

International Monetary Fund Country Focus. (2020, May 28). *Jamaica ramps up social and economic support in COVID-19 Response*. https://www.imf.org/en/News/Articles/2020/05/27/na052720-jamaica-ramps-up-social-and-economic-support-in-covid-19-response.

Jackson, S. (2020, April 15). Jamaican economy to shrink by 5.6%—IMF. *Jamaica Gleaner*.

Jamaica Information Service. (2020a, January 15). *Cabinet holds retreat Jan. 16 to 18*. https://jis.gov.jm/cabinet-holds-retreat-jan-16-to-18/.

Jamaica Information Service. (2020b, March 3). *PIOJ reports gains under Vision 2030*. https://jis.gov.jm/pioj-reports-gains-under-vision-2030/.

Jamaica Observer. (2018, November 20). One in two high skilled Caribbean citizens migrating, says UNESCO report. *Jamaica Observer*.

Leslie, G. (2010). Background: Violent crime in Jamaica. In G. Leslie (Ed.), *Confronting the Don* (pp. 5–9). Small Arms Survey.

Loop News. (2020, January 31). *Jamaica bans China travel; Quarantine for those who break rule*. https://www.loopjamaica.com/content/jamaica-bans-china-travel-quarantine-those-who-break-rule.

McIntosh, D. (2020, June 1). *$3.6billion transferred to persons under CARE Programme*. https://jis.gov.jm/3-6-billion-transferred-to-persons-under-care-programme/.

McPherse, T. (2017, May 30). Brain Drain in Jamaica more evident among women. *Jamaica Gleaner*.

Ministry of Health and Wellness. (2020). *Infection prevention and control guidelines*. Kingston: Ministry of Health and Wellness.

Negron, R. (2012). Personal networks and migration decision: The case of Jamaican brain drain. *Journal of Identity and Migration Studies*, 43–63.

Overseas Security Advisory Council. (2019, May 30). *Jamaica 2019 crime and safety report*. https://www.osac.gov/Country/Jamaica/Content/Detail/Report/1d98b2df-fd4b-485f-aa62-15f4aed245ef#:~:text=In%202017%2C%20Jamaica's%20homicide%20rate,for%20women%20travelers%20in%202017.

Planning Institute of Jamaica. (2020a, May 27). *The Planning Institute of Jamaica*. https://www.pioj.gov.jm/wp-content/uploads/2020/05/DGs_QPB_244-speaking-notes-revised-27-5-20-FINAL_1.pdf.

Planning Institute of Jamaica. (2020b, September 9). *Review of economic performance, April–June 2020 Media Brief*. Kingston: Planning Institute of Jamaica.

Planning Institute of Jamaica. (2020c, September). *Media and speeches*. https://www.pioj.gov.jm/wp-content/uploads/2020/09/Five-Years-of-Action-in-Implementing-the-SDGs_website-version.pdf.

Planning Institute of Jamaica. (2020d). *Review of economic performance July–September 2020*. Kingston: Planning Institute of Jamaica.

Ricketts, M. (2020, April 5). Government must call in the IMF. *The Jamaica Gleaner*.

Statistical Institute of Jamaica. (2020a, November 19). *Main labour force indicators*. https://statinja.gov.jm/LabourForce/NewLFS.aspx.

Statistical Institute of Jamaica. (2020b, November 19). *Year over year change of value added by industry at constant (2007) prices (seasonally unadjusted)*. https://statinja.gov.jm/NationalAccounting/Quarterly/NewQuarterlyGDP.aspx.

The Ministry of Finance and the Public Service. (2020, November 20). *We care*. https://www.wecare.gov.jm/.

Torero, M., Robles, M., Hernandez, M., De la Roca, J., Webber, M., & Thomas, D. (2006). *The informal sector in Jamaica*. Washington, DC: Inter-American Development Bank (IDB).

World Health Organisation. (2020, November 19). *WHO Coronavirus disease (COVID-19) dashboard*. https://covid19.who.int/table?tableChartType=heat.

Index

C. Clarke and C. Nelson, *Jamaica's Evolving Relationship with the IMF*,
https://doi.org/10.1007/978-3-030-59204-2

M

N

Q

R

S

The manufacturer's authorised representative in the EU is Springer Nature Customer Service Centre GmbH, Europaplatz 3, 69115 Heidelberg, Germany. If you have any concerns regarding our products, please contact ProductSafety@springernature.com

Printed and bound by CPI Group (UK) Ltd, Croydon, CR0 4YY
23/09/2026
02221520-0013